Plea Bargaining Across Borders

ASPEN PUBLISHERS

Plea Bargaining Across Borders

Criminal Procedure

Jenia I. Turner

Southern Methodist University

Hiram E. Chodosh

Series Editor

AUSTIN BOSTON CHICAGO NEW YORK THE NETHERLANDS

Aspen Publishers
Attn: Permissions Department
76 Ninth Avenue, 7th Floor
New York, NY 10011-5201

To contact Customer Care, e-mail customer.care@aspenpublishers.com, call 1-800-234-1660, fax 1-800-901-9075, or mail correspondence to:

Aspen Publishers
Attn: Order Department
PO Box 990
Frederick, MD 21705

Printed in the United States of America.

1 2 3 4 5 6 7 8 9 0

ISBN 978-0-7355-7571-4

Library of Congress Cataloging-in-Publication Data

Turner, Jenia I.
Plea bargaining across borders : criminal procedure / Jenia I. Turner.
p. cm.
ISBN 978-0-7355-7571-4
1. Plea bargaining. I. Title.
K5458.T87 2010
345'.072—dc22

2009032625

About Wolters Kluwer Law & Business

Wolters Kluwer Law & Business is a leading provider of research information and workflow solutions in key specialty areas. The strengths of the individual brands of Aspen Publishers, CCH, Kluwer Law International and Loislaw are aligned within Wolters Kluwer Law & Business to provide comprehensive, in-depth solutions and expert-authored content for the legal, professional and education markets.

CCH was founded in 1913 and has served more than four generations of business professionals and their clients. The CCH products in the Wolters Kluwer Law & Business group are highly regarded electronic and print resources for legal, securities, antitrust and trade regulation, government contracting, banking, pension, payroll, employment and labor, and healthcare reimbursement and compliance professionals.

Aspen Publishers is a leading information provider for attorneys, business professionals and law students. Written by preeminent authorities, Aspen products offer analytical and practical information in a range of specialty practice areas from securities law and intellectual property to mergers and acquisitions and pension/benefits. Aspen's trusted legal education resources provide professors and students with high-quality, up-to-date and effective resources for successful instruction and study in all areas of the law.

Kluwer Law International supplies the global business community with comprehensive English-language international legal information. Legal practitioners, corporate counsel and business executives around the world rely on the Kluwer Law International journals, loose-leafs, books and electronic products for authoritative information in many areas of international legal practice.

Loislaw is a premier provider of digitized legal content to small law firm practitioners of various specializations. Loislaw provides attorneys with the ability to quickly and efficiently find the necessary legal information they need, when and where they need it, by facilitating access to primary law as well as state-specific law, records, forms and treatises.

Wolters Kluwer Law & Business, a unit of Wolters Kluwer, is headquartered in New York and Riverwoods, Illinois. Wolters Kluwer is a leading multinational publisher and information services company.

Summary of Contents

Contents

Acknowledgments

I thank my SMU colleagues, especially Anthony Colangelo, Nathan Cortez, Jeff Kahn, Fred Moss, and Beth Thornburg, for their helpful comments on various parts of this project. I am also grateful to the many other colleagues and friends who offered invaluable comments and suggestions: Professor Cynthia Alkon, Till Gut, Judge Yohei Okamoto, Leigha Simonton, Professor Thomas Weigend, and a Japanese judge to whom I promised anonymity. The entire chapter on Germany would not have been possible without the support of Professor Weigend, who hosted me at the University of Cologne's Institute on Foreign and International Criminal Law during the summer of 2004 and helped me arrange interviews with German judges, prosecutors, and defense attorneys. Philipp Esser and his family kindly hosted me in their home in Cologne and also helped me contact interviewees. I am also grateful to the many interviewees themselves—judges, prosecutors, and defense attorneys—in Germany and Bulgaria, who generously shared their insights into the practice of plea bargaining in their respective countries. I also thank the anonymous reviewers of the book, who offered thoughtful comments and greatly helped me improve the project.

Many other people provided critical support for different parts of the project: my research assistants, Becky Bailey, Zhiyuan Chen, Gemma Galeoto, Gregory Shannon, and Mei Zhang; my former student Yan Xiang; Foreign and International Law Librarian Tom Kimbrough; and my assistant Jan Spann. I am grateful to the SMU Dedman School of Law for the award of a summer research grant in support of this project. My thanks also go to Dean Hiram Chodosh and to Aspen Publishers for inviting me to take part in the Law Across Borders series.

Finally, I owe a debt of gratitude to my husband, John Turner, who read through several drafts of the book and offered invaluable comments and steadfast support.

I thank the following authors and copyright holders for permission to use their works:

Albert Alschuler, *Implementing the Criminal Defendant's Right to Trial*, 50 U. Chi. L. Rev. 931, 932-934 (1983). Copyright © by the University of Chicago Law Review. Reprinted with permission of the author and the University of Chicago Law Review.

Mirjan Damaška, *Negotiated Justice in International Criminal Courts*, 2 J. Int'l Crim. Just. 1018, 1037, 1038-1039 (2004). Reprinted with permission of the author and the Journal of International Criminal Justice.

Markus Dirk Dubber, *American Plea Bargains, German Lay Judges, and the Crisis of Criminal Procedure*, 49 Stan. L. Rev. 547, 604-605 (1997). Reprinted with permission of the author and the Stanford Law Review.

Frank H. Easterbrook, *Plea Bargaining as Compromise*, 101 Yale L.J. 1969, 1975 (1992). Reprinted with permission of the Yale Law Journal.

Jenia Iontcheva Turner, *Judicial Participation in Plea Negotiations: A Comparative View*, 54 Am. J. Comp. L. 199 (2006). Reprinted with permission of the American Journal of Comparative Law.

Thomas Weigend, *The Decay of the Inquisitorial Ideal: Plea Bargaining Invades German Criminal Procedure*, in John Jackson et al., Crime, Procedure and Evidence in a Comparative and International Context 39 (2008). Reprinted with permission of the author and Hart Publishers.

Plea Bargaining Across Borders

Introduction

Over the last three decades, a quiet revolution has occurred in criminal justice systems around the world. Plea bargaining has been introduced in systems that had long opposed the practice. The term "plea bargaining," as I use it in this book, means the process of negotiation and explicit agreement between the defendant, on one hand, and the prosecution, the court, or both, on the other, whereby the defendant confesses, pleads guilty, or provides other assistance to the government in exchange for more lenient treatment. Plea bargaining has now reached nations as diverse as Germany, Russia, India, Taiwan, South Africa, Australia, and Argentina, and is being considered by others, including China and Indonesia.

Despite the recent advance of plea bargaining globally, the practice remains controversial in the country where it originated and where it is most entrenched—the United States. American scholars have long expressed concerns about the fairness of plea negotiations. Some have even compared the coercive aspects of plea bargaining to the procedures of medieval inquisitions.[1] Plea bargaining has been criticized for its potential to undermine the search for truth in criminal prosecutions, and it is blamed for interfering with victims' rights.[2] Moreover, the lack of transparency in plea negotiations is said to reduce the public legitimacy of the criminal justice system.[3]

---

[1] *See* John Langbein, *Torture and Plea Bargaining*, 46 U. Chi. L. Rev. 3 (1978).

[2] Michael M. O'Hear, *Victims and Plea Bargaining: From Consultation to Guidelines*, 91 Marq. L. Rev. 323 (2007); Sarah N. Welling, *Victim Participation in Plea Bargains*, 65 Wash. U. L.Q. 301, 304 (1987).

[3] Stephanos Bibas, *Transparency and Participation in Criminal Procedure*, 81 N.Y.U. L. Rev. 911 (2006).

But even as its merits continue to be debated in the nation of its origin, the spread of plea bargaining to new territories suggests that the practice will play a significant role in criminal justice around the world for the foreseeable future. This is an ideal moment to study the forms that plea bargaining is taking as it is being transposed into new systems. What can countries learn from one another as they observe these developments? Are plea bargaining practices in different countries converging, or are they being heavily modified to conform to the existing features of each new justice system?[4] And what do the responses to plea bargaining reveal about the underlying principles of various criminal justice systems?

To assess the directions that plea bargaining might take as it spreads across the globe, this book focuses on five approaches to the subject.

Chapter 1, Traditions of Plea Bargaining, presents the United States as an example of a system in which plea bargaining is well developed and extensively regulated. This chapter focuses on the federal system, with some attention to the systems of individual states as necessary. The different approaches to plea bargaining in American federal and state jurisdictions and the long history of plea bargaining in the United States provide a wealth of experience and valuable insights. In addition, American plea bargaining has served as an example for a number of other countries considering adoption of the practice. Therefore, any discussion of the global rise of plea bargaining must necessarily examine the American model.

In Chapter 2, Informal Plea Bargaining, I turn to Germany as a paradigmatic example of this type of plea bargaining. By "informal," I mean plea bargaining introduced without legislative authorization by practitioners responding pragmatically to an overburdened court system. Until recently, the German Criminal Procedure Code did not provide for plea bargaining or even for guilty pleas, even though forms of consensual disposition of cases had been commonly used since at least the early 1990s. The practice was first tacitly and then openly approved by the German higher courts, but it was not formally regulated by the legislature until May 2009. German courts sanctioned the practice despite its tensions with the traditional German principles of mandatory prosecution and independent judicial investigation. Plea bargaining managed to take hold despite these formal obstacles because of the practical needs of the Ger-

---

[4] Máximo Langer, *From Legal Transplants to Legal Translations: The Globalization of Plea Bargaining and the Americanization Thesis in Criminal Procedure*, 45 Harv. Int'l L.J. 1 (2004).

man system—primarily the need to process a large number of increasingly complex cases more efficiently. Although there was no deliberate attempt to import plea bargaining from abroad, the familiarity of German lawyers with plea bargaining in other jurisdictions likely influenced its adoption and acceptance indirectly.

In Chapter 3, Introducing Plea Bargaining as Part of Comprehensive Legal Reform, I describe the open embrace of plea bargaining by Eastern European jurisdictions such as Russia and Bulgaria. The deliberate adoption of plea bargaining in Eastern European countries was part of broader criminal procedure reforms, which were driven both by changing domestic needs and by international demands. As economic interaction between East and West increased after the collapse of the Iron Curtain, the European Union and the United States pressed for criminal procedure reform in Eastern Europe, and adoption of plea bargaining was one of the results. The Russian and Bulgarian plea bargaining regimes deliberately combine features from inquisitorial and adversarial regimes and can provide useful information about the feasibility of legal transplants in criminal procedure. The chapter analyzes the legitimacy and effectiveness of plea bargaining transplants in Eastern Europe and raises questions about the desirability of importing bargaining in countries with relatively weak judicial systems.

Chapter 4, Alternatives to Plea Bargaining, focuses on Japan and China. These two jurisdictions—and others in Asia—present a challenge to the thesis that systems around the world are converging toward explicit adoption of plea bargaining. The chapter focuses primarily on the Japanese system, which remains resistant to explicit recognition of plea bargaining, even in the face of an increasingly overburdened criminal justice system. Japan has responded to the need to process criminal cases more efficiently through alternative methods, such as introducing a simpler form of summary procedure for less serious cases; providing for a "pretrial arrangement procedure," in which the parties and the court attempt to limit the issues to be adjudicated at trial; and encouraging prosecutors to screen cases more thoroughly at the outset to ensure that each case is serious and warrants prosecutorial resources. But even in Japan, the system has arguably come to condone implicit forms of the plea bargaining. It is now common for a Japanese defendant to confess to a crime and cooperate with the authorities with the aim of receiving a sentencing discount, earlier release on bail, or suspended prosecution. Courts and prosecutors have acquiesced in these tacit exchanges and have even encouraged them at times. As Japanese criminal dockets face increasing caseloads, such exchanges are likely to become more frequent and perhaps more explicit. A similar move from simplified trial procedures toward explicit plea bargaining may also occur in China. But as in Eastern Europe, the potential introduction of plea bargaining in a system whose regard for the rule of law and for defense rights remains the subject of international criticism raises serious concerns.

Chapter 5, Plea Bargaining in International Courts, reviews the rise of plea bargaining at international criminal courts such as the International Criminal Tribunals for the former Yugoslavia (ICTY) and for Rwanda (ICTR). These courts were created to try three categories of crimes of special concern to the international community: genocide, war crimes, and crimes against humanity committed in Rwanda and the former Yugoslavia. The tribunals' statutes and their early rules of procedure did not provide for plea bargaining, and although the ICTY and ICTR received guilty pleas in each of their first cases, these pleas did not appear to rest on any promises of leniency by the prosecution or the court. But the considerable cost of the prosecutions and the length of the proceedings soon led to demands for greater efficiency, which in turn spurred the introduction of plea bargaining at these tribunals. The practice has been controversial. Some commentators view plea bargaining as an inappropriate tool for resolving crimes as heinous as those prosecuted in the ICTY and ICTR, and argue that it undermines the objective of creating an accurate historical record of the atrocities. Moreover, many victims are outraged that some defendants have received more lenient sentences as a result of "deals" with the prosecution. The experience of the international tribunals thus raises many of the same questions that plea bargaining confronts at the domestic level, but does so with even greater intensity. Significantly, it calls into question whether some classes of cases are so extreme or politically significant that plea bargaining, even if appropriate for the vast majority of offenses, is inappropriate for them.

Finally, the Conclusion reviews lessons from the experience with plea bargaining around the world, and offers tentative predictions for its future. In particular, it predicts that plea bargaining will continue to spread globally, as part of law-reform movements or in response to practical needs. As plea bargaining is introduced in new territories, it will also change form to adapt to local circumstances. The chapter advocates that policy makers should study these new forms of plea bargaining to identify practices that are most likely to be fair, legitimate, and effective. These practices can then be considered for adoption both by countries with long traditions of plea bargaining, such as the United States, and by those who have just recently introduced or are about to introduce plea bargaining.

Each chapter concludes with a set of problems structured around two representative types of crimes in which plea bargaining may be used. The first is drug trafficking, a relatively common offense that is ordinarily regarded as less serious than most violent crimes. The second is the serious violent crime of homicide. (Given the limited jurisdiction of the international criminal tribunals, the focus in Chapter 5 will be solely on violent crimes.) In each of the national systems discussed in this book, plea bargaining will typically be handled quite differently, and used for different reasons, in the cases of these two crimes. In the case of drug trafficking, plea bargaining is most commonly used for the sake of efficiency and for the purpose of obtaining the defendant's cooperation in preventing or uncovering other crimes. In homicide cases, plea bargaining is used primarily as a way to deal with weak or insufficient evidence—where prosecution witnesses may not be fully credible, for example, or where a colorable legal defense may exist. In some countries, plea bargaining cannot be used at all in homicide cases, although other mechanisms may be available for shortening the proceedings when the defendant confesses guilt.

The various approaches to plea bargaining described in this book will rarely come into direct conflict with one another. Unlike transnational problems examined in other books in the Law Across Borders series, issues of criminal procedure rarely raise choice-of-law questions or involve international treaties. But the different approaches to plea bargaining around the world have and will continue to influence one another subtly and indirectly. As plea bargaining spreads, an understanding of its many variations, and their successes and failures, will be helpful in making informed choices that promote criminal justice systems that are efficient, fair, and legitimate.

CHAPTER 1

Traditions of Plea Bargaining

The United States

INTRODUCTION

Plea bargaining is the predominant method of resolving criminal cases in the United States. Over 90 percent of convictions are obtained through a guilty plea, and the vast majority of guilty pleas are the product of bargaining.[1] Plea bargaining has been practiced in the United States for more than a century and a half, and it is now recognized and supported by courts as an important tool in the efficient administration of criminal justice. Despite its long history and prevalence, plea bargaining remains controversial. In response to critiques about the fairness, accuracy, and legitimacy of negotiated pleas, federal and state legislatures and courts have regulated a number of aspects of the plea bargaining process. Still, calls for reform and even outright abolition continue.

Given the entrenched position of plea bargaining in the United States and the extensive debate surrounding it, a thorough understanding of the American practice is essential to any examination of plea bargaining from a comparative or international perspective. American-style plea bargaining has been considered and adopted (with some modification) by many countries pursuing criminal law reform, ranging from Italy to Bulgaria to India. It has also influenced developments at the international criminal tribunals for Rwanda and the former Yugoslavia, whose

[1] Bureau of Justice Statistics, Federal Criminal Case Processing (2002), *at* http://www.ojp.usdoj.gov/bjs/abstract/fccp02.htm (showing that federal prosecutors declined to prosecute 27 percent of all matters investigated in 2002, that 89 percent of those whose criminal cases were concluded in federal district court were convicted, and that 96 percent of those convicted pleaded guilty or no contest); *see also* Bureau of Justice Statistics, Felony Defendants in Large Urban Counties 24 tbl. 23 (2002) (showing that 61 percent of arrest charges in large-county state courts were resolved through a guilty plea).

criminal procedure rules have relied heavily on the adversarial model of criminal justice. The experience of these tribunals is in turn likely to shape procedure at the International Criminal Court. For all of these reasons, American plea bargaining is an appropriate place to begin our discussion.

HISTORY OF PLEA BARGAINING IN THE UNITED STATES

Confessions of guilt by an accused have, of course, existed since ancient times. The "guilty plea"—that is, a defendant's declaration that he will waive a trial and allow himself to be punished immediately—is a somewhat newer invention, but has also existed for centuries under the common law. It has been present since at least the Middle Ages in England and since colonial times in America.[2]

Still, a number of scholars, most notably Albert Alschuler, have argued that, until the nineteenth century, guilty pleas were relatively rare and treated with suspicion by courts in both England and the United States.[3] Given that a guilty plea to a felony quite often meant that the defendant would be executed, judges worried that defendants who pleaded guilty were doing so because they were coerced or uninformed.[4] Judges therefore commonly encouraged defendants to exercise the right to trial.

Plea bargaining itself—that is, negotiation between prosecutors and defendants giving rise to a guilty plea—was virtually unknown in the United States until the nineteenth century. Before that time, jury trials were brief affairs, with minimal attention to the formalities of evidence and procedure, and were often conducted without lawyers representing either side.[5] A number of influential studies have pointed to these features and have contended that little pressure existed to promote development of a system of plea bargaining before the nineteenth century.

---

[2] Albert W. Alschuler, *Plea Bargaining and Its History*, 13 Law & Soc'y Rev. 211, 214-215 (1979).

[3] *Id.* at 214-215.

[4] *Id.* at 214-217.

[5] John H. Langbein, *Understanding the Short History of Plea Bargaining*, 13 Law & Soc'y Rev. 261, 261-270 (1979) (discussing the practice in England); Lawrence Friedman, Crime and Punishment in American History 237-238 (1993) (discussing the United States).

These scholars have argued that changes in these characteristics led to the rise of plea bargaining.[6]

Between the mid-nineteenth and early twentieth centuries, the United States went from being a nation where plea bargaining did not exist to one in which plea bargaining was the method by which a majority of criminal prosecutions were resolved.[7] This transformation occurred largely without legislative action or formal judicial sanction. Its initial adoption appears to have been driven principally by prosecutors responding to heavier caseloads in larger American cities such as New York, Chicago, and Boston. The increase in caseloads was due in large part to increases in population and crime rates.[8] In addition, the greater complexity of jury trials and professionalization of criminal justice likely placed further burdens upon state systems.[9] Plea bargaining appears to have been a primary solution to the problems created by prosecutors' offices that no longer had the time or resources to contemplate full trials in all criminal cases.[10]

Even as it became common, plea bargaining came under criticism from many quarters. Some public authorities in the early twentieth century denounced it as resulting in excessively lenient treatment and sending the wrong message to criminals.[11] A few observers worried that it coerced some potentially innocent defendants to "confess crime . . . through hope of reward or fear of extreme punishment."[12] Yet others argued that, through plea bargaining, inexperienced prosecutors had replaced judges as the true decision makers in the criminal justice system.

But such objections did not slow the growth of the practice during the twentieth century. For a variety of reasons—growing caseloads, a due process revolution giving more bargaining chips to defendants, and a greater comfort level with the practice by lawyers and judges—plea

---

[6] Friedman, *supra* note 5, at 237-238; Malcolm Feeley, *Plea Bargaining and the Structure of the Criminal Process*, 7 Just. Sys. J. 338, 345-350 (1982); Langbein, *supra* note 5, at 265.

[7] Mike McConville & Chester L. Mirsky, Jury Trials and Plea Bargaining 1 (2005); *see also* Lawrence Friedman, *Plea Bargaining in Historical Perspective*, 13 Law & Soc'y Rev. 247 (1979).

[8] George Fischer, *Plea Bargaining's Triumph*, 109 Yale L.J. 857, 865 (2000).

[9] *See* Friedman, *supra* note 5, at 237-238; Langbein, *supra* note 5, at 262.

[10] Fischer, *supra* note 8, at 865.

[11] Alschuler, *supra* note 2, at 232.

[12] *Id.* at 233 (citing Justin Miller, *The Compromise of Criminal Cases*, 1 S. Cal. L. Rev. 1, 23 (1927)).

bargaining continued to grow, and it gradually became the dominant mode of conviction in the United States. By 2004, more than 95 percent of convictions in federal court and a similar number in state systems were resolved through no-contest or guilty pleas.[13]

LAW RELATED TO PLEA BARGAINING IN THE UNITED STATES

Although plea bargaining was taking place routinely in the United States in the late nineteenth and early twentieth centuries, it was generally conducted informally and without explicit judicial recognition. Appellate courts often denounced the practice even as prosecutors and defense attorneys in urban courts persisted in it, confident that it would rarely attract judicial review.[14] It was not until 1970 that the Supreme Court itself first acknowledged and expressly approved its use. In *Brady v. United States*, the Court held that plea bargaining did not in itself undermine the voluntariness of guilty pleas. The decision legitimated the practice and at the same time opened the way to a new era of regulation by courts and legislatures.

Brady v. United States, 397 U.S. 742 (1970)

Mr. Justice White delivered the opinion of the Court.

In 1959, petitioner was charged with kidnaping in violation of 18 U.S.C. §1201(a). Since the indictment charged that the victim of the kidnaping was not liberated unharmed, petitioner faced a maximum penalty of death if the verdict of the jury should so recommend. Petitioner, represented by competent counsel throughout, first elected to plead not guilty. Apparently because the trial judge was unwilling to try the case without a jury, petitioner made no serious attempt to reduce the possibility of a death penalty by waiving a jury trial. Upon learning that his codefendant, who had confessed to the authorities, would plead guilty and be available to testify against him, petitioner changed his plea to guilty. His plea was accepted after the trial judge twice questioned him

---

[13] Bureau of Justice Statistics, Compendium of Federal Justice Statistics, 2004, at 1, 59 (2004), *at* http://www.ojp.usdoj.gov/bjs/pub/pdf/cfjs0404.pdf.

[14] Alschuler, *supra* note 2, at 224-227.

as to the voluntariness of his plea. Petitioner was sentenced to 50 years' imprisonment, later reduced to 30.

In 1967, petitioner sought relief under 28 U.S.C. §2255, claiming that his plea of guilty was not voluntarily given because §1201(a) operated to coerce his plea, because his counsel exerted impermissible pressure upon him, and because his plea was induced by representations with respect to reduction of sentence and clemency. It was also alleged that the trial judge had not fully complied with Rule 11 of the Federal Rules of Criminal Procedure. [. . .]

I

[. . .] That a guilty plea is a grave and solemn act to be accepted only with care and discernment has long been recognized. Central to the plea and the foundation for entering judgment against the defendant is the defendant's admission in open court that he committed the acts charged in the indictment. He thus stands as a witness against himself and he is shielded by the Fifth Amendment from being compelled to do so—hence the minimum requirement that his plea be the voluntary expression of his own choice. But the plea is more than an admission of past conduct; it is the defendant's consent that judgment of conviction may be entered without a trial—a waiver of his right to trial before a jury or a judge. Waivers of constitutional rights not only must be voluntary but must be knowing, intelligent acts done with sufficient awareness of the relevant circumstances and likely consequences. On neither score was Brady's plea of guilty invalid.

II

The trial judge in 1959 found the plea voluntary before accepting it; the District Court in 1968, after an evidentiary hearing, found that the plea was voluntarily made; the Court of Appeals specifically approved the finding of voluntariness. We see no reason on this record to disturb the judgment of those courts. Petitioner, advised by competent counsel, tendered his plea after his codefendant, who had already given a confession, determined to plead guilty and became available to testify against petitioner. It was this development that the District Court found to have triggered Brady's guilty plea.

The voluntariness of Brady's plea can be determined only by considering all of the relevant circumstances surrounding it. One of these circumstances was the possibility of a heavier sentence following a guilty verdict after a trial. It may be that Brady, faced with a strong case against him and recognizing that his chances for acquittal were slight, preferred to plead guilty and thus limit the penalty to life imprisonment rather than to elect a jury trial which could result in a death penalty. But even if we assume that Brady would not have pleaded guilty except for the death penalty provision of §1201(a), this assumption merely identifies the penalty provision as a "but for" cause of his plea. That the statute caused the plea in this sense does not necessarily prove that the plea was coerced and invalid as an involuntary act.

The State to some degree encourages pleas of guilty at every important step in the criminal process. For some people, their breach of a State's law is alone sufficient reason for surrendering themselves and accepting punishment. For others, apprehension and charge, both threatening acts by the Government, jar them into admitting their guilt. In still other cases, the post-indictment accumulation of evidence may convince the defendant and his counsel that a trial is not worth the agony and expense to the defendant and his family. All these pleas of guilty are valid in spite of the State's responsibility for some of the factors motivating the pleas; the pleas are no more improperly compelled than is the decision by a defendant at the close of the State's evidence at trial that he must take the stand or face certain conviction.

Of course, the agents of the State may not produce a plea by actual or threatened physical harm or by mental coercion overbearing the will of the defendant. But nothing of the sort is claimed in this case; nor is there evidence that Brady was so gripped by fear of the death penalty or hope of leniency that he did not or could not, with the help of counsel, rationally weigh the advantages of going to trial against the advantages of pleading guilty. Brady's claim is of a different sort: that it violates the Fifth Amendment to influence or encourage a guilty plea by opportunity or promise of leniency and that a guilty plea is coerced and invalid if influenced by the fear of a possibly higher penalty for the crime charged if a conviction is obtained after the State is put to its proof.

Insofar as the voluntariness of his plea is concerned, there is little to differentiate Brady from (1) the defendant, in a jurisdiction where the judge and jury have the same range of sentencing power, who pleads guilty because his lawyer advises him that the judge will very probably be more lenient than the jury; (2) the defendant, in a jurisdiction where the judge alone has sentencing power, who is advised by counsel that the judge is normally more lenient with defendants who plead guilty than with those who go to trial; (3) the defendant who is permitted by prosecutor and judge to plead guilty to a lesser offense included in the offense charged; and (4) the defendant who pleads guilty to certain counts with the understanding that other charges will be dropped. In each of these situations,[15] as in Brady's case, the defendant might never plead guilty absent the possibility or certainty that the plea will result in a lesser penalty than the sentence that could be imposed after a trial and a verdict of guilty. We decline to hold, however, that a guilty plea is compelled and invalid under the Fifth Amendment whenever motivated by the defendant's desire to accept the certainty or probability of a lesser penalty rather than face a wider range of possibilities extending from acquittal to conviction and a higher penalty authorized by law for the crime charged.

The issue we deal with is inherent in the criminal law and its administration because guilty pleas are not constitutionally forbidden, because the criminal law characteristically extends to judge or jury a range of choice in setting the sentence in individual cases, and because both the State and the defendant often find it advantageous to preclude the possibility of the maximum penalty authorized by law. For a defendant who sees slight possibility of acquittal, the advantages of pleading guilty and limiting the probable penalty are obvious—his exposure is reduced, the correctional processes can begin immediately, and the practical burdens of a trial are eliminated. For the State there are also advantages—the more promptly imposed punishment after an admission of guilt may more effectively attain the objectives of punishment; and with the avoidance of trial, scarce judicial and prosecutorial resources are conserved for those cases in which there is a substantial issue of the defendant's guilt or in which there is substantial doubt that the State can sustain its burden of proof. It is this mutuality of advantage that perhaps explains the fact that at present well over three-fourths of the criminal convictions in this country rest on pleas of guilty, a great many of them no doubt motivated at least in part by the hope or assurance of a lesser penalty than might be imposed if there were a guilty verdict after a trial to judge or jury.

[. . .]

Brady first pleaded not guilty; prior to changing his plea to guilty he was subjected to no threats or promises in face-to-face encounters

---

[15] [Footnote in original] We here make no reference to the situation where the prosecutor or judge, or both, deliberately employ their charging and sentencing powers to induce a particular defendant to tender a plea of guilty. In Brady's case there is no claim that the prosecutor threatened prosecution on a charge not justified by the evidence or that the trial judge threatened Brady with a harsher sentence if convicted after trial in order to induce him to plead guilty.

with the authorities. He had competent counsel and full opportunity to assess the advantages and disadvantages of a trial as compared with those attending a plea of guilty; there was no hazard of an impulsive and improvident response to a seeming but unreal advantage. His plea of guilty was entered in open court and before a judge obviously sensitive to the requirements of the law with respect to guilty pleas. Brady's plea [. . .] was voluntary.

The standard as to the voluntariness of guilty pleas must be essentially that defined by Judge Tuttle of the Court of Appeals for the Fifth Circuit:

> "(A) plea of guilty entered by one fully aware of the direct consequences, including the actual value of any commitments made to him by the court, prosecutor, or his own counsel, must stand unless induced by threats (or promises to discontinue improper harassment), misrepresentation (including unfulfilled or unfulfillable promises), or perhaps by promises that are by their nature improper as having no proper relationship to the prosecutor's business (e.g. bribes)."[16]

Under this standard, a plea of guilty is not invalid merely because entered to avoid the possibility of a death penalty.

III

The record before us also supports the conclusion that Brady's plea was intelligently made. He was advised by competent counsel, he was made aware of the nature of the charge against him, and there was nothing to indicate that he was incompetent or otherwise not in control of his mental faculties; once his confederate had pleaded guilty and became available to testify, he chose to plead guilty, perhaps to ensure that he would face no more than life imprisonment or a term of years. Brady was aware of precisely what he was doing when he admitted that he had kidnaped the victim and had not released her unharmed.

It is true that Brady's counsel advised him that §1201(a) empowered the jury to impose the death penalty and that nine years later in *United States v. Jackson*, *supra*, the Court held that the jury had no such power as long as the judge could impose only a lesser penalty if

[16] [Footnote in original] Shelton v. United States, 246 F.2d 571, 572 n.2 (5th Cir. 1957) (en banc), *rev'd on confession of error on other grounds*, 356 U.S. 26 (1958).

trial was to the court or there was a plea of guilty. But these facts do not require us to set aside Brady's conviction.

Often the decision to plead guilty is heavily influenced by the defendant's appraisal of the prosecution's case against him and by the apparent likelihood of securing leniency should a guilty plea be offered and accepted. Considerations like these frequently present imponderable questions for which there are no certain answers; judgments may be made that in the light of later events seem improvident, although they were perfectly sensible at the time. The rule that a plea must be intelligently made to be valid does not require that a plea be vulnerable to later attack if the defendant did not correctly assess every relevant factor entering into his decision. A defendant is not entitled to withdraw his plea merely because he discovers long after the plea has been accepted that his calculus misapprehended the quality of the State's case or the likely penalties attached to alternative courses of action. More particularly, absent misrepresentation or other impermissible conduct by state agents [. . .], a voluntary plea of guilty intelligently made in the light of the then applicable law does not become vulnerable because later judicial decisions indicate that the plea rested on a faulty premise. A plea of guilty triggered by the expectations of a competently counseled defendant that the State will have a strong case against him is not subject to later attack because the defendant's lawyer correctly advised him with respect to the then existing law as to possible penalties but later pronouncements of the courts, as in this case, hold that the maximum penalty for the crime in question was less than was reasonably assumed at the time the plea was entered.

The fact that Brady did not anticipate *United States v. Jackson*, *supra*, does not impugn the truth or reliability of his plea. We find no requirement in the Constitution that a defendant must be permitted to disown his solemn admissions in open court that he committed the act with which he is charged simply because it later develops that the State would have had a weaker case than the defendant had thought or that the maximum penalty then assumed applicable has been held inapplicable in subsequent judicial decisions.

This is not to say that guilty plea convictions hold no hazards for the innocent or that the methods of taking guilty pleas presently employed in this country are necessarily valid in all respects. This mode of conviction is no more foolproof than full trials to the court or to the jury. Accordingly, we take great precautions against unsound results, and we should continue to do so, whether conviction is by plea or by trial. We would have serious doubts about this case if the encouragement of guilty pleas by offers of leniency substantially increased the likelihood that defendants, advised by competent counsel, would falsely condemn themselves. But our view is to the contrary and is based on our expectations that courts will satisfy themselves that pleas of guilty are voluntarily and intelligently made by competent defendants with adequate advice of counsel and that there is nothing to question the accuracy and reliability of the defendants' admissions that they committed the crimes with which they are charged. In the case before us, nothing in the record impeaches Brady's plea or suggests that his admissions in open court were anything but the truth.

Although Brady's plea of guilty may well have been motivated in part by a desire to avoid a possible death penalty, we are convinced that his plea was voluntarily and intelligently made and we have no reason to doubt that his solemn admission of guilt was truthful. [. . .]

Notes and Questions:

1. The defendant Brady ultimately received a sentence of 30 years following his guilty plea, but he was facing the possibility of a death sentence if he had opted for a jury trial. Is this sentencing discount so large as to be potentially coercive? Might an innocent person plead guilty when faced with that choice? Should the Court have addressed the question of whether inordinately large sentencing discounts could be coercive? How would one determine what qualifies as a coercive discount? Should plea bargaining in death-penalty cases be prohibited, on the grounds that it is inherently coercive?

   Consider the following scenario:

   > Imagine that you are a defense attorney and you represent a man charged with kidnapping and forcible rape. You believe that the defendant is innocent and, after investigating the case, you believe that a jury would acquit him. The prosecutor appears to share your opinion that the case is weak and offers to allow a guilty plea to simple battery. Conviction on this charge would lead to a sentence of up to thirty days imprisonment, and there is a strong possibility that the defendant would receive probation. When you inform your client of the offer, you emphasize that conviction at trial is highly improbable. But your client responds: "I can't take the chance."[17]

[17] Albert W. Alschuler, *The Prosecutor's Role in Plea Bargaining*, 36 U. Chi. L. Rev. 50, 61 (1968) (reporting an actual case).

Would you try to persuade your client not to take the deal? Why or why not? Should the system's rules be changed so as not to allow such bargains?

2. As discussed in later chapters, some foreign jurisdictions that have introduced plea bargaining have limited the sentencing discount that a defendant may receive in return for a guilty plea. England, Italy, and Russia, for example, set a discount of about one-third of either the expected or the maximum sentence for the charged offense.[18] In federal court in the United States, courts regularly give an acceptance-of-responsibility reduction to defendants who plead guilty, which reduces the expected post-trial sentence by one-fourth to one-third.[19] But even this discount is not entirely "fixed" because charge and fact bargaining, as well as departures for cooperation with the prosecution, can increase the discount significantly. Should American jurisdictions adopt clear fixed discounts to reduce the coerciveness of plea bargaining? Would such fixed discounts be able to take into consideration the various factors that might affect the verdict (e.g., how sympathetic the victim is; how sympathetic the defendant is; how credible the witnesses are)? Would fixed discounts be enforceable, particularly in systems that allow charge and fact bargaining?
3. There was evidence that Brady's plea was entered, at least in part, out of fear that he could receive the death penalty. Nine years after Brady pleaded guilty, and while his case was being reviewed on habeas, the Supreme Court struck down the death penalty provision in Section 1201(a) of the Federal Kidnapping Act, meaning that Brady would not have received the death penalty in any event. Brady therefore argued that his plea was invalid because it rested on a faulty premise—in other words, an incorrect assumption about the applicable law. How did the Court

---

[18] Sentencing Guidelines Council, Reduction in Sentence for a Guilty Plea 5-6 (2007), *at* http://www.sentencing-guidelines.gov.uk/docs/Reduction%20in%20Sentence-final.pdf (providing guidelines for English courts); Nicola Boari & Gianluca Fiorentini, *An Economic Analysis of Plea Bargaining: The Incentives of the Parties in a Mixed Penal System*, 21 Int'l Rev. L. & Econ. 213, 216 (2001) (discussing the Italian requirement that the discount be no more than one-third of the anticipated post-trial sentence); Russ. Code Crim. Proc. §316 (7) (2001, with amendments through 2005), *translation available at* http://www.legislationline.org/upload/legislations/9a/eb/3a4a5e98a67c25d4fe5eb5170513.htm (setting a maximum discount of one-third of the statutory maximum for the charged offense).

[19] *E.g.*, Stephen J. Schulhofer & Ilene H. Nagel, *Negotiated Pleas Under the Federal Sentencing Guidelines: The First Fifteen Months*, 27 Am. Crim. L. Rev. 231, 244-245 (1989).

respond to this argument? Was this response adequate in your view?

A year after *Brady* was decided, in *Santobello v. New York*, the Court affirmed its support for plea bargaining, calling it "not only an essential part of the process but a highly desirable part for many reasons." It also held that the prosecution's failure to keep its promise made under a plea agreement was grounds for vacating the judgment.

Santobello v. New York, 404 U.S. 260 (1971)

[Santobello was indicted on two felony counts of promoting gambling in the first degree and possessing gambling records in the first degree. After negotiations, the prosecutor agreed to allow Santobello to plead to possessing gambling records in the second degree, which would carry a maximum of one-year imprisonment. The prosecutor agreed to make no recommendation as to the sentence. Santobello pleaded guilty, and the court accepted the plea. Before the sentencing hearing took place, Santobello acquired new defense counsel. The new counsel moved to withdraw the guilty plea, alleging that Santobello did not know at the time of his guilty plea that evidence against him had been seized illegally. The court denied the motion and proceeded to sentence Santobello. At sentencing, a different prosecutor than the one who had negotiated the plea with Santobello represented the government. The new prosecutor recommended the maximum one-year sentence and referred to Santobello's criminal record and associations with organized crime. Defense counsel objected, pointing to the promise by the state not to make any sentence recommendation. The judge nonetheless sentenced Santobello to one year of imprisonment and stated that the prosecutor's recommendation had not influenced the sentence. The judge explained that he was instead influenced by evidence in the probation report, which portrayed Santobello as a "professional criminal" who was "unamenable to supervision in the community." The question before the Supreme Court was whether the government's breach of its promise not to recommend a sentence required a new trial.]

Mr. Chief Justice BURGER delivered the opinion of the Court.

We granted certiorari in this case to determine whether the State's failure to keep a commitment concerning the sentence recommendation on a guilty plea required a new trial. [. . .]

The disposition of criminal charges by agreement between the prosecutor and the accused, sometimes loosely called "plea bargaining," is an essential component of the administration of justice. Properly administered, it is to be encouraged. If every criminal charge were subjected to a full-scale trial, the States and the Federal Government would need to multiply by many times the number of judges and court facilities.

Disposition of charges after plea discussions is not only an essential part of the process but a highly desirable part for many reasons. It leads to prompt and largely final disposition of most criminal cases; it avoids much of the corrosive impact of enforced idleness during pre-trial confinement for those who are denied release pending trial; it protects the public from those accused persons who are prone to continue criminal conduct even while on pretrial release; and, by shortening the time between charge and disposition, it enhances whatever may be the rehabilitative prospects of the guilty when they are ultimately imprisoned. *See* Brady v. United States, 397 U.S. 742, 751-752 (1970).

However, all of these considerations presuppose fairness in securing agreement between an accused and a prosecutor. [. . .]

This phase of the process of criminal justice, and the adjudicative element inherent in accepting a plea of guilty, must be attended by safeguards to insure the defendant what is reasonably due in the circumstances. Those circumstances will vary, but a constant factor is that when a plea rests in any significant degree on a promise or agreement of the prosecutor, so that it can be said to be part of the inducement or consideration, such promise must be fulfilled.

On this record, petitioner "bargained" and negotiated for a particular plea in order to secure dismissal of more serious charges, but also on condition that no sentence recommendation would be made by the prosecutor. It is now conceded that the promise to abstain from a recommendation was made, and at this stage the prosecution is not in a good position to argue that its inadvertent breach of agreement is immaterial. The staff lawyers in a prosecutor's office have the burden of "letting the left hand know what the right hand is doing" or has done. That the breach of agreement was inadvertent does not lessen its impact.

We need not reach the question whether the sentencing judge would or would not have been influenced had he known all the details of the negotiations for the plea. He stated that the prosecutor's recommendation did not influence him and we have no reason to doubt that. Nevertheless, we conclude that the interests of justice and appropriate recognition of the duties of the prosecution in relation to promises made in the negotiation of pleas of guilty will be best served by remanding the case to the state courts for further consideration. The ultimate relief to which petitioner is entitled we leave to the discretion of the state court, which is in a better position to decide whether the circumstances of this case require only that there be specific performance of the agreement on the plea, in which case petitioner should be resentenced by a different judge, or whether, in the view of the state court, the circumstances require granting the relief sought by petitioner, i.e., the opportunity to withdraw his plea of guilty.[20] We emphasize that this is in no sense to question the fairness of the sentencing judge; the fault here rests on the prosecutor, not on the sentencing judge.

The judgment is vacated and the case is remanded for reconsideration not inconsistent with this opinion.

Mr. Justice DOUGLAS, concurring.

[. . .] Where the "plea bargain" is not kept by the prosecutor, the sentence must be vacated and the state court will decide in light of the circumstances of each case whether due process requires (a) that there be specific performance of the plea bargain or (b) that the defendant be given the option to go to trial on the original charges. One alternative may do justice in one case, and the other in a different case. In choosing a remedy, however, a court ought to accord a defendant's preference considerable, if not controlling, weight inasmuch as the fundamental rights flouted by a prosecutor's breach of a plea bargain are those of the defendant, not of the State.

Mr. Justice MARSHALL, with whom Mr. Justice BRENNAN and Mr. Justice STEWART join, concurring in part and dissenting in part.

I agree with much of the majority's opinion, but conclude that petitioner must be permitted to withdraw his guilty plea. This is the relief petitioner requested and, on the facts set out by the majority, it is a form of relief to which he is entitled.

There is no need to belabor the fact that the Constitution guarantees to all criminal defendants the right to a trial by judge or jury, or, put another way, the "right not to plead guilty." [. . .] This and other federal rights may be waived through a guilty plea, but such waivers are not lightly presumed and, in fact, are viewed with the "utmost solicitude." [. . .] Given this, I believe that where the defendant presents a

---

[20] [Footnote in original] If the state court decides to allow withdrawal of the plea, the petitioner will, of course, plead anew to the original charge on two felony counts.

reason for vacating his plea and the government has not relied on the plea to its disadvantage, the plea may be vacated and the right to trial regained at least where the motion to vacate is made prior to sentence and judgment. In other words, in such circumstances I would not deem the earlier plea to have irrevocably waived the defendant's federal constitutional right to a trial.

Here, petitioner never claimed any automatic right to withdraw a guilty plea before sentencing. Rather, he tendered a specific reason why, in his case, the plea should be vacated. His reason was that the prosecutor had broken a promise made in return for the agreement to plead guilty. When a prosecutor breaks the bargain, he undercuts the basis for the waiver of constitutional rights implicit in the plea. This, it seems to me, provides the defendant ample justification for rescinding the plea. Where a promise is "unfulfilled," *Brady v. United States*, 397 U.S. 742, 755 (1970), specifically denies that the plea "must stand." Of course, where the prosecutor has broken the plea agreement, it may be appropriate to permit the defendant to enforce the plea bargain. But that is not the remedy sought here. Rather, it seems to me that a breach of the plea bargain provides ample reason to permit the plea to be vacated.

It is worth noting that in the ordinary case where a motion to vacate is made prior to sentencing, the government has taken no action in reliance on the previously entered guilty plea and would suffer no harm from the plea's withdrawal. More pointedly, here the State claims no such harm beyond disappointed expectations about the plea itself. At least where the government itself has broken the plea bargain, this disappointment cannot bar petitioner from withdrawing his guilty plea and reclaiming his right to a trial.

I would remand the case with instructions that the plea be vacated and petitioner given an opportunity to replead to the original charges in the indictment.

Notes and Questions:

1. Why do you think Santobello requested that his plea be vacated instead of asking for the remedy of specific performance? Would he have been better off if his plea agreement had been rescinded and his guilty plea vacated? Are defendants on average more likely to prefer specific performance or rescission as a remedy for prosecutorial breach of the plea agreement?
2. Given that the sentencing judge in *Santobello* specifically stated that he was not influenced by the prosecutor's recommendation, why wasn't the prosecutorial breach a harmless error?

3. While courts have imposed only broad limits on plea bargaining, more extensive rules regulate the acceptance of a guilty plea by the court. In federal court, Rule 11 of the Federal Rules of Criminal Procedure governs the procedures that a judge must follow to ensure that a plea is validly entered.[21] The key requirements for accepting a guilty plea are discussed later in this chapter.

PRACTICE OF PLEA BARGAINING IN THE UNITED STATES

PARTICIPANTS

In most cases in the United States, the only participants in plea bargaining are the prosecutor and defense attorney, who in turn consults with his or her client. The negotiations are usually conducted on the phone, in the prosecutor's office, or in the courtroom. In most jurisdictions, victims play no role in plea bargaining. Only a few states by statute or case law require prosecutors to inform or consult the victims about plea agreements with the defendant.[22] There are two indirect ways in which a victim may influence the outcome of plea negotiations, however. For example, some jurisdictions, including federal courts, require the preparation of pre-sentence reports, which are prepared by probation officers and include victim impact statements. These reports may influence a court's decision to accept or reject the plea bargain and the sentence recommendation attached to it. In addition, some states mandate restitution to victims as part of the punishment and prohibit the bargaining away of restitution.

The defendant is often absent from the negotiations between the defense attorney and the prosecutor, but ethical rules instruct defense attorneys to inform their clients of a proposed plea agreement.[23] Commentators have called for greater checks on defense representation dur-

---

[21] For a discussion of the history of the Rule, as well as a critique of the Rule, see Julian A. Cook, III, *Federal Guilty Pleas Under Rule 11: The Unfulfilled Promise of the Post-*Boykin *Era*, 77 Notre Dame L. Rev. 597 (2002).

[22] Ind. Code §35-35-3-5; Me. Rev. Stat. tit. 15, §812, tit. 17-A, §§1172, 1173; R.I. Gen. Laws §§12-28-3(14); 12-28-4.1; State v. Casey, 44 P.3d 756, 762-763 (Utah 2002); W. Va. Code §61-11A-6(a). *See generally* U.S. Dept. of Justice, Victim Input into Plea Agreements (2002), *at* http://www.ojp.usdoj.gov/ovc/publications/bulletins/legalseries/bulletin7/ncj189188.pdf.

[23] Model Rules of Prof'l Conduct R. 4.1; ABA Standards for Criminal Justice: Defense Function §4-6.2(a), (b), *at* http://www.abanet.org/crimjust/standards/dfunc_blk.html#6.2.

ing the plea bargaining process, because resource constraints provide an incentive for overburdened defense attorneys to urge their clients to plead guilty even when this may not be in the client's best interest.[24] Prosecutors have a similar incentive to resolve cases as quickly as possible, which could lead to unduly favorable plea agreements. Prosecutorial guidelines attempt to place limits on charge bargaining and other prosecutorial concessions during negotiations, but it is unclear how successful such guidelines have been in constraining prosecutorial behavior in practice.[25] Although both the defense and the prosecution also have an incentive to "bluff" during plea negotiations, ethical rules prevent both sides from knowingly making false statements during the negotiations.[26]

Judges are generally not involved in plea negotiations. A number of jurisdictions specifically prohibit their participation.[27] One reason for this prohibition is the concern that by participating in the negotiations, judges may compromise their impartiality. Moreover, because judges are the ultimate arbiters of the punishment the defendant will receive, their participation in the negotiations would raise concerns about coercion of the defendant's plea decision.[28]

While judges generally do not take part in the actual negotiations, they do review the validity of the guilty plea. In a hearing held in open court, the judge examines the defendant and evidence related to the case to ensure that the guilty plea is intelligent, knowing, voluntary, and based on the facts of the case.[29] Judges also decide whether to accept or

---

[24] *E.g.*, Stephanos Bibas, *Plea Bargaining Outside the Shadow of the Law*, 117 Harv. L. Rev. 2463, 2470-2482 (2004).

[25] *See* David Boerner & Roxanne Lieb, *Sentencing Reform in the Other Washington*, 28 Crime & Just. 71, 73 (2001) (suggesting that prosecutorial guidelines are unlikely to be successful); Julie R. O'Sullivan, *In Defense of the U.S. Sentencing Guidelines' Modified Real-Offense System*, 91 Nw. U. L. Rev. 1342, 1425-1432 (1997) (same). *But see* Stephen J. Schulhofer, *Is Plea Bargaining Inevitable?*, 97 Harv. L. Rev. 1037, 1038 (1984) (arguing that prosecutorial policy limiting plea bargaining is likely to be fairly effective).

[26] Model Rules of Prof'l Conduct R. 4.1; ABA Standards for Criminal Justice §§3-4.1(c), 4-6.2.

[27] Fed. R. Crim. Proc. 11(e)(1); Jenia Iontcheva Turner, *Judicial Participation in Plea Negotiations: A Comparative View*, 54 Am. J. Comp. L. 199, 202 n.6 (2006) (listing state jurisdictions that prohibit judicial participation).

[28] *E.g.*, State v. Bouie, 817 So. 2d 48, 53-54 (La. 2002); Richard Klein, *Due Process Denied: Judicial Coercion in the Plea Bargaining Process*, 32 Hofstra L. Rev. 1349 (2004).

[29] Judges' ability to perform a thorough review is limited by their dependence on the parties to present them with evidence related to the case. Because the parties have already agreed on a deal, they are unlikely to present any evidence that might disturb it.

reject the plea agreement. Unless the prosecution and the defense have agreed to a specific sentence[30]—something that occurs rarely, because judges dislike such agreements—judges retain the ultimate sentencing discretion. Although the prosecution will typically make a sentencing recommendation pursuant to the plea agreement, judges are not bound by it.[31]

The sentencing discretion of judges has important consequences for plea bargaining. The greater the judge's discretion, the less able prosecutors are to make firm commitments about sentencing when negotiating with the defense. In the United States, judges have relatively narrow sentencing discretion. A number of American states, as well as the federal system, have laws requiring that judges impose mandatory minimum sentences for certain offenses. In addition, a number of jurisdictions have advisory or binding sentencing guidelines, which further narrow judicial sentencing discretion. Such laws and guidelines allow the parties to predict more accurately the range in which defendants might be sentenced (based on the charges filed), and to bargain accordingly. As subsequent chapters discuss, in civil-law countries, prosecutors are less able to manipulate sentencing outcomes through their charging decisions, in large part because of the broad sentencing discretion of civil-law judges.

Notes and Questions:

1. A number of commentators have argued that prosecutors, defense counsel, and judges may all have an incentive to conclude plea bargains even when those bargains are not in the best interests of the defendant or the public. What pressures on defense attorneys, prosecutors, and judges may distort plea bargaining outcomes?[32] What protections can be enacted to ensure that defense attorneys act in their clients' best interests and prosecutors and judges act in the public interest when deciding whether to recommend, enter, or approve a plea agreement?
2. What role should victims play in plea bargaining? Should they have a veto over any proposed plea agreement?[33] Should prosecutors be required to consult with victims before entering into a plea

---

[30] *See* Fed. R. Crim. Proc. 11(c)(1)(C).

[31] *See* Fed. R. Crim. Proc. 11(c)(1)(B).

[32] *See, e.g.*, Bibas, *supra* note 24, at 2470-2482.

[33] George P. Fletcher, With Justice for Some: Victims' Rights in Criminal Trials 248 (1995).

agreement?[34] What are the disadvantages to such victim involvement? Are there ways in which victim satisfaction with the plea bargaining process might be improved?[35]

3. Should judges be more involved in the plea discussions? What are the advantages and disadvantages of increased judicial participation?
4. Should all prosecutors' sentencing recommendations made pursuant to a plea agreement be binding on the judge? Or is the current system, wherein (in the absence of an agreement upon a specific sentence) the judge has the ultimate sentencing discretion, the better approach? What are the advantages and disadvantages of each?
5. Should prosecutors' offices promulgate plea bargaining guidelines? What form might these take? Consider the following provisions in the Department of Justice's U.S. Attorney's Manual (2007), which provides guidelines for federal prosecutors:

9-16.300 Plea Agreements—Federal Rule of Criminal Procedure 11(e)

Federal Rule of Criminal Procedure 11(e) recognizes and codifies the concept of plea agreements. Plea agreements should honestly reflect the totality and seriousness of the defendant's conduct, and any departure to which the prosecutor is agreeing, and must be accomplished through appropriate Sentencing Guideline provisions. [. . .] The Department's policy is to stipulate only to facts that accurately represent the defendant's conduct. [. . .]

9-27.300 Selecting Charges—Charging Most Serious Offenses

Except as provided in USAM 9-27.330, (precharge plea agreements), once the decision to prosecute has been made, the attorney for the government should charge, or should recommend that the grand jury charge, the most serious offense that is consistent with the nature of the defendant's conduct, and that is likely to result in a sustainable conviction. If mandatory minimum sentences are also involved, their effect must be considered, keeping in mind the fact that a mandatory minimum is

[34] Sarah N. Welling, *Victim Participation in Plea Bargains*, 65 Wash. U. L.Q. 301, 304 (1987).

[35] *See, e.g.*, Michael M. O'Hear, *Victims and Plea Bargaining: From Consultation to Guidelines*, 91 Marq. L. Rev. 323, 324-326 (2007).

statutory and generally overrules a guideline. The "most serious" offense is generally that which yields the highest range under the sentencing guidelines. [. . .]

9-27.320 Additional Charges

Except as hereafter provided, the attorney for the government should also charge, or recommend that the grand jury charge, other offenses only when, in his/her judgement, additional charges:

Are necessary to ensure that the information or indictment:
- Adequately reflects the nature and extent of the criminal conduct involved; and
- Provides the basis for an appropriate sentence under all the circumstances of the case; or
- Will significantly enhance the strength of the government's case against the defendant or a codefendant.

9-27.420 Plea Agreements—Considerations to Be Weighed

In determining whether it would be appropriate to enter into a plea agreement, the attorney for the government should weigh all relevant considerations, including:

- The defendant's willingness to cooperate in the investigation or prosecution of others;
- The defendant's history with respect to criminal activity;
- The nature and seriousness of the offense or offenses charged;
- The defendant's remorse or contrition and his/her willingness to assume responsibility for his/her conduct;
- The desirability of prompt and certain disposition of the case;
- The likelihood of obtaining a conviction at trial;
- The probable effect on witnesses;
- The probable sentence or other consequences if the defendant is convicted;
- The public interest in having the case tried rather than disposed of by a guilty plea;
- The expense of trial and appeal;
- The need to avoid delay in the disposition of other pending cases; and
- The effect upon the victim's right to restitution.

9-27.440 Plea Agreements When Defendant Denies Guilt

The attorney for the government should not, except with the approval of the Assistant Attorney General with supervisory responsibility over the subject matter, enter into a plea agreement if the defendant maintains his/her innocence with respect to the charge or charges to which he/she offers to plead guilty. In a case in which the defendant tenders a plea of guilty but denies committing the offense to which he/she offers to plead guilty, the attorney for the government should make an offer of proof of all facts known to the government to support the conclusion that the defendant is in fact guilty.

Do the DOJ guidelines adequately limit prosecutorial discretion to enter into plea bargains that are unfair or otherwise contrary to the public interest? Do you believe it is possible to draft guidelines that would be more effective in attaining these objectives? What would such guidelines look like?

6. Sentencing rules have an important influence on the extent and nature of plea bargaining in a particular jurisdiction. Until recently, in U.S. federal courts, mandatory statutory minimum sentences combined with binding sentencing guidelines to limit the sentencing discretion of judges and to give prosecutors great influence over the sentence through their charging and bargaining decisions. But in a 2005 case, *United States v. Booker*, the Supreme Court held that judicial sentencing under mandatory sentencing guidelines was unconstitutional and that the federal sentencing guidelines had to be construed as being merely advisory.[36] Commentators have suggested that *Booker* has shifted influence over sentencing from prosecutors back to judges, decreased the predictability of sentencing, and lowered the sentencing differential between trials and guilty pleas.[37] Consequently, some have argued, defendants are more likely to choose to go to trial and less likely to plead guilty. By affirming judicial authority to sentence outside the guidelines, *Booker* and its progeny are also likely to influence the nature of plea bargaining discussions. Because judges are freer to consider the various individual circumstances of defendants, plea discussions are more likely to focus on those individual characteristics, rather than merely on the nature of the offense and the prior record of the defendant.[38]

---

[36] 543 U.S. 220, 244 (2005).

[37] *E.g.*, Stephanos Bibas, *White-Collar Plea Bargaining and Sentencing After* Booker, 47 Wm. & Mary L. Rev. 721, 731 (2005).

[38] Laurie L. Levenson, *A Guide to Negotiating Federal Guilty Pleas in a Post-*Gall *Sentencing World*, 23 Crim. Just. 40, 42 (2008).

TIMING

Plea bargains may be reached either before or after the charges are filed. Typically, plea bargains occur before trial, but it is possible to reach an agreement during trial, during jury deliberations, or even after trial.[39] Prosecutors typically prefer to make bargains as early in the process as possible, in the interest of saving time and resources.

SUBJECT MATTER

Some jurisdictions limit the types of cases in which plea bargaining can occur. For example, California and Mississippi do not permit plea bargaining in serious violent and sexual assault cases.[40] Other states restrict "charge bargaining"[41]—promises by the prosecution to dismiss or modify charges in exchange for a guilty plea or cooperation by the defendant. Yet other jurisdictions limit the sentence reductions that may result from a plea bargain in certain serious cases.[42] But such restrictions are the exception rather than the rule. On the whole, plea bargaining in the United States occurs in all kinds of cases and with little regulation of its scope.

The bargain may concern a wide variety of concessions on each side. As part of a "charge bargain," the prosecutor may offer to drop certain counts, to reduce charges, or not to file charges in the future against the defendant or a third party. Under a "sentence bargain," the prosecutor may agree to recommend a particular sentence or a sentence cap to the judge, or to make no sentencing recommendation. Unlike in some civil-law countries like Italy and Russia, there is no established sentencing discount for a guilty plea.[43] Research of federal sentencing practices places the average sentencing discount for pleading guilty at around 35 percent for all cases (meaning that the sentence imposed after a plea bargain is 35 percent shorter than the sentence given to defendants who are convicted after trial), or 50 percent for cases in which the defendant

---

[39] G. Nicholas Herman, Plea Bargaining 69, §6:10 (2d ed. 2004).

[40] Cal. Pen. Code §1192.7(2)-(3); Miss. Stat. §43-21-555.

[41] Nev. Rev. Stat. §§483.560 (2)(c); 484.3792 (4).

[42] N.Y. Crim. Proc. Law §220.10.

[43] Indeed, such a standard discount for pleading guilty may be unconstitutional because it may unduly burden the right to jury trial. *Cf.* Corbitt v. New Jersey, 439 U.S. 212, 226-228 (1978) (Stewart, J., concurring).

also cooperates with the prosecution.[44] These statistics, however, do not account for the effects of charge bargaining on the ultimate sentence. A recent study of charge bargaining in North Carolina state courts found that charge bargaining itself results in sentence reductions as high as 79 percent of the post-trial sentences for certain crimes.[45] In addition to offering standard charging or sentencing concessions, the prosecutor may also negotiate about the location where the sentence will be served, the conditions to be imposed for probation or supervised release, and other collateral consequences of the guilty plea (e.g., sex offender registration).[46]

In exchange for concessions by the prosecutor, the defendant agrees to plead guilty and waive a number of trial-related rights. Courts have allowed defendants to waive their rights to trial even while refusing to admit guilt (the so-called no contest or nolo contendere pleas) or actively professing innocence (the so-called *Alford* pleas[47]). In *North Carolina v. Alford*, the Supreme Court explained the constitutionality of "nolo contendere" and *Alford* pleas as follows:

> Implicit in the nolo contendere cases is a recognition that the Constitution does not bar imposition of a prison sentence upon an accused who is unwilling expressly to admit his guilt but who, faced with the grim alternatives, is willing to waive his trial and accept the sentence. . . . The fact that [Alford's] plea was denominated a plea of guilty rather than a plea of nolo contendere is of no constitutional significance. . . . Thus, while most pleas of guilty consist of both a waiver of trial and an express admission of guilt, the latter element is not a constitutional requisite to the imposition of a criminal penalty. An individual accused of crime may voluntarily, knowingly, and understandingly consent to the imposition of a prison sentence even if he is unwilling or unable to admit his participation in the acts constituting the crime.

---

[44] U.S. Sentencing Commission, Preliminary Post-*Kimbrough/Gall* Data Report tbl.5A, *at* http://www.ussc.gov/USSC_Kimbrough_Gall_Report_May_08_Final.pdf [hereinafter *Kimbrough/Gall* Report]; Bibas, *supra* note 24, 2488-2489; O'Sullivan, *supra* note 25, at 1415 & n.274.

[45] Ronald F. Wright & Rodney L. Engen, *The Effects of Depth and Distance in a Criminal Code on Charging, Sentencing, and Prosecutor Power*, 84 N.C. L. Rev. 1935, 1971-1972 & tbl. 7 (2006) (noting also that "charge reductions prior to sentencing have a much greater impact on sentence duration than does the choice among sentencing options under the grid").

[46] Michael M. O'Hear & Andrea Kupfer Schneider, *Dispute Resolution in Criminal Law*, 91 Marq. L. Rev. 1, 3 (2007).

[47] North Carolina v. Alford, 400 U.S. 25, 36 (1970).

Although the Court found no contest and *Alford* pleas to be constitutional, it noted that judges ought to be especially careful in assessing the factual basis for a plea when the defendant refuses to admit guilt. In other words, even if the defendant refuses to admit guilt, courts are charged with determining that sufficient facts exist to demonstrate that the defendant did, in fact, commit the crime. Such scrutiny is needed to protect innocent defendants from pleading guilty and to ensure that plea decisions are made intelligently and knowingly.

Defendants may also enter a "conditional plea" of guilty or nolo contendere. Under Federal Rule of Criminal Procedure 11(a)(2), a defendant may, with the consent of the court and the government, plead guilty or no contest, but reserve in writing the right to appeal an adverse determination of a specified trial motion, such as a motion to suppress evidence obtained in violation of the Constitution. A defendant who prevails on appeal may then withdraw the plea.

Cooperation Agreements. In addition to agreeing to plead guilty, defendants may also agree to cooperate with the government in the investigation and prosecution of other defendants or crimes. In the United States, the plea and sentencing hearings are separate proceedings. There is thus a time lag between the hearing at which the defendant pleads guilty and the hearing at which he is sentenced. This provides an opportunity for the defendant to provide assistance in time to receive a sentencing credit. Rules such as Federal Rule of Criminal Procedure 35(B) offer an additional opportunity for crediting assistance rendered after sentencing:

> (b) Reducing a Sentence for Substantial Assistance.
>
> (1) In General. Upon the government's motion made within one year of sentencing, the court may reduce a sentence if the defendant, after sentencing, provided substantial assistance in investigating or prosecuting another person.
>
> (2) Later Motion. Upon the government's motion made more than one year after sentencing, the court may reduce a sentence if the defendant's substantial assistance involved:
>
> (A) information not known to the defendant until one year or more after sentencing;
>
> (B) information provided by the defendant to the government within one year of sentencing, but which did not become useful to the government until more than one year after sentencing; or
>
> (C) information the usefulness of which could not reasonably have been anticipated by the defendant until

> more than one year after sentencing and which was promptly provided to the government after its usefulness was reasonably apparent to the defendant.

In the federal system, the court cannot grant the defendant a sentence reduction for his cooperation unless and until the prosecutor files a motion stating that the defendant has provided substantial assistance in the investigation or prosecution of another person who has committed an offense.[48] A prosecutorial motion certifying that the defendant provided substantial assistance may allow judges to impose a sentence below the (now advisory) Sentencing Guidelines range[49] and even below any applicable mandatory statutory minimums.[50] These "substantial assistance departures" offer significant benefits to defendants. A 2005 report by the Sentencing Commission found that "offenders receiving a substantial assistance departure experienced the largest reduction among all types of below range sentences. Sentences for offenders receiving substantial assistance reductions [. . .] had a median 28-month sentence reduction from the minimum of the applicable guideline range.

---

[48] Wade v. United States, 504 U.S. 181 (1992) (citing U.S.S.G. 5K1.1. and requiring a government motion to depart from a Sentencing Guidelines range on the basis of the defendant's cooperation with the government); U.S.S.G. §5K1.1; 18 U.S.C. §3553(e) (requiring a specific government motion to depart from an applicable mandatory minimum sentence on the basis of the defendant's cooperation with the government).

[49] Section 5K1.1 of the United States Sentencing Guidelines authorizes a downward departure from the Guidelines range for "substantial assistance":

> Upon motion of the government stating that the defendant has provided substantial assistance in the investigation or prosecution of another person who has committed an offense, the court may depart from the guidelines.
>
> (a) The appropriate reduction shall be determined by the court for reasons stated that may include, but are not limited to, consideration of the following:
>
> (1) the court's evaluation of the significance and usefulness of the defendant's assistance, taking into consideration the government's evaluation of the assistance rendered;
>
> (2) the truthfulness, completeness, and reliability of any information or testimony provided by the defendant;
>
> (3) the nature and extent of the defendant's assistance;
>
> (4) any injury suffered, or any danger or risk of injury to the defendant or his family resulting from his assistance;
>
> (5) the timeliness of the defendant's assistance.

U.S.S.G. §5K1.1.

[50] 18 U.S.C. §3553 (e). The prosecutor must file separate motions under U.S.S.G. §5K1.1 and 18 U.S.C. §3553(e) for the defendant to receive both benefits.

This results in a 50.0 percent median decrease in the otherwise applicable guideline minimum."[51]

While a prosecutor will typically recommend a particular sentencing discount for the defendant's cooperation, the court, again, retains ultimate sentencing discretion.[52] Apart from filing substantial assistance motions with the court, the prosecution may reward cooperation by dropping or reducing charges, which often results in a significantly lower sentence.[53]

A study by the Federal Sentencing Commission reports the percentage of federal criminal cases that involved the granting of substantial assistance motions between 2005 and 2007.[54] Substantial assistance departures from the Guidelines were granted in 14.5 percent of all criminal cases. The rates are significantly higher for certain offenses, as detailed in the chart below. Moreover, these numbers do not include cases in which prosecutors rewarded cooperation with a charge reduction.

§5K1.1 SUBSTANTIAL ASSISTANCE MOTIONS GRANTED BETWEEN FISCAL YEAR 2005, POST-*BOOKER*,[55] AND 2007 IN U.S. FEDERAL COURT (AS PERCENT OF ALL CASES IN EACH OFFENSE CATEGORY)[56]

Drug trafficking	25.9%
Arson	27%
Kidnapping/hostage taking	35.3%
Bribery	31.8%
Racketeering/extortion	23.5%
Money laundering	25.6%
Antitrust	57.9%

The same study confirmed that substantial assistance departures yield significant sentence reductions for defendants. For the same

---

[51] U.S. Sentencing Commission, 2005 Annual Report ch.5, *at* http://www.ussc.gov/ANNRPT/2005/chpt5_05.pdf.

[52] *See, e.g.*, United States v. Saenz, 429 F. Supp. 2d 1081 (N.D. Iowa 2006).

[53] *See, e.g.*, United States v. Hammer, 940 F.2d 1141 (8th Cir. 1991) (J. Heaney, concurring).

[54] *Kimbrough/Gall* Report, *supra* note 44, at tbl. 3A.

[55] That is, after January 12, 2005, the date of the *Booker* decision.

[56] *Kimbrough/Gall* Report, *supra* note 44, at tbl. 3A.

reporting period, the median substantial assistance departure was 29 months, or 48.2 percent.[57] These numbers varied by offense, as follows:

§5K1.1 SUBSTANTIAL ASSISTANCE CASES: DEGREE OF DECREASE FOR OFFENDERS IN EACH PRIMARY OFFENSE CATEGORY, BETWEEN FISCAL YEAR 2005, POST-*BOOKER*, AND 2007[58]

Offense Type	Median Decrease in Months from Guideline Minimum	Median Percent Decrease from Guideline Minimum
Drug trafficking	40.0	43.9%
Arson	28.0	47.3%
Kidnapping/hostage taking	76.5	44.0%
Bribery	18.0	86.7%
Racketeering/extortion	31.0	51.4%
Money laundering	23.0	59.9%
Antitrust	10.0	72.2%

Plea agreements that condition a sentencing discount on the defendant's cooperation are often quite vague. They typically state simply that the defendant will cooperate with the government in a particular case or that he will testify truthfully in a certain proceeding. Such agreements ordinarily leave the prosecution with the sole discretion to decide whether to move the court for a sentence reduction pursuant to the bargain.[59] If the agreement does leave such discretion with the prosecution, when a dispute about the defendant's performance under the plea agreement arises, and the prosecution believes that the defendant did not cooperate sufficiently in order to receive the bargained-for sentencing benefit, the defendant may not have the opportunity to argue otherwise to the court.[60]

[57] *Id.* at tbl. 5A.

[58] *Id.*

[59] *See, e.g.*, United States v. Garcia-Bonilla, 11 F.3d 45, 47 (5th Cir. 1993).

[60] The only exception to this rule is when the prosecutorial decision was completely arbitrary or when an unconstitutional motive underlay the government's refusal to credit the defendant's performance. Wade v. United States, 504 U.S. 181 (1992); *Garcia-Bonilla*, 11 F.3d at 45.

Prosecutors view cooperation agreements as indispensable tools in the prosecution of organized crime. Defendants who participate in organized crime face a number of real risks if they assist the government, and they would rarely agree to cooperate if not for an incentive like a substantially lower sentence. Prosecutors point out that, without the cooperation of insiders, it would be very difficult, if not impossible, to bring down large-scale or sophisticated conspiracies. Prosecutors further argue that "substantial assistance" sentence reductions are justified on a moral level, because the cooperating defendant is helping bring down a criminal organization of which he was a part, which arguably reduces his culpability or shows that he is more likely to be rehabilitated.[61]

Yet other commentators have criticized cooperation agreements on a number of grounds. First, because such agreements are generally open-ended, they are said to leave too much discretion in the hands of prosecutors.[62] Cooperation agreements are also criticized for producing unwarranted sentencing disparities between similarly situated defendants. The Sentencing Commission has repeatedly found inconsistency in the way substantial assistance motions are used. A 1994 report concluded that substantial assistance rates varied greatly by judicial circuit and district, and that they varied for several defendant demographic characteristics, most notably race and citizenship status.[63] More generally, commentators have criticized the lack of public scrutiny over the propriety and fairness of cooperation agreements.[64]

---

[61] I thank prosecutors at the U.S. Attorney's Office of the Northern District of Texas for raising these points.

[62] *See, e.g.*, Daniel C. Richman, *Cooperating Clients*, 56 Ohio St. L.J. 69, 96-110 (1995); Alexandra Natapoff, *Snitching: The Institutional and Communal Consequences*, 73 U. Cin. L. Rev. 645, 666 (2004) ("While written cooperation agreements are enforceable, many aspects of a cooperation remain unwritten, discretionary, and impossible to litigate. More broadly, informant deals are contingent upon police or prosecutor satisfaction with an informant's usefulness, and therefore the benefits to be conferred remain indeterminate and discretionary. Ironically, one of the most powerful protections available to informants may not be the court but the market: police who "burn" their snitches or prosecutors whose rewards are meager may have difficulty recruiting future informants.").

[63] Linda Drazga Maxfield & John H. Kramer, Substantial Assistance: An Empirical Yardstick Gauging Equity in Current Federal Policy and Practice 5 (U.S. Sent. Comm'n 1998), *at* http://www.ussc.gov/publicat/5kreport.pdf. The most recent study of substantial assistance departures granted in different federal circuits shows that at least geographic disparities continue. *Kimbrough/Gall* Report, *supra* note 44. *See generally* Ian Weinstein, *Regulating the Market for Snitches*, 47 Buff. L. Rev. 563, 564 (1999).

[64] Maxfield & Kramer, *supra* note 63, at 20; Daniel Richman, *Cooperating Defendants: The Costs and Benefits of Purchasing Information from Scoundrels*, 8 Fed. Sent. Rep. 292, 294 (1996); Ellen Yaroshefsky, *Cooperation with Federal Prosecutors: Experiences*

Ad Hoc Plea Bargaining. Under so-called ad hoc plea bargaining, defendants may accept a punishment that the judge would not be authorized to impose after a contested trial.[65] For example, a defendant may agree to (1) contribute a specified sum of money to a governmental agency or a charity; (2) surrender collateral rights, such as the right to certain property, right to raise his children, or right to engage in a particular profession; (3) submit to a shaming punishment; or (4) leave the jurisdiction.[66] Such plea bargains are commonly struck, even though they are often of doubtful legality.[67]

Waiving Rights. As part of a plea agreement, the defendant agrees to waive a number of rights. Certain waivers are inherent in the decision to plead guilty. When a defendant pleads guilty, he waives the right to a jury trial, to confront adverse witnesses, to be protected from compelled self-incrimination, to testify and present evidence, and to compel the attendance of witnesses. In addition, courts have held that defendants may agree to waive certain other rights, including the right to appeal their conviction;[68] the right not to be placed in double jeopardy;[69] the right not to have statements made during plea negotiations admitted into evidence at a later trial;[70] the right to be free from prosecution of any crime for which the statute of limitation has expired; [71] the right to interview the victim;[72] the right to be represented by counsel at the plea hearing;[73] and the right to file a civil action related to the investigation or prosecution of their case.[74]

---

of Truth Telling and Embellishment, 68 Fordham L. Rev. 917, 927 (1999); Natapoff, *supra* note 62, at 646.

[65] Joseph A. Colquitt, *Ad Hoc Plea Bargaining*, 75 Tul. L. Rev. 695 (2001).

[66] *Id.* at 716-735.

[67] *Id.* at 697.

[68] United States v. Guevara, 941 F.2d 1299 (4th Cir. 1991); State v. Ethington, 592 P.2d 768 (Ariz. 1979).

[69] United States v. Broce, 488 U.S. 563 (1989); Novaton v. State, 634 So. 2d 607 (Fla. 1994); People v. Allen, 658 N.E.2d 1012 (N.Y. 1995).

[70] United States v. Mezzanatto, 513 U.S. 196 (1995); United States v. Burch, 156 F.3d 1315 (D.C. Cir. 1998).

[71] Cowan v. Superior Court, 926 P.2d 438 (Cal. 1996).

[72] State v. Draper, 784 P.2d 259 (Ariz. 1989).

[73] Iowa v. Tovar, 541 U.S. 77 (2004).

[74] Newton v. Rumery, 480 U.S. 386, 394 (1987) (holding that release-dismissal agreements—plea agreements in which a criminal defendant released his right to file a civil

Defendants cannot bargain away all rights, however.[75] For example, they cannot waive their right to appeal on the grounds that they received ineffective assistance of counsel, that they were sentenced on the basis of race, or that their sentence exceeded the statutory maximum. In some jurisdictions, defendants also cannot waive their right to appeal a constitutional speedy trial claim.[76]

Package Deals. At times, bargains involve concessions that have been challenged as undermining the voluntariness of the guilty plea. A common example of such bargains is the so-called package deal or wired plea. In a package deal, the government offers to dismiss or reduce charges or recommend a more lenient sentence for one suspect in exchange for a plea agreement with one or more other suspects. Thus, the plea agreements are one package or "wired" to one another. Courts have repeatedly held that wired pleas are not involuntary even where defendants enter the pleas in order to secure more lenient treatment of a relative or loved one.[77] As long as the prosecution has probable cause to arrest and prosecute both the pleading defendant and the other suspects in a related crime, and "there is no suggestion that the government conducted itself in bad faith in an effort to generate additional leverage over the defendant,"[78] wired pleas are constitutional.

Notes and Questions:

1. As later chapters discuss, many foreign jurisdictions limit the categories of cases in which plea bargaining can occur. Most prohibit plea bargaining in cases of homicide and other serious

---

action under 42 U.S.C. §1983 in return for a prosecutor's dismissal of pending criminal charges—are not per se unconstitutional).

[75] Nancy Jean King, *Priceless Process: Nonnegotiable Features of Criminal Litigation*, 47 UCLA L. Rev. 113 (1999).

[76] People v. Callahan, 604 N.E.2d 108, 113 (N.Y. 1992) (holding that "a bargained-for waiver of the right to appeal is ineffective to the extent it impairs the defendant's ability to obtain appellate review of a constitutional speedy trial claim").

[77] This is the case even where the spouse/relative/loved one is sick or pregnant. *E.g.*, United States v. Pollard, 959 F.2d 1011 (1992); United States v. Clark, 931 F.2d 292, 294-295 (5th Cir. 1991) (holding that the defendant was not coerced to enter guilty plea even where the government threatened to indict his "sick, pregnant, and innocent" wife; there was no evidence that the government was insincere in considering the prosecution of the wife); United States v. Marquez, 909 F.2d 738, 742 (2d Cir. 1990) (citing cases from several circuits).

[78] *Pollard*, 959 F.2d at 1011.

violent crimes. Would such limitations be useful in the American context? Why or why not?

2. Should American jurisdictions prohibit certain kinds of plea bargains, such as package deals, charge bargains, or fact bargains? What are their costs and benefits, and do the benefits outweigh the costs?
3. Should prosecutors be able to "buy" witness testimony by promising leniency? What does this do to the accuracy of the testimony? In *United States v. Stapleton*, a Tenth Circuit panel held that prosecutors had violated a federal anti-bribery statute by promising leniency to a prospective witness in exchange for his testimony.[79] The Tenth Circuit sitting *en banc* reversed the decision, holding that the federal statute prohibiting bribery of witnesses does not apply to U.S. attorneys.[80] Do you agree with the outcome of the appellate panel decision or the *en banc* decision in *Stapleton*? If it is wrong to pay for testimony, why is it permissible to procure it through sentence or charge discounts? Consider that many countries do not allow bargains for testimony (see, e.g., the case of *Enomoto v. Japan*, discussed in Chapter 4).

CONDITIONS FOR VALIDITY OF A GUILTY PLEA

After the prosecutor and defense reach a plea agreement, the defendant appears in court to enter a guilty plea. Judges are required to examine the guilty plea carefully for its validity. Because the guilty plea involves the waiver of a number of rights and privileges, the court must ascertain that this waiver is voluntary and knowing.[81] The court must also develop a record supporting this conclusion.[82] Rules of procedure impose additional requirements for a valid plea. The court must inform the defendant of the rights the defendant is giving up by pleading guilty and of some of the consequences of the guilty plea. Finally, to minimize the possibility that an innocent defendant pleads guilty to a crime he did not commit, rules require that the guilty plea rests on a factual basis. These requirements are examined in greater detail below.

[79] 144 F.3d 1343 (1998).

[80] 165 F.3d 1297 (1999).

[81] Boykin v. Alabama, 395 U.S. 238 (1969).

[82] *Id.*

VOLUNTARINESS AND KNOWLEDGE

A voluntary plea cannot be produced by physical or mental coercion, deception, or improper promises.[83] But the mere possibility of a more severe sentence upon conviction after trial will not invalidate a guilty plea.[84] Courts do not presume coercion even when the defendant maintains his innocence at the plea hearing and asserts that he is pleading guilty merely to avoid the possibility of a substantially harsher sentence after trial. As long as a sufficient factual basis exists for the plea, it will not be considered involuntary.[85] Similarly, if the defendant is facing several charges for the same act, as a result of a prosecutorial decision to "overcharge" and gain leverage in bargaining, this does not render the plea involuntary, as long as the prosecutor has probable cause to file each charge.[86] Even where the prosecutor expressly threatens to bring additional charges against a defendant if the defendant refuses to accept a plea offer, this is not likely to invalidate the resulting guilty plea, unless the prosecutor lacks probable cause to bring the additional charges or is acting on an unjustifiable basis such as race, religion or another arbitrary classification.[87]

A guilty plea entered in response to a threat by the prosecutor to indict the defendant's wife or children may also pass the voluntariness test. As discussed above, as long as the prosecutor has probable cause to prosecute all of the persons involved and is not acting in bad faith, the guilty plea will be upheld, although the court will conduct "a more searching inquiry" into the voluntariness of the plea.[88] Similarly, if the

---

[83] "(A) plea of guilty entered by one fully aware of the direct consequences, including the actual value of any commitments made to him by the court, prosecutor, or his own counsel, must stand unless induced by threats (or promises to discontinue improper harassment), misrepresentation (including unfulfilled or unfulfillable promises), or perhaps by promises that are by their nature improper as having no proper relationship to the prosecutor's business (e.g. bribes)." Shelton v. United States, 246 F.2d 571, 572 n.2 (5th Cir. 1957) (*en banc*), *rev'd on confession of error on other grounds*, 356 U.S. 26 (1958).

[84] Brady v. United States, 397 U.S. 742, 755 (1970). (holding that "a plea of guilty is not invalid merely because entered to avoid the possibility of a death penalty").

[85] North Carolina v. Alford, 400 U.S. 25 (1970).

[86] *See* Bordenkircher v. Hayes, 434 U.S. 357 (1978).

[87] *Id.* The defendant in *Bordenkircher* did not plead guilty, and the opinion did not squarely address the voluntariness of a guilty plea. But when read together with *Brady*, *Bordenkircher* suggests that if a defendant pleads guilty and then claims that his plea was involuntary because it was based on a prosecutorial threat to bring additional charges, he is unlikely to prevail. *See* Wayne R. LaFave et al., Principles of Criminal Procedure: Post-Investigation 442-443 (2004).

[88] United States v. Pollard, 959 F.2d 1011 (D.C. Cir. 1992).

prosecutor requires that multiple co-defendants all agree to plead guilty as part of a package deal, the resulting guilty pleas are likely to be upheld. Courts have recognized, however, that "a careful inquiry into the totality of circumstances surrounding [such] plea[s]" is necessary because such pleas are "fraught with danger."[89]

In a number of jurisdictions, involvement of the judge in plea negotiations can render the guilty plea involuntary.[90] The Federal Rules of Criminal Procedure specifically prohibit judicial involvement in plea negotiations. The Federal Rules Advisory Committee explained this decision by pointing primarily to the potential coercive effect of judicial involvement: "[The judge's] awesome power to impose a substantially longer or even maximum sentence in excess of that proposed is present whether referred to or not. A defendant needs no reminder that if he rejects the proposal, stands upon his right to trial and is convicted, he faces a significantly longer sentence."[91]

To be voluntary and knowing, the plea must be entered by a defendant who is mentally competent to understand the nature and consequences of the plea. The standard for competence to enter a plea is the same as the standard for competence to stand trial—whether the defendant "has sufficient present ability to consult with his lawyer with a reasonable degree of rational understanding, and whether he has a rational as well as factual understanding of the proceedings against him."[92] If a judge has any doubt about the defendant's competence, the judge must conduct a hearing to examine the defendant's competence.[93]

In reviewing the plea, the judge must also ensure that the defendant understands the charges to which he is pleading. The Supreme Court held in *Henderson v. Morgan* that "the plea could not be voluntary in the sense that it constituted an intelligent admission that he [the defendant] committed the offense unless the defendant received 'real notice of the true nature of the charge against him, the first and most universally recognized requirement of due process.'"[94] At the plea colloquy,

---

[89] State v. Solano, 724 P.2d 17 (Ariz. 1986); United States v. Caro, 997 F.2d 657 (9th Cir. 1993).

[90] *E.g.*, State v. Bouie, 817 So. 2d 48 (La. 2002).

[91] Fed. R. Crim. Proc. 11, advisory committee's note (1974 amendment) (quoting United States *ex rel.* Elksnis v. Gilligan, 256 F. Supp. 244, 254 (S.D.N.Y. 1966)).

[92] Godinez v. Moran, 509 U.S. 389 (1993).

[93] *See* 21 Am. Jur. 2d Criminal Law §605 (2008).

[94] 426 U.S. 637 (1976).

therefore, the judge must inform the defendant of at least the critical elements of the offense to which the defendant pleads guilty.

To ensure that the plea is knowing, the court must further determine the defendant's understanding of the rights he is waiving by pleading guilty, such as the privilege against self-incrimination, the right to trial by jury, and the right to confront one's accusers, or, if applicable, the right to appeal or to be represented by counsel at the plea hearing.[95] To ensure that the plea is informed, the court must also tell the defendant about the maximum possible punishment for the charged offense. Many jurisdictions, including the federal system, require judges to provide additional sentencing information to the defendant, including information about any applicable mandatory minimum penalty.

The Supreme Court held in *United States v. Ruiz*, however, that the Constitution does not require that the defendant have complete knowledge of all the circumstances related to pleading guilty and waiving various constitutional rights.[96] A guilty plea may be voluntary and intelligent, for example, even if the prosecution has failed to reveal evidence that serves to impeach the credibility of government witnesses.[97]

In this respect, American practice is quite different from other systems that have adopted plea bargaining. Whereas civil-law countries generally allow the defense full access to the investigative file—which contains all of the information gathered by the police and prosecutor for introduction at trial—U.S. jurisdictions typically fail to provide for full pre-plea discovery to the defense. American prosecutors have a constitutional duty to disclose at most evidence that is materially exculpatory and relates to factual innocence.[98] Some jurisdictions provide for disclosure of certain items material to the preparation of the defense, even if they are not exculpatory, after an indictment has been filed.[99] But this information does not extend to witness names and statements, or to

---

[95] Boykin v. Alabama, 395 U.S. 238 (1969); *see also* Iowa v. Tovar, 541 U.S. 77 (2004).

[96] 536 U.S. 622 (2002).

[97] *Id.* at 629.

[98] *Id.* at 630. Although the Supreme Court in *Ruiz* left unsettled the question whether information related to factual innocence ought to be disclosed in plea negotiations before trial, some lower courts have required such disclosure. Sanchez v. United States, 50 F.3d 1448 (9th Cir. 1995); Ferrara v. United States, 384 F. Supp. 2d 384 (D. Mass. 2005).

[99] *E.g.*, Fed. R. Crim. Proc. 16.

materials relevant to sentencing.[100] Nor do prosecutors have to disclose such information in pre-indictment plea negotiations.[101] Some prosecutors follow the recommendation of the federal sentencing and prosecutorial guidelines and disclose to the defense all sentencing-related facts.[102] Others, however, disclose such information only after the pre-sentencing report has been prepared, long after plea bargaining has ended.[103] Courts have approved the practice of providing sentence-related information just before sentencing, rather than before the plea colloquy.[104]

FACTUAL BASIS[105]

As mentioned above, many jurisdictions require that, in addition to reviewing whether a plea is voluntary and intelligent, courts determine whether the plea accurately reflects the facts of the case. The factual basis requirement furthers the truth-seeking function of the criminal justice system and protects defendants from pleading guilty to crimes they did not commit.

The factual basis requirement is not a very stringent one, however. The rules typically do not specify the amount of proof that must be presented. One court has defined the standard of proof as "sufficient evidence at the time of the plea upon which the court may reasonably determine that the defendant likely committed the offense."[106] Others have simply required "some factual basis."[107] Mere admissions of guilt by the defendant may be sufficient to support a guilty plea.[108] In practice, the inquiry into the factual basis has become a mere formality, as many courts have allowed judges to read the indictment to the defendant and

---

[100] *Id.* States vary widely in their discovery rules, but the denial of discovery of witness statements is common. Stephen A. Saltzburg & Daniel J. Capra, American Criminal Procedure 987-988 (7th ed. 2004).

[101] Fed. R. Crim. Proc. 16; Brown v. Appelman, 672 N.Y.S.2d 373, 377 (App. Div. 1998).

[102] *See* U.S. Sentencing Guidelines Manual §6B1.2 cmt.; U.S. Attorneys' Manual §9-27.750.

[103] Herman, *supra* note 39, at 151.

[104] *E.g.*, United States v. Brewster, 1 F.3d 51, 53 (1st Cir. 1993).

[105] This Section is based on Turner, *supra* note 27, at 212-213.

[106] United States v. Marks, 38 F.3d 1009, 1012 (8th Cir. 1994).

[107] United States v. Fountain, 777 F.2d 351, 357 (7th Cir. 1985).

[108] United States v. Deal, 678 F.2d 1062, 1067 (11th Cir. 1982) (holding that factual basis was established when defendant twice admitted in court to knowing that goods transported across state line were stolen).

then merely to inquire whether he committed the acts in question.[109] In other courts, the prosecutor's summary of the evidence or submission of a probable cause affidavit is enough.[110] Even where a defendant pleads guilty while protesting his innocence,[111] the standard of proving the plea's factual basis is not reasonable doubt, but something closer to a "high probability of conviction."[112]

Notes and Questions:

1. Should courts be more demanding in their review of the voluntariness and knowingness of the guilty plea? Should courts hold that a disproportionately high plea discount renders the plea involuntary? That certain types of pleas (pleas in capital cases, package deals, deals waiving the right to appeal) are inherently coercive? That failure by the prosecution to disclose evidence material to the defense renders a guilty plea uninformed?
2. In *Bordenkircher v. Hayes*, the Supreme Court held that a prosecutor did not violate due process when he carried out a threat made during plea negotiations to have the accused, Hayes, reindicted on more serious charges when he refused to plead guilty to the offense with which he was originally charged.[113] Under the original charges for forging a check of $88.30, Hayes would have faced a two- to ten-year sentence; as part of the negotiations, the prosecutor had offered to recommend a sentence of five years in exchange for a guilty plea. After Hayes refused to plead guilty, the prosecutor filed habitual criminal charges, which carried a mandatory life sentence. Because Hayes had two prior felony convictions, the jury convicted him of the habitual criminal charges, and the judge imposed the mandatory life sentence. In holding that the prosecutor's behavior did not violate due process, the Supreme

---

[109] *E.g.*, Paradiso v. United States, 482 F.2d 409, 415-416 (3d Cir. 1973); *see also* United States v. Guichard, 779 F.2d 1139, 1146 (5th Cir. 1986) (holding that a guilty plea was properly accepted where the defendant agreed to and signed a recitation of events); State v. Campbell, 488 P.2d 968, 970 (Ariz. 1971).

[110] John G. Douglass, *Fatal Attraction? The Uneasy Courtship of* Brady *and Plea Bargaining*, 50 Emory L.J. 437, 473-474 (2001).

[111] North Carolina v. Alford, 400 U.S. 25, 38 (1970).

[112] John L. Barkai, *Accuracy Inquiries for All Felony and Misdemeanor Pleas: Voluntary Pleas but Innocent Defendants?*, 126 U. Pa. L. Rev. 88, 126 (1977); *see also* United States v. Tunning, 69 F.3d 107, 111-112 (6th Cir. 1995) ("[S]trong evidence of actual guilt is not necessary to satisfy Rule 11(f), even where a defendant protests his innocence.").

[113] Bordenkircher v. Hayes, 434 U.S. 357 (1978).

Court emphasized that the recidivist charge was supported by the evidence at the time of the original indictment and that, "[a]s a practical matter . . . , this case would be no different if the grand jury had indicated Hayes as a recidivist from the outset, and the prosecutor had offered to drop that charge as part of the plea bargaining." Do you agree that there is no difference between (1) charging Hayes as a recidivist at the outset, and offering to drop that charge as part of the plea bargaining; and (2) indicting Hayes on the less serious charges originally, and then threatening to add the habitual criminal charge if he refused to plead guilty? Can the Supreme Court's holding in *Bordenkircher* be reconciled with *Brady*'s holding that guilty pleas cannot be procured through threats?

3. Many commentators believe that the factual basis requirement has become largely a formality. The parties have little incentive to provide judges with information that might disturb the validity of the plea, and courts have not demanded a high standard of proof. How could a more stringent factual basis requirement be implemented? In order for a more thorough review to take place, what materials should judges have at their disposal? Would judges have to be given access to the prosecutors' files, as they are in inquisitorial systems? Would the parties have to call some of their witnesses, particularly when the credibility of witness testimony is crucial to the case? Should judges be precluded from accepting stipulations to the factual basis (i.e., waivers of factual basis review)? If these features were to be introduced, would the judge have to recuse herself from presiding over a trial if the plea bargain fails? If the plea hearing were changed to entail a thorough review of the facts by the judge, would it be better to have short bench trials, discussed below at pp. 57-58? (As subsequent chapters discuss, other countries, including Italy, Japan, and Bulgaria, use simplified bench trials instead of or in addition to plea bargaining to expedite proceedings.)
4. It is important to understand the distinction between a guilty plea and a plea bargain. A defendant can plead guilty without entering into a plea agreement with the prosecution. In a number of districts around the country, defendants often plead guilty without a plea agreement. They do so because they believe that, in return for their "acceptance of responsibility," the court will reduce their sentence even in the absence of a bargain with the prosecution. What are the advantages and disadvantages of pleading guilty without entering into a plea agreement?

WITHDRAWAL OF A GUILTY PLEA AND BREACH OF A PLEA AGREEMENT

WITHDRAWAL

A defendant may withdraw his plea any time before the judge has accepted it. After the court has accepted the guilty plea, the defendant may withdraw the plea if the court has rejected the plea agreement between the parties, or if the defendant shows a "fair and just reason."[114] In determining whether the defendant has provided a fair and just reason, the court will examine factors such as the possibility that the defendant might be innocent or might have entered an invalid plea and balance these against competing considerations, such as the likely prejudice to the government.[115] After sentencing, the defendant may not withdraw the guilty plea unless he can show that withdrawal must be permitted to avoid "manifest injustice."[116] These rather vague standards reveal the courts' efforts to maintain a balance between the efficiency of the process and the need to protect defendants from unfair and unjust plea bargains.[117]

BREACH

A plea agreement is generally enforceable as a contract. Both prosecutors and defendants will be held to their promises under plea agreements that have been accepted by the court.[118] As the Supreme Court stated in *Santobello v. New York*, excerpted above, "when a plea rests in any significant degree on a promise or agreement of the prosecutor, so that it can be said to be part of the inducement or consideration, such promise must be fulfilled."[119] *Santobello* identified specific performance or rescission of the agreement as possible remedies for breach by the prosecution. But the Court held further that the remedy remains within

---

[114] *E.g.*, United States v. Jones, 168 F.3d 1217, 1219 (10th Cir. 1999).

[115] *Id.*

[116] LaFave et al., *supra* note 87, at 478.

[117] *See* Saltzburg & Capra, *supra* note 100, at 1085.

[118] Mabry v. Johnson, 467 U.S. 504 (1984) (holding that a plea agreement is not binding until the guilty plea is entered and accepted by a court, and that the prosecutor can withdraw from the agreement before then). But some states hold the government to its bargain even before that point. *E.g.*, *Ex parte* Yarber, 437 So. 2d 1330, 1334 (Ala. 1983); State v. Brockman, 357 A.2d 376, 381 (Md. 1976).

[119] 404 U.S. 257, 262 (1971).

the trial court's discretion, although four Justices supported the proposition that in choosing the remedy, "a court ought to accord a defendant's preference considerable, if not controlling, weight."[120]

If a defendant fails to carry out an obligation under a plea agreement, for example, by failing to cooperate, the government will be entitled to rescind the agreement or seek specific performance.[121] If the agreement is rescinded, the government may prosecute the defendant anew, even on dropped charges.[122] The government may also opt to hold the defendant to his guilty plea, while ignoring its own agreement not to seek a higher sentence.[123] At the government's request, the court may also order specific performance. Although specific performance is rarely requested by the government, courts have at times ordered defendants to perform certain obligations under their plea agreements, such as surrendering disputed assets[124] or promising not to argue for departures from the Federal Sentencing Guidelines.[125]

A case in which the defendant's refusal to continue cooperating with the government proved very costly to the defendant is *Ricketts v. Adamson*. In that case, the defendant Adamson was charged with first-degree murder, but had his charges reduced to second-degree murder in exchange for a promise that he would testify against his associates.[126] Adamson did testify, and his associates were convicted. But their convictions were later reversed, and Adamson refused to testify at their second trial. Adamson's lawyer wrote to the prosecutor that Adamson had fulfilled his end of the plea agreement and that he would testify again only if certain conditions were met, including that he be released from custody after his testimony. The state responded that it deemed Adamson in breach of the original agreement. After Adamson refused to testify, invoking his privilege against self-incrimination, the state

---

[120] *Id.* at 267 (Douglas, J., concurring). Justice Douglas explained that this was justified because "the fundamental rights flouted by the prosecutor's breach of a plea bargain are those of the defendant, not of the state." *Id.*

[121] United States v. Cimino, 381 F.3d 124, 127 (2d Cir. 2004).

[122] *See id.*

[123] *Id.* In some cases, the plea agreement itself may on its terms foreclose plea withdrawal by the defendant. *Remedy for Broken Bargain*, 5 Crim. Proc. §21.2 (E) (2008). At least one court has allowed the government to prosecute the defendant on dropped charges while holding the defendant to his guilty plea. United States v. Holbrook, 368 F.3d 415 (4th Cir. 2004).

[124] United States v. Alexander, 869 F.2d 91, 94 (2d Cir. 1989).

[125] United States v. Williams, 510 F.3d 416, 428 (3d Cir. 2007).

[126] 483 U.S. 1 (1987).

charged Adamson with first-degree murder and obtained a conviction and a death sentence. Adamson argued that the second conviction violated the Double Jeopardy Clause, and the court of appeals agreed. But the Supreme Court reversed, holding that the defendant's prosecution on the original murder charges did not violate double jeopardy because his breach of the plea agreement removed the double jeopardy bar.

> The agreement specifies in two separate paragraphs the consequences that would flow from respondent's breach of his promises. Paragraph 5 provides that if respondent refused to testify, "this entire agreement is null and void and the original charge will be automatically reinstated." [. . .] Similarly, Paragraph 15 of the agreement states that "[i]n the event this agreement becomes null and void, then the parties shall be returned to the positions they were in before this agreement." [. . .] Respondent unquestionably understood the meaning of these provisions. At the plea hearing, the trial judge read the plea agreement to respondent, line by line, and pointedly asked respondent whether he understood the provisions in Paragraphs 5 and 15. Respondent replied "Yes, sir," to each question. [. . .] The terms of the agreement could not be clearer: in the event of respondent's breach occasioned by a refusal to testify, the parties would be returned to the status quo ante, in which case respondent would have no double jeopardy defense to waive. And, an agreement specifying that charges may be reinstated given certain circumstances is, at least under the provisions of this plea agreement, precisely equivalent to an agreement waiving a double jeopardy defense. The approach taken by the Court of Appeals would render the agreement meaningless: first-degree murder charges could not be reinstated against respondent if he categorically refused to testify after sentencing even if the agreement specifically provided that he would so testify, because, under the Court of Appeals' view, he never waived his double jeopardy protection. [. . .]
>
> We are also unimpressed by the Court of Appeals' holding that there was a good-faith dispute about whether respondent was bound to testify a second time and that until the extent of his obligation was decided, there could be no knowing and intelligent waiver of his double jeopardy defense. But respondent knew that if he breached the agreement he could be retried, and it is incredible to believe that he did not anticipate that the extent of his obligation would be decided by a court. Here he sought a construction of the agreement in the Arizona Supreme Court, and that court found that he had failed to live up to his promise. The result was that respondent was returned to the position he occupied prior to execution of the plea bargain: he stood charged with first-degree murder. [. . .]
>
> Finally, it is of no moment that following the Arizona Supreme Court's decision respondent offered to comply with the terms of the

agreement. At this point, respondent's second-degree murder conviction had already been ordered vacated and the original charge reinstated. The parties did not agree that respondent would be relieved from the consequences of his refusal to testify if he were able to advance a colorable argument that a testimonial obligation was not owing. The parties could have struck a different bargain, but permitting the State to enforce the agreement the parties actually made does not violate the Double Jeopardy Clause.

Justice Brennan, joined by Justices Marshall, Blackmun, and Stevens, dissented.

Adamson's interpretation of the agreement—that he was not required to testify at the retrials of [his confederates]—was reasonable. Nothing in the plea agreement explicitly stated that Adamson was required to provide testimony should retrials prove necessary. Moreover, the agreement specifically referred in two separate paragraphs to events that would occur only after the conclusion of all testimony that Adamson would be required to give. Paragraph 8 stated that Adamson "will be sentenced at the conclusion of his testimony in all of the cases referred to in this agreement and Exhibits A and B, which accompany it." [. . .] At the time that the State demanded that Adamson testify in the retrials, he had been sentenced. Paragraph 18 stated that "[t]he defendant is to remain in the custody of the Pima County Sheriff from the date of the entry of his plea until the conclusion of his testimony in all of the cases in which the defendant agrees to testify as a result of this agreement." [. . .] At the time the State demanded that Adamson testify in the retrials, Adamson had been transferred from the custody of the Pima County Sheriff. Adamson therefore could reasonably conclude that he had provided all the testimony required by the agreement, and that, as he communicated to the State by letter of April 3, 1980, the testimony demanded by the State went beyond his duties under the agreement. [. . .]

This Court has yet to address in any comprehensive way the rules of construction appropriate for disputes involving plea agreements. Nevertheless, it seems clear that the law of commercial contract may in some cases prove useful as an analogy or point of departure in construing a plea agreement, or in framing the terms of the debate. [. . .] It is also clear, however, that commercial contract law can do no more than this, because plea agreements are constitutional contracts. The values that underlie commercial contract law, and that govern the relations between economic actors, are not coextensive with those that underlie the Due Process Clause, and that govern relations between criminal defendants and the State. Unlike some commercial contracts, plea agreements must be construed in light of the rights and obligations created by the Constitution.

The State argues and the Arizona Supreme Court seems to imply that a breach occurred when Adamson sent his letter of April 3, 1980, to the prosecutor in response to the State's demand for his testimony at the retrials of Dunlap and Robison. [. . .] In this letter, Adamson stated that, under his interpretation of the agreement, he was no longer obligated to testify, and demanded additional consideration for any additional testimony. [. . .]

Neither the State, the state courts, nor this Court has attempted to explain why this letter constituted a breach of the agreement. Of course, it could not plausibly be argued that merely sending such a letter constituted a breach by nonperformance, for nothing in the plea agreement states that Adamson shall not disagree with the State's interpretation of the plea agreement, or that Adamson shall not send the State a letter to that effect. But one might argue that, in the language of commercial contract law, the letter constituted a breach by anticipatory repudiation. [. . .] Such a breach occurs when one party unequivocally informs the other that it no longer intends to honor their contract. "[W]here the contract is renounced before performance is due, and the renunciation goes to the whole contract, is absolute and unequivocal, the injured party may treat the breach as complete and bring his action at once." [. . .]

In the conventional case of anticipatory repudiation, therefore, the announcement of an intention to default on the contract constitutes a breach. In his letter of April 3, however, Adamson did not announce such an intention. To the contrary, Adamson invoked the integrity of that agreement as a defense to what he perceived to be an unwarranted demand by the prosecutor that he testify at the retrials of [his confederates]. And in insisting that he had no obligation to perform as the State demanded, Adamson advanced an objectively reasonable interpretation of his contract. [. . .]

Of course, far from being a commercial actor, Adamson is an individual whose "contractual" relation with the State is governed by the Constitution. The determination of Adamson's rights and responsibilities under the plea agreement is controlled by the principles of fundamental fairness imposed by the Due Process Clause. To grant to one party—here, the State—the unilateral and exclusive right to define the meaning of a plea agreement is patently unfair. Moreover, such a grant is at odds with the basic premises that underlie the constitutionality of the plea-bargaining system. Guilty pleas are enforceable only if taken voluntarily and intelligently. [. . .] It would be flatly inconsistent with these requirements to uphold as intelligently made a plea agreement which provided that, in the future, the agreement would mean whatever the State interpreted it to mean. Yet the Court upholds today the equivalent of such an agreement. The logic of the plea-bargaining system requires acknowledgment and protection of the defendant's right to advance against the State a reasonable interpretation of the plea agreement.

This right requires no exotic apparatus for enforcement. Indeed, it requires nothing more than common civility. If the defendant offers an interpretation of a plea agreement at odds with that of the State, the State should notify the defendant of this fact, particularly if the State is of the view that continued adherence to defendant's view would result in breach of the agreement. If the State and the defendant are then unable to resolve their dispute through further discussion, a ready solution exists—either party may seek to have the agreement construed by the court in which the plea was entered. [. . .]

The unfairness of the Court's decision does not end here. Even if one assumes, arguendo, that Adamson breached his plea agreement by offering an erroneous interpretation of that agreement, it still does not follow that the State was entitled to retry Adamson on charges of first-degree murder. [. . .] [I]mmediately following the decision of the Arizona Supreme Court adopting the State's construction of the plea agreement, Adamson sent a letter to the State stating that he was ready and willing to testify. At this point, there was no obstacle to proceeding with the retrials of Dunlap and Robison; each case had been dismissed without prejudice to refiling, and only about one month's delay had resulted from the dispute over the scope of the plea agreement. Thus, what the State sought from Adamson—testimony in the Dunlap and Robison trials—was available to it.

The State decided instead to abandon the prosecution of Dunlap and Robison, and to capitalize on what it regarded as Adamson's breach by seeking the death penalty against him. No doubt it seemed easier to proceed against Adamson at that point, since the State had the benefit of his exhaustive testimony about his role in the murder of Don Bolles. But even in the world of commercial contracts it has long been settled that the party injured by a breach must nevertheless take all reasonable steps to minimize the consequent damage. [. . .]

Here it is macabre understatement to observe that the State needlessly exacerbated the liability of its contractual partner. The State suffered a 1-month delay in beginning the retrial of Dunlap and Robison, and incurred litigation costs. For these "losses," the State chose to make Adamson pay, not with a longer sentence, but with his life. A comparable result in commercial law, if one could be imagined, would not be enforced. The fundamental unfairness in the State's course of conduct here is even less acceptable under the Constitution.

Notes and Questions:

1. Does the holding in *Ricketts* mean that a defendant is precluded from "advanc[ing] against the State a reasonable interpretation

of the plea agreement," as the dissent argues? What can defense counsel do in negotiating a plea agreement to ensure that the defendant has recourse to argue for a different interpretation of the plea agreement, before the prosecution deems the defendant in breach of the agreement?

2. In *Santobello v. New York*, discussed earlier, the government's alleged breach of its plea agreement occurred after the defendant had pleaded guilty. In that case, the Court held that a defendant is entitled to relief when the prosecutor breaches the plea agreement. Should the rule be different when the government breaches before the defendant has pleaded guilty? Consider the approach taken by the Illinois Supreme Court in *People v. Navarroli*, 521 N.E.2d 891 (Ill. 1988). In *Navarroli*, the defendant acted as an informant in various drug investigations in exchange for the state's promise to reduce the charges against him and to agree to a sentence of probation and fine. The defendant alleged that after he had cooperated with the police, but before he was to plead guilty, the prosecutor refused to reduce the charges. The court held that the state's repudiation of the agreement had not deprived the defendant of any constitutional rights. The defendant had not pleaded guilty in reliance on the agreement and had therefore not been deprived of his liberty interest. Because the defendant's performance had not implicated his constitutional rights, the court refused to enforce the agreement. Is this approach consistent with the logic of *Santobello*? For an example of a case disagreeing with *Navarroli*, see *Watkins v. Commonwealth*, 491 S.E.2d 755 (Va. App. 1997).

ARGUMENTS FOR AND AGAINST PLEA BARGAINING IN THE UNITED STATES

According to defenders of plea bargaining, plea agreements are valuable to all sides involved and should therefore be respected: "The defendant saves the anxiety and cost of litigation, and the prosecutor frees up resources to pursue other criminals."[127] Consider the following defense of the practice by Judge Frank Easterbrook:

> Plea bargains are preferable to mandatory litigation—not because the analogy to contract is overpowering, but because compromise is bet-

[127] Frank H. Easterbrook, *Criminal Procedure as a Market System*, 12 J. Legal Stud. 289, 297 (1983).

ter than conflict. Settlements of civil cases make both sides better off; settlements of criminal cases do so too. Defendants have many procedural and substantive rights. By pleading guilty, they sell these rights to the prosecutor, receiving concessions they esteem more highly than the rights surrendered. Rights that may be sold are more valuable than rights that must be consumed, just as money (which may be used to buy housing, clothing, or food) is more valuable to a poor person than an opportunity to live in public housing.

Defendants can use or exchange their rights, whichever makes them better off. So plea bargaining helps defendants. Forcing them to use their rights at trial means compelling them to take the risk of conviction or acquittal; risk-averse persons prefer a certain but small punishment to a chancy but large one. Defendants also get the process over sooner, and solvent ones save the expense of trial. Compromise also benefits prosecutors and society at large. In purchasing procedural entitlements with lower sentences, prosecutors buy that most valuable commodity, time. With time they can prosecute more criminals. When eight percent of defendants plead guilty, a given prosecutorial staff obtains five times the number of convictions it could achieve if all went to trial. Even so, prosecutors must throw back the small fish. The ratio of prosecutions (and convictions) to crimes would be extremely low if compromises were forbidden. Sentences could not be raised high enough to maintain deterrence, especially not when both economics and principles of desert call for proportionality between crime and punishment.[128]

Many scholars disagree with Judge Easterbrook about the value of plea bargaining. Professor Alschuler has offered vigorous criticism of the practice:

Albert W. Alschuler, *Implementing the Criminal Defendant's Right to Trial*, 50 U. Chi. L. Rev. 931, 932-934 (1983).

Plea bargaining makes a substantial part of an offender's sentence depend, not upon what he did or his personal characteristics, but upon a tactical decision irrelevant to any proper objective of criminal proceedings. In contested cases, it substitutes a regime of split-the-difference for a judicial determination of guilt or innocence and elevates a concept of partial guilt above the requirement that criminal responsibility be established beyond a reasonable doubt. This practice also deprecates the value of human liberty and the purposes of the criminal sanction by treating these things as commodities to be traded for economic

---

[128] Frank H. Easterbrook, *Plea Bargaining as Compromise*, 101 Yale L.J. 1969, 1975 (1992).

savings—savings that, when measured against common social expenditures, usually seem minor.

Plea bargaining leads lawyers to view themselves as judges and administrators rather than as advocates; it subjects them to serious financial and other temptations to disregard their clients' interests; and it diminishes the confidence in attorney-client relationships that can give dignity and purpose to the legal profession and that is essential to the defendant's sense of fair treatment. In addition, this practice makes figureheads of court officials who typically prepare elaborate presentence reports only after the effective determination of sentence through prosecutorial negotiations. Indeed, it tends to make figureheads of judges, whose power over the administration of criminal justice has largely been transferred to people of less experience, who commonly lack the information that judges could secure, whose temperaments have been shaped by their partisan duties, and who have not been charged by the electorate with the important responsibilities that they have assumed. Moreover, plea bargaining perverts both the initial prosecutorial formulation of criminal charges and, as defendants plead guilty to crimes less serious than those that they apparently committed, the final judicial labeling of offenses.

The negotiation process encourages defendants to believe that they have "sold a commodity and that [they have], in a sense, gotten away with something." It sometimes promotes perceptions of corruption. It has led the Supreme Court to a hypocritical disregard of its usual standards of waiver in judging the most pervasive waiver that our criminal justice system permits. The practice of plea bargaining is inconsistent with the principle that a decent society should want to hear what an accused person might say in his defense—and with constitutional guarantees that embody this principle and other professed ideals for the resolution of criminal disputes. Moreover, plea bargaining has undercut the goals of legal doctrines as diverse as the fourth amendment exclusionary rule, the insanity defense, the right of confrontation, the defendant's right to attend criminal proceedings, and the recently announced right of the press and the public to observe the administration of criminal justice. This easy instrument of accommodation has frustrated both attempts at sentencing reform and some of the most important objectives of the due process revolution.

Plea bargaining provides extraordinary opportunities for lazy lawyers whose primary goal is to cut corners and to get on to the next case; it increases the likelihood of favoritism and personal influence; it conceals other abuses; it maximizes the dangers of representation by inexperienced attorneys who are not fully versed in an essentially secret system of justice; it promotes inequalities; it sometimes results in unwarranted leniency; it merges the tasks of adjudication, sentencing, and administration into a single amorphous judgment to the detriment of all three; it treats almost every legal right as a bargaining chip to be traded for a discount in sentence; and it almost certainly increases the number of innocent defendants who are convicted. In short, an effort to describe comprehensively the evils that plea bargaining has wrought requires an extensive tour of the criminal justice system.

Notes and Questions:

1. Judge Easterbrook believes that plea bargaining makes all parties better off—the defendant, the prosecution, and society as a whole. Even if this is true, would the public have any grounds for limiting or even prohibiting plea bargaining? What are these grounds? Does Professor Alschuler accept the premise that plea bargaining makes all parties better off? In what circumstances might that not be the case?
2. Kenneth Kipnis tries to illustrate the impropriety of plea bargaining by comparing it to the idea of "grade bargaining." He asks us to imagine a grade bargain between a "grade-conscious student" and an overburdened instructor:

   > A term paper has been submitted and, after glancing at the first page, the instructor says that if he were to read the paper carefully, applying his usually rigid standards, he would probably decide to give the paper the grade of D. But if the student were to waive his right to a careful reading and conscientious critique, the instructor would agree to a grade of B. The grade-point average being more important to him than either education or justice in grading, the student happily accepts the B, and the instructor enjoys a reduced workload.[129]

   Would such a practice be proper? Would your answer be different if you knew that the university was severely underfunded and had to impose an unmanageable workload on instructors, leading to year-long delays in grading? Does this hypothetical provide any insights into the propriety of plea bargaining? What do you think of Kipnis's argument that, like academia, the criminal justice system is a setting "in which persons are justly given, not what they have bargained for, but what they deserve, irrespective of their position"?
3. The possibility that an innocent defendant may plead guilty has preoccupied many scholars. Stephen Schulhofer has argued that

[129] Kenneth Kipnis, *Criminal Justice and the Negotiated Plea*, 86 Ethics 93, 104-105 (1976).

innocent defendants should not be permitted to plead guilty, even if that is their preference:[130]

> [T]he innocent defendant, facing a small possibility of conviction on a serious charge, [may] consider[] it in his interest to accept conviction and a small penalty. The defendant's choice to plead guilty can be rational from his private perspective, but it imposes costs on society by undermining public confidence that criminal convictions reflect guilt beyond a reasonable doubt. An "efficient" system of voluntary contracting for pleas would convict large numbers of defendants who had a high probability of acquittal at trial; indeed, to the extent that innocent defendants are likely to be more risk averse than guilty ones, the former are likely to be overrepresented in the pool of "acquittable" defendants who are attracted by prosecutorial offers to plead guilty. To deal seriously with these problems we must consider complete abolition of plea bargaining. [. . .] [A]n innocent's preference for bargaining cannot be decisive when his conviction would impose serious costs on others.

Do you believe that we should ban plea bargaining so as to protect innocent defendants? Why or why not?

4. Confirming concerns by scholars like Albert Alschuler and Stephen Schulhofer, a recent empirical study of exonerations shows that at least some innocent defendants have pleaded guilty.[131] In *Exonerations in the United States, 1989 Through 2003,* a team of researchers led by Samuel Gross found that, in about 6 percent of cases in their database, innocent persons had pleaded guilty and had been convicted:[132] Fifteen innocent murder defendants and four innocent rape defendants pleaded guilty in exchange for long prison sentences in order to avoid the risk of life imprisonment or

---

[130] Stephen J. Schulhofer, *Plea Bargaining as a Disaster*, 101 Yale L.J. 1979, 2000, 2001 (1992).

[131] The connection between this study and plea bargaining was first made by Scott Howe, *The Value of Plea Bargaining*, 58 Okla. L. Rev. 599 (2005), and this discussion draws on Howe's.

[132] The researchers classified as an exoneration "an official act declaring a defendant not guilty of a crime for which he or she had previously been convicted." Samuel Gross et al., Exonerations in the United States, 1989 Through 2003, at 1 (2004), *at* http://www.soros.org/initiatives/usprograms/focus/justice/articles_publications/publications/exonerations_20040419/exon_report.pdf. To qualify, the acquittal also had to be based on "strong evidence of factual innocence," and there had to be no evidence that the defendant played a role in the crime. *Id.* at 1-2 & n.4. Almost half of the exonerations presented in the study rested on DNA evidence analysis. *Id.* at 1.

the death penalty.[133] In addition, Gross and his colleagues found that two cases of mass exonerations due to large-scale police perjury involved very large proportions of convictions based on guilty pleas. One was the Rampart scandal in Los Angeles,[134] and the other was the scandal in Tulia, Texas.[135] The researchers noted that "the majority of the 100 or more exonerated defendants in the Rampart scandal" pleaded guilty to offenses they did not commit, as did "31 of the 39 Tulia defendants."[136]

These numbers may understate how many innocent defendants may plead guilty. As Scott Howe explains, "[p]leading guilty, as opposed to being convicted after trial, likely makes subsequent exoneration more difficult. . . . In addition, while the [Gross et al.] study focused only on cases involving death or a long prison term (where exoneration efforts generally focus), more innocent offenders may enter bargained guilty pleas in minor cases."[137]

5. Advocates of plea bargaining acknowledge that some innocent people might plead guilty, but argue that some innocent defendants are also likely to be convicted after a contested trial. They question whether trials are better than guilty pleas in separating the innocent from the guilty:

> Some innocent persons nonetheless are prosecuted. An eyewitness may have made a mistaken identification. The guilty person

---

133 *Id.* at 12.

134 The Rampart Scandal arose out of the testimony of an officer in the Rampart division of the L.A. police department who testified that officers in one of the program's units ("Community Resources Against Street Hoodlums" or CRASH) "routinely lied in arrest reports, shot and killed or wounded unarmed suspects and innocent bystanders, planted guns on suspects after shooting them, fabricated evidence, and framed innocent defendants. In the aftermath of this scandal, at least 100 criminal defendants who had been framed by Rampart CRASH officers—and possibly as many as 150—had their convictions vacated and dismissed by Los Angeles County judges in late 1999 and 2000. The great majority were young Hispanic men who had pleaded guilty to false felony gun or drug charges." *Id.* at 10.

135 The Tulia scandal relates to drug offense convictions of 39 defendants, in 1999 and 2000, in Tulia, Texas, on the uncorroborated word of a dishonest undercover narcotics agent: "In 2003, 35 of them were pardoned when it was shown that the undercover officer had systematically lied about these cases, and charged the defendants with drug sales that had never occurred. (The remaining 4 Tulia defendants were not eligible for pardons because their convictions had been dismissed, or because they were also imprisoned on unrelated charges.)" *Id.* at 11.

136 *Id.* at 12.

137 Howe, *supra* note 131, at n.172 (quoting Gross et al., *supra* note 132, at 12) ("It is well known, for example, that many defendants who can't afford bail plead guilty in return for short sentences, often probation and credit for time served, rather than stay in jail for months and then go to trial and risk much more severe punishment if convicted.").

may have accused an innocent one to divert suspicion. It is hard to assess the worth of testimony. Juries give eyewitness testimony more credence than it deserves. Guilt may depend on the defendant's mental state, which is elusive. Some defendants are innocent in the sense that the prosecutor has overstepped the reach of the criminal law: the defendant has committed a moral rather than legal offense, or has broken a contract but not the criminal law, or has broken a state but not a federal law. Sometimes efforts to enlarge the scope of criminal responsibility will succeed at trial, sometimes not; it may be hard to predict the judicial reaction. When judges and juries cannot separate the guilty from the innocent, that failure has repercussions in bargaining.

Scott and Stuntz have identified a problem with plea bargaining only if negotiation is inferior to trial at distinguishing guilt from innocence. But why should that be? Trials come with a variety of rules that exclude probative evidence thought to mislead jurors who may not be perfect Bayesians. During bargaining the parties can consider all the evidence that will come in at trial, and then some. The persons doing the considering are knowledgeable; prosecutors are more likely than jurors to discount eyewitness accounts, and prosecutors know from experience which details are most likely to separate guilt from innocence. The full panoply of information plus sophisticated actors are the standard ingredients of adroit decisionmaking.[138]

6. Supporters of plea bargaining also maintain that the practice is indispensable for the effective functioning of the criminal justice system. By contrast, those who have proposed the abolition of plea bargaining have tried to show that there are alternative ways to ensure the efficient administration of justice.

   In his study of plea bargaining in Philadelphia in the early 1980s, Stephen Schulhofer found that plea bargaining was relatively rare in Philadelphia courts, but that the system had not been overwhelmed with cases. Instead, caseloads remained manageable because a large number of defendants opted for bench trials.[139]

   Three factors accounted for the low rate of guilty pleas in Philadelphia. First, the District Attorney's office limited the ability of prosecutors to negotiate charge bargains or agreements to

[138] Frank H. Easterbrook, *Plea Bargaining as Compromise*, 101 Yale L.J. 1969, 1975 (1992).

[139] Stephen J. Schulhofer, *Is Plea Bargaining Inevitable?*, 97 Harv. L. Rev. 1037 (1984).

recommend a sentence.[140] Second, judges rarely rewarded guilty pleas with sentencing concessions. Therefore, when defendants did plead guilty, it was typically because either they or their attorneys believed that it would be futile to take the case to trial.[141] Finally, defendants had the option to waive their right to a jury trial and to choose a bench trial instead, and unlike guilty pleas, bench trials were rewarded with sentencing concessions by the judges.[142] Therefore, most defendants did claim a trial, but this was usually a bench, not a jury trial.

Schulhofer and his research team observed these bench trials closely and concluded that they were not merely "slow guilty pleas," but instead were "genuinely contested adversary proceedings," albeit shorter and less formal than jury trials. Whereas a plea colloquy lasted on average about 20 minutes, a bench trial lasted about 45 minutes.[143] At the bench trial, the prosecutor did call witnesses, and the defense cross-examined them and sometimes called its own witnesses. The parties generally adopted an adversarial posture. Finally, the parties did skip certain formalities, such as opening arguments, and the judge often intervened to ask questions of the witnesses.[144] In sum, the bench trials were much shorter and somewhat less formal than jury trials, but they were also more adversarial than guilty pleas.

Schulhofer concluded that Philadelphia's experience with bench trials cast doubt on the argument that caseload pressures make plea bargaining inevitable:

> First, the data indicate that bargaining by trial prosecutors is not inevitable. The Philadelphia prosecutors complied with office policy that prevented bargaining in nearly all cases. Our observations strongly suggest, moreover, that office policy could have effectively foreclosed the few areas remaining for negotiation. Second, tacit judicial sentencing concessions in exchange for guilty pleas are likewise not inevitable. The Philadelphia judges generally did not extend such concessions, and the criminal defense bar was fully aware of this. Third, failures of adversariness are

[140] Some charge bargains were prohibited, while others required specific approval by the unit chief or his deputy. Similar approval was necessary for agreements to recommend a sentence. *Id.* at 1058.

[141] *Id.* at 1061.

[142] *Id.* at 1062-1063.

[143] *Id.* at 1066.

[144] *Id.* at 1065, 1070-1071.

> not inevitable on the defense side. In the absence of incentives to cooperate, Philadelphia defense counsel made the bench trial a genuinely contested proceeding. Finally, contested trials will not inevitably create unmanageable case pressure; the study showed that large numbers of contested cases did not overwhelm the trial capacity of the system.[145]

Do you agree with Schulhofer's assessment? Should more American jurisdictions encourage short bench trials in lieu of guilty pleas? Would it be feasible to ban plea bargains and rely exclusively on bench trials, jury trials, and non-negotiated guilty pleas?

7. What would be the effect upon innocent defendants were plea bargaining to be abolished in favor of summary proceedings such as those used in Philadelphia? Consider the argument by Professors Robert Scott and William Stuntz:

> Unfortunately, abolition would likely only worsen innocent defendants' plight. In order to accommodate the dramatic increase in trials, the trial process itself would have to be truncated, as Stephen Schulhofer's famous discussion of the Philadelphia process shows. The mini-trials that took the place of bargaining in Philadelphia were brief affairs, most lasting no more than an hour; the pretrial preparation on both sides was minimal. Altering the trial process in this way necessarily increases the error rate (unless our current trial system is nonsensical), meaning that it raises the rate at which innocent defendants are convicted. That, in turn, alters prosecutors' incentives when making decisions about which cases to take to trial. Indeed, it may alter police incentives when making arrests. Police officers and prosecutors alike can afford to be less careful in screening their cases if the trial "backstop" becomes more casual.
>
> In short, prohibiting plea bargaining would likely raise the proportion of innocents who are convicted of crimes.[146]

8. Discussions of plea bargaining often assume the inevitability of the practice. Yet two jurisdictions—Alaska and El Paso County, Texas—formally abolished plea bargaining and were successful in

---

[145] *Id.* at 1093.

[146] Robert E. Scott & William J. Stuntz, *Plea Bargaining as Contract*, 101 Yale L.J. 1909, 1950 (1992).

maintaining the ban for a number of years. Consider the following evaluation of the effectiveness of the Alaska ban:

> Plea bargaining effectively was prohibited in most Alaska cases for about ten years. The prohibition did not, as far as could be measured, cause major disruption to the justice system. The screening portion of the policy resulted in better police investigations and stronger cases. . . . [C]harge bargaining, but not sentencing bargaining, returned to most areas of the state after about 1985. The return of bargaining appeared to be related to changes in personnel in the attorney general's office and to declines in state revenues.[147]

Alaska formally ended its ban on plea bargaining in 1993. As the excerpt above indicates, the ban did not significantly increase the burden on courts, but this was in part because a form of implicit bargaining continued even after the ban, whereby defendants who went to trial generally received higher sentences than those who pleaded guilty. By contrast, in El Paso County, Texas, a plea bargaining ban resulted in a significant increase in trial rates, forcing a reorganization of the court system to supply more judges for criminal cases.[148] In both jurisdictions, plea bargaining was substantially curtailed for a number of years, but for various reasons, the bans did not have a lasting success and did not spread to other jurisdictions (although a number of other jurisdictions have introduced partial bans of plea bargaining, with greater success).[149]

9. Proponents of plea bargaining have argued that our criminal justice system could not afford to abolish plea bargaining and handle the resulting increase in jury trials. But advocates of abolition have suggested that other reforms can be implemented to make the criminal justice system more efficient, without sacrificing fairness and accuracy in the way that plea bargaining does.

   In the article excerpted above, *Implementing the Criminal Defendant's Right to Trial: Alternatives to the Plea Bargaining*

---

[147] Teresa White Carns & John A. Kruse, *Alaska's Ban on Plea Bargaining Reevaluated*, 75 Judicature 310, 317 (1992).

[148] Robert A. Weininger, *The Abolition of Plea Bargaining: A Case Study of El Paso County, Texas*, 35 UCLA L. Rev. 265, 270 (1987).

[149] Oren Gazal-Ayal, *Partial Ban on Plea Bargains*, 27 Cardozo L. Rev. 2295 (2006).

System, Albert Alschuler offers several such proposals.[150] First, he advocates the introduction of a "penal order" procedure in misdemeanor cases. This procedure is used in a number of continental European legal systems, including Germany. Under the penal order procedure, the prosecutor proposes, in a draft order sent to the defendant in writing, a specific sanction not involving imprisonment. The courts routinely approve the orders in *ex parte* proceedings. If the defendant fails to object within a certain period, the order becomes final. If he does object, he gets an ordinary trial, and his sentence is no higher than it would have been had he accepted the draft penal order.[151]

Alschuler proposes several other ways in which the criminal justice system can resolve more serious cases efficiently, without resorting to plea bargaining. He advocates simplifying evidentiary rules and other trial procedures to make trials more expeditious, limiting the size of juries, simplifying jury selection procedures, using court capacity more effectively, limiting the availability of postconviction remedies, and screening cases more carefully at the charging stage. Finally, commenting favorably on the Philadelphia practice of relying extensively on bench trials rather than plea bargains (discussed above in Note 6), Alschuler argues that jurisdictions trying to reduce full-blown jury trials should encourage bench trials rather than plea bargains.

In your opinion, which of these reforms are most likely to succeed and which are most likely to produce fair and accurate outcomes (or at least outcomes that are likely to be fairer and more accurate than plea bargains)?

10. The debate about whether to keep or abolish plea bargaining may have created a false dilemma. As Ronald Wright and Marc Miller explain in *The Screening/Bargaining Tradeoff*:[152]

> This dilemma about plea bargaining—take it or leave it—is a false one. It is based on a false dichotomy. It errs in assuming that criminal trials are the only alternative to plea bargains. In this erroneous view, fewer plea bargains lead inexorably to more trials; indeed, the whole point in limiting plea bargains is to produce more trials.

---

[150] Albert W. Alschuler, *Implementing the Criminal Defendant's Right to Trial*, 50 U. Chi. L. Rev. 931 (1983).

[151] *Id.* at 957-959.

[152] 55 Stan. L. Rev. 29, 31-33 (2002).

Instead, Wright and Miller argue for prosecutorial screening as an alternative to plea bargaining. They argue that a "more structured and reasoned charge selection process than is typical in most prosecutors' offices in this country" would reduce the caseload sufficiently to eliminate the need for plea bargaining. The authors describe how such prosecutorial screening would work:

> First, the prosecutor's office must make an early and careful assessment of each case, and demand that police and investigators provide sufficient information before the initial charge is filed. Second, the prosecutor's office must file only appropriate charges. Which charges are "appropriate" is determined by several factors. A prosecutor should only file charges that the office would generally want to result in a criminal conviction and sanction. In addition, appropriate charges must reflect reasonably accurately what actually occurred. They are charges that the prosecutor can very likely prove in court. Third, and critically, the office must severely restrict all plea bargaining, and most especially charge bargains. Prosecutors should also recognize explicitly that the screening process is the mechanism that makes such restrictions possible. Fourth, the kind of prosecutorial screening we advocate must include sufficient training, oversight, and other internal enforcement mechanisms to ensure reasonable uniformity in charging and relatively few changes to charges after they have been filed.
>
> . . . A prosecutor who makes a realistic and early evaluation of the case will no longer need to depend on negotiations with defense counsel to sort the wheat from the chaff. The screening decisions make possible a decrease in the number of negotiated guilty pleas, especially charge bargains.[153]

11. The articles by Professors Scott, Stuntz, Wright, and Miller are examples of a shift in the literature on plea bargaining from arguing for the outright abolition of the practice to suggesting ways in which it can be better regulated. One of Scott and Stuntz's proposals is to make sentencing agreements between prosecutors and defendants binding, not mere recommendations that can be disregarded by the judge.[154] Many of the other reforms proposed by scholars have focused on reducing the agency costs of plea bargaining. These include providing greater information about

---

[153] *Id.*

[154] Scott & Stuntz, *supra* note 146, at 1950-1951.

the case to the defendant before plea negotiations,[155] providing more resources to public defender's offices,[156] promulgating prosecutorial plea bargaining guidelines,[157] consulting victims before entering into a plea agreement,[158] strengthening judicial review of the plea's voluntariness and factual basis,[159] and even greater involvement of judges in the negotiations themselves.[160]

In an effort to make plea bargaining send more honest and straightforward moral messages, one author has further proposed that courts and legislatures abolish *Alford* and no contest pleas, so that defendants will either admit guilt and accept responsibility, or have their guilt or innocence determined in jury trials.[161] Finally, a number of proposals have focused on sentencing and have called for reduced harshness of sentencing laws,[162] a uniform sentencing discount for pleading guilty (allowing minor modifications on a case-by-case basis),[163] and reducing overbroad criminal statutes carrying mandatory sentences (thus reducing the possibility that prosecutors will manipulate these statutes to coerce defendants into pleading guilty).

Which of the proposed reforms seem most desirable to you? Can you think of other plea bargaining reforms that would promote more just and accurate results?

HYPOTHETICALS

Consider the two hypothetical situations below, representing plea bargaining scenarios that could arise in the American system. The hypotheti-

[155] Bibas, *supra* note 24, at 2531.

[156] *Id.* at 2539-2540.

[157] O'Hear, *supra* note 35, at 325.

[158] *Id.* at 332; Welling, *supra* note 34, at 304.

[159] Susan Klein, *Enhancing the Judicial Role in Criminal Plea and Sentence Bargaining*, 84 Tex. L. Rev. 2023 (2006); Nancy King, *Judicial Oversight of Negotiated Sentences in a World of Bargained Punishment*, 58 Stan. L. Rev. 293 (2005).

[160] Turner, *supra* note 27.

[161] Stephanos Bibas, *Bringing Moral Values into a Flawed Plea Bargaining System*, 88 Cornell L. Rev. 1425 (2003).

[162] Maximo Langer, *Rethinking Plea Bargaining: The Practice and Reform of Prosecutorial Adjudication in American Criminal Procedure*, 33 Am. J. Crim. L. 223 (2006).

[163] Albert W. Alschuler, *The Trial Judge's Role in Plea Bargaining*, 76 Colum. L. Rev. 1059, 1124-1128 (1976).

cals are not intended to represent the average plea bargained case, but are instead offered to illustrate some of the difficult questions and problems that may occasionally arise under that system.

Plea Bargaining in a Drug Trafficking Case in the United States[164]

Jamie Duke

Jamie Duke and Marvin Strong were partners in a drug conspiracy. They smuggled from Florida into the Virgin Islands about 100 grams of methamphetamine hydrochloride a week during a four-month period in 2004. Duke and Strong split profits equally. Duke had been convicted of rape in 1986 and of possessing two grams of cocaine with intent to sell in 1994.[165]

Duke was arrested in Florida in 2005 for his role in the conspiracy to smuggle drugs into the Virgin Islands. Originally, he was charged with conspiracy to import over 500 grams of methamphetamine hydrochloride, a.k.a. "ice," "into the United States from a place outside thereof" in violation of 21 U.S.C. §§952(a), 960, and 963, as well as conspiracy to distribute over 500 grams of methamphetamine hydrochloride in violation of 21 U.S.C. §§841(a)(1) and 846.[166]

He entered into a plea agreement with the federal authorities as part of which he promised to help the government in apprehending other members of the conspiracy and to testify against those persons. In return, the government agreed that if Duke pleaded guilty to conspiring to import 100 grams of "ice" into the United States in violation of 21 U.S.C. §§952(a) and 960, the government would dismiss the remaining charges against him. The decision to reduce the charged drug quantity from "over 500 grams" to 100 grams decreased Duke's statutory minimum sentence from 20 to 10 years.

The government further promised that it would file a motion under USSG §5K1.1, stating that Duke had provided the government with substantial assistance, and would recommend a sentence of ten years for the importing offenses. If the government had not agreed to file a 5K1.1 motion, Duke would be subject to a minimum of 151 months (about 12 1/2

[164] This hypothetical is based on several real cases: United States v. Saenz, 429 F. Supp. 2d 1081 (N.D. Iowa 2006); United States v. Hammer, 940 F.2d 1141 (8th Cir. 1991); United States v. Transfiguracion, 442 F.3d 1222 (9th Cir. 2007).

[165] He served a prison sentence of 14 months for this offense.

[166] The government suspected, but did not believe it could prove, that Duke and Strong imported as much as 1.6kg of "ice"; therefore, it charged both men for importing over 500 grams of "ice."

years) in prison under the (advisory, but typically observed) Sentencing Guidelines.[167]

In addition, the U.S. Attorney's office in the Virgin Islands agreed that it would not bring any additional charges in the Virgin Islands. If these additional charges were brought, Duke would likely be facing a sentence of 30 years to life imprisonment under the Guidelines.

The plea agreement with Duke read as follows:

PLEA AGREEMENT

The United States of America and Jamie Duke ("defendant") hereby enter into the following Plea Agreement pursuant to Rule 11(c)(1)(B) of the Federal Rules of Criminal Procedure:

1. The defendant agrees to waive indictment pursuant to Rule 7(b) of the Federal Rules of Criminal Procedure and enter a guilty plea to an Information charging him with importation of 100 grams net weight of methamphetamine hydrochloride, in violation of 21 U.S.C. §§952(a) and 960. The government will move to dismiss Counts I and VI against him in CR ## 05-000555 upon sentencing.

   The defendant further agrees to fully and truthfully cooperate with federal and local law enforcement agents concerning their investigation of the importation, possession, and distribution of controlled substances, and related unlawful activities, including the disposition of profits from and assets relating to such activities. He agrees to testify fully and truthfully before any grand juries and at any trials or proceedings against any co-conspirators if called upon to do so for the United States, subject to prosecution for perjury for not testifying truthfully. The United States will make this cooperation known to the Court prior to the defendant's sentencing. The defendant further understands that he remains liable and subject to prosecution for any non-violent Federal or Territorial offenses of which he does not fully advise the United States, or for any material omissions in this

[167] This assumes that the probation officer, who is supposed to independently investigate facts related to sentencing, and the court, with whom the probation officer files a pre-sentencing report, would accept the parties' stipulation that Duke imported only 100g and not over 500 g. Even when the parties agree to these facts, the court is able, under the so-called relevant conduct provisions, to consider the actual amount imported (here, over 500 g). In practice, however, probation officers and courts tend to accept the stipulations of the parties.

regard. In return for this cooperation, the United States agrees not to prosecute defendant in the Southern District of Florida or the District of the Virgin Islands for any other non-violent offenses now known to the government or which he reveals to the federal authorities. [. . .]

6. If, in its discretion, the government determines that the defendant has provided full, truthful, and substantial assistance to investigating federal agencies, the government will move the Court, as provided by Section 5K1.1, United States Sentencing Guidelines, for a downward departure from the Guidelines. The defendant agrees that the decision whether to file such a motion rests within the sole discretion of the United States.
7. The defendant understands that to establish a violation of importation of 100 grams of methamphetamine hydrochloride, a.k.a., "ice," the government must prove beyond a reasonable doubt the following elements: 1) defendant knowingly brought 100 grams net weight of methamphetamine hydrochloride into the United States from a place outside thereof; and 2) defendant knew it was methamphetamine hydrochloride. [. . .]
9. The defendant understands that this plea agreement depends on the fullness and truthfulness of his cooperation. Defendant understands and agrees that if he should fail to fulfill completely each and every one of his obligations under this plea agreement, or make material omissions or intentional misstatements or engage in criminal conduct after the entry of his plea agreement and before sentencing, the government will be free from its obligations under the plea agreement. Defendant, in addition to standing guilty of the matters to which he has pleaded guilty pursuant to this agreement, shall also be fully subject to criminal prosecution for other crimes, and for the counts which were to be dismissed. In any such prosecution, the prosecuting authorities, whether Federal, State, or Local, shall be free to use against him, without limitation, any and all information, in whatever form, that he has provided pursuant to this plea agreement or otherwise; the defendant shall not assert any claim under the U.S. Constitution, any statute, Rule 11(e)(6) of the Federal Rules of Criminal Procedure, Rule 410 of the Federal Rules of Evidence, or any other provision of law, to attempt to bar such use of information.
10. The defendant seeks to waive any right to appeal or to collaterally attack this conviction. The defendant reserves the right to appeal the sentence actually imposed in this case.

11. If defendant's guilty plea is rejected, withdrawn, vacated, or reversed at any time, the United States will be free to prosecute defendant for all charges of which it then has knowledge, and any charges that have been dismissed will be automatically reinstated or may be represented to a grand jury with jurisdiction over the matter. In such event, defendant waives any objections, motions, or defenses based upon the Statute of Limitations, Speedy Trial Act, or constitutional restrictions as to the time of the bringing of such charges.

Duke pleaded guilty and cooperated with the government, as outlined in the plea agreement. In turn, the government dismissed some of the charges, filed a 5K1.1 motion for substantial assistance, and made a recommendation that Duke receive a ten-year sentence. The court followed the recommendation and sentenced Duke to ten years.

Marvin Strong

Marvin Strong, Jamie Duke's partner, did not have a prior criminal history. But he did not cooperate with the government and did not plead guilty. After a three-day trial, at which Jamie Duke testified against him, Strong was convicted of conspiracy to import over 500 grams of methamphetamine hydrochloride "into the United States from a place outside thereof" in violation of 21 U.S.C. §§952(a), 960, and 963, as well as of conspiracy to distribute over 500 grams of methamphetamine hydrochloride in violation of 21 U.S.C. §§841(a)(1) and 846. Under these statutes, Strong was subject to a mandatory minimum sentence of ten years for the amount of drugs he imported.[168] Under the guidelines, his sentencing range would be 292-365 months, so the court sentenced him to 25 years in prison.

Lauren Little

Lauren Little was Marvin Strong's girlfriend, and she was heavily involved in the drug distribution ring. She frequently acted as a drug courier and was involved in the purchase and delivery of 500 grams of methamphetamine hydrochloride in Florida. She was originally charged with (1) aiding and abetting an attempt to possess 500 grams of methamphetamine hydrochloride; and (2) conspiring to distribute more than 500 grams of methamphetamine hydrochloride. Both of these offenses were in viola-

[168] Although Strong did not have a criminal history, he was subject to the same mandatory minimum as Duke, because he was charged with importing a larger quantity of methamphetamine hydrochloride.

tion of 21 U.S.C. §§841(a)(1) and 846. Little also had a prior drug possession conviction from 2000, for which she had served six months in prison. If she had been convicted on the two charges above, she would be facing a statutory minimum of 20 years and a guideline sentence range of 262-327 months (a minimum of 21 years and 10 months).

But the government offered her a favorable plea bargain. In exchange for her cooperation, the charges against her would be dropped, and she would instead have to plead guilty to violating the "drug house" statute, 21 U.S.C. §856(a)(1). No mandatory minimum applies to this violation. As a result, her sentencing range would be 210-262 months (i.e., a minimum of 17 1/2 years). The prosecution further agreed to move for a downward departure under §5K1.1 of the Sentencing Guidelines and to recommend a sentence of 144 months (12 years), about a 30 percent departure below the minimum sentence applicable.

In discussing the reasons for its 5K1.1 motion with the court, the government stated that Lauren Little talked to law enforcement officers about her co-conspirators on the same day that she was arrested; provided information within a day or two, which assisted in preparing affidavits in support of criminal complaints; testified at the trial and sentencing hearings of co-conspirators; and attempted to cooperate with Drug Enforcement Administration agents in Miami while on pretrial release, including providing information used to procure one search warrant, although the information Little provided was outdated, and the search pursuant to the warrant did not lead to any arrests or seizures.

While the government recommended a 30 percent downward departure for Little's assistance, the defense argued for a greater sentence reduction. It argued that Little was exceptionally timely in her cooperation, that there was no indication that she was anything but totally truthful, complete, and reliable, and that she gave the government all the information she could. Pointing out that the median substantial assistance departure from the applicable sentencing guidelines minimum was 50 percent, the defense argued for a greater-than-50-percent reduction and a sentence of eight years. The court agreed with the defense and sentenced Little to eight years.

Vicki Lewis

Vicki Lewis was also a drug courier and facilitator of the conspiracy, though she did not make sales on her own (unlike Lauren Little). Lewis offered to cooperate with the government with respect to other co-conspirators, but her offer was rejected as untimely. She also offered to cooperate by providing self-incriminating information to help with the investigation of her own case, but the prosecution stated that such information does not constitute "substantial assistance" for purposes of Section 5K1.1. In the end, Lewis pleaded guilty to conspiring to distribute more than 500 grams of methamphetamine hydrochloride and received a 135-month sentence (11 years and 3 months), without the benefit of a substantial assistance departure.

Notes and Questions:

1. Compare the culpability of the defendants and the bargains they reached with the prosecutor. Are the sentencing disparities among the defendants fair and justified? As you respond to this question, consider also that, in their study of the use of substantial assistance departures with respect to members of drug trafficking conspiracies, Linda Maxfield and John Kramer found that "more than one-third (38.1%) of the [30] conspiracies had more culpable defendants receiving sentences shorter than or equal to a least one less culpable defendant, usually (in six out of eight instances) because the more culpable defendants received §5K1.1 departures)." The authors further acknowledged the common criticism by scholars and practitioners alike that "highly-culpable drug traffickers can provide substantial assistance and thus receive a sentence equal to or less than co-conspirators with significantly less culpable roles in the offense."[169]
2. Consider the sentencing discounts that Jamie Duke and Lauren Little received, when the charging concessions by the prosecution are included: at least 20 years, or two-thirds off the minimum applicable sentence in Duke's case, and at least 13 years and 10 months, or about two-thirds, in Little's case. Do you believe that either of these discounts is too large and therefore potentially coercive? Is there a point at which an innocent person might plead guilty in order to avoid the possibility of a much more severe sentence after trial? How should courts evaluate claims that a discount for pleading guilty is so significant as to render the guilty plea involuntary? Consider again the Supreme Court's opinion in *Brady v. United States*.
3. In entering the agreements with Jamie Duke and Lauren Little, the prosecution stipulated to certain facts about the crime, which significantly reduced Duke's and Little's exposure. Yet even when the parties agree to certain facts in a plea agreement, a federal court may, under the so-called relevant conduct provisions of the

[169] Maxfield & Kramer, *supra* note 63, at 16.

Federal Sentencing Guidelines, review the facts independently. To do so, the court may rely on the independent investigation of the facts by a probation officer (these facts are contained in a pre-sentencing report that the probation officer files with the court). After an independent investigation of the facts in Duke's case, a probation officer might find that Duke imported more than 500 grams of "ice," rather than the mere 100 grams to which the parties stipulated. Such a finding would clearly unsettle the parties' expectations under the plea bargain. In practice, however, probation officers and courts often accept the stipulations of the parties and do not disturb bargained-for stipulations of fact.[170] What is the value of the "relevant conduct" provision of the Sentencing Guidelines, and should this provision trump the results of bargaining about the relevant facts? Should fact bargaining be allowed at all? Note that the policy of the Department of Justice is that federal prosecutors should "stipulate only to facts that accurately represent the defendant's conduct,"[171] yet despite this policy, as part of plea bargaining, prosecutors often do stipulate to facts that do not fully reflect the defendant's criminal conduct.

4. Consider the following variation on the hypothetical. The government and Jamie Duke reach an agreement that the prosecution would file a 5K1.1 "substantial assistance" motion if Duke cooperates with the government by providing information about several crime figures. Duke does provide some information, but the government decides that this information is of no value to it because it is limited in scope and merely confirms facts that the government has already obtained from other sources. The prosecution therefore refuses to file a "substantial assistance" motion under USSG §5K1.1. Duke's lawyer files a motion challenging the government's failure to file such a motion as a breach of the agreement. How should the court rule? Compare the American rule to that of German and international criminal courts, in which the defendant may receive a sentencing reduction even if the prosecution has not made a motion to that effect. Note also that in these courts, it is judges who make the ultimate judgment about whether the defendant has cooperated substantially and what reduction his cooperation warrants, although judges usually defer to prosecutorial recommendations on these matters.

---

[170] *E.g.*, Frank O. Bowman, III & Michael Heise, *Quiet Rebellion? Explaining Nearly a Decade of Declining Federal Drug Sentences*, 86 Iowa L. Rev. 1043, 1122-1124 (2001).

[171] U.S. Attorneys' Manual §9-16.300.

5. Consider the following variation on the hypothetical. After Jamie Duke's guilty plea, Duke cooperates as promised with the government. But just before his sentencing, the Eleventh Circuit Court of Appeals (the court of appeals for the Southern District of Florida) decides a case in which it holds that the smuggling of drugs from Florida to the U.S. Virgin Islands does not constitute the crime of importation of a controlled substance "into the United States from any place outside thereof," as defined in 21 U.S.C. §952(a). The court concludes that the statute does not prohibit the transportation of drugs between two domestic locations within the United States, even if the travel includes a flight through international airspace. In light of this opinion, Jamie Duke moves to dismiss the importation information filed against him. He does not seek to withdraw his guilty plea to these charges. The defendant also moves to dismiss the indictment in criminal case # 05-000555. How should the court rule on the defendant's motions? *See United States v. Transfiguracion*, 442 F.3d 1222 (9th Cir. 2007).
6. Consider the following variation on the hypothetical. While Lauren Little was incarcerated in Florida pending sentencing, she was harassed and threatened by associates of Vicki Lewis, who were detained in the same jail. Several of these inmates called Little a "snitch" and threatened her and her children. During the period that she was in the jail's general population, she suffered threats and harassment almost daily whenever she was out of her cell. After three weeks in general population, jail officials determined that Little was at risk from other inmates and placed her in protective segregation for the next three months until she began serving her sentence at a different facility. Should these threats be taken into account when the court considers what sentencing benefit to award Little for her cooperation with the government?
7. Was the government justified in rejecting Vicki Lewis's offer to cooperate as untimely? Was the government correct in refusing to consider Lewis's self-incriminating statements as cooperation qualified for a substantial assistance motion? Consider the following finding by researchers at the U.S. Sentencing Commission who interviewed U.S. attorneys about their practice in moving for a substantial assistance departure when the defendant offers self-incriminating information: "The U.S. attorneys split almost evenly over whether this type of assistance would be considered in making a §5K1.1 motion; just under half of the districts (48.9%) used self-incriminating information in considering substantial assistance. This difference suggests that, depending upon the sentencing jurisdiction, one defendant may receive a sentence

reduction for such behavior, while a similarly situated defendant in another district would not. Further, as self-incriminating assistance by itself does not appear to meet the criteria of either 18 U.S.C. §3553(e) or §5K1.1, motions based solely on such cooperation may be illegal."[172]

Plea Bargaining in a Homicide Case in the United States[173]

Pat Vaughn and Raymond Jones were friends who lived in Dallas, Texas. After an altercation, Vaughn stabbed Jones twice and killed him. Vaughn was charged with murder, but after a plea deal, the prosecutor agreed to recommend probation if Vaughn pleaded guilty. Vaughn pleaded guilty, the prosecutor made the recommendation, and the judge accepted it. Consider each of the following elaborations on the scenario and discuss whether the prosecutor's decision to offer the deal would be justified.

Notes and Questions:

1. The prosecutor made the deal because there was no physical evidence linking Vaughn to the murder. The only witness, one of Vaughn's neighbors, was a drug addict, who had had numerous brushes with the law himself, had a longstanding dispute with Vaughn, and was not likely to be credible before a jury. Vaughn's girlfriend was also willing to testify that he was with her at the time the murder took place. Faced with weak evidence, the prosecutor estimated his chances of winning the case at 40 percent. Because Vaughn had no prior record, the sentence he would face if convicted would be probation to life imprisonment. Should the prosecutor have made the plea deal with Vaughn? Why or why not?
2. The prosecutor made the deal because Vaughn had a strong self-defense claim. On the night of the murder, Vaughn was alone with Jones's ex-girlfriend at a friend's trailer. Jones showed up and broke into the trailer, confronting Vaughn and starting to beat him. After Jones's ex-girlfriend ran out of the trailer and after

[172] *Id.* at 9.

[173] These hypotheticals are loosely based on cases discussed in a multi-part series of reports in the Dallas Morning News about the plea bargaining practices of the Dallas District Attorney's office in murder cases. Reese Dunklin & Brooks Egerton, *Unequal Justice: Prosecutors' Ploy in Shaky Cases*, Dallas Morning News, Nov. 14, 2007, at 1A; Brooks Egerton & Reese Dunklin, *This Case Cannot Be Proven: Though They Knew Guilt Was Far from Certain, Prosecutors Played to Win*, Dallas Morning News, Nov. 14, 2007, at 13A; Reese Dunklin & Brooks Egerton, *In Some Cases, It's High Crime, No Time*, Dallas Morning News, Nov. 12, 2007, at 1A; *see also* Ronald F. Wright & Marc L. Miller, *Dead Wrong*, 2008 Utah L. Rev. 89.

Jones had repeatedly punched Vaughn, Vaughn got a hold of a knife and stabbed Jones twice, killing him. The relevant statutory provisions on self-defense read:

Self-Defense.

(a) Except as provided in Subsection (b), a person is justified in using force against another when and to the degree the actor reasonably believes the force is immediately necessary to protect the actor against the other's use or attempted use of unlawful force. The actor's belief that the force was immediately necessary as described by this subsection is presumed to be reasonable if the actor:

(1) knew or had reason to believe that the person against whom the force was used:

(A) unlawfully and with force entered, or was attempting to enter unlawfully and with force, the actor's occupied habitation, vehicle, or place of business or employment; [. . .]

(2) did not provoke the person against whom the force was used; and

(3) was not otherwise engaged in criminal activity, other than a Class C misdemeanor that is a violation of a law or ordinance regulating traffic at the time the force was used.

(b) The use of force against another is not justified:

(1) in response to verbal provocation alone [. . .][174]

Based on your assessment of the law and the facts, should the prosecutor have made the deal with Vaughn? Why or why not?

3. The prosecutor made the deal because Raymond Jones had been a habitual criminal himself, prone to violent outbursts, while Pat Vaughn was a nice old lady who the prosecutor thought did not deserve to go to prison. Jones was also known by neighbors to have hit Vaughn on numerous occasions, although he had not been convicted of these assaults. Vaughn told the prosecutor that she stabbed Jones because he was yelling at her and threatening to hit her, as he had done in the past. Should the prosecutor have made the deal with Vaughn? Why or why not?
4. After reviewing these cases in which the prosecution bargained with defendants in murder cases, do you believe that American jurisdictions ought to ban or at least limit plea bargaining in homicide cases, as many foreign jurisdictions do? Why or why not?

[174] Tex. Pen. Code §9.31.

CHAPTER 2

Informal Bargaining

Germany

INTRODUCTION

Germany's adoption of "plea bargaining" illustrates how a legal practice can spread to new territory without any deliberate attempt to import it from abroad. Plea bargaining in Germany developed informally rather than being introduced through legislation. It was neither adopted as part of a large-scale criminal procedure reform nor modeled on a foreign system. The emergence of plea bargaining did, however, occur in the background of the well-developed system already present in the United States. Although there is no specific reference to the American practice in German opinions or in proposed legislation, scholars in Germany have long been familiar with American plea bargaining and have discussed it in some of their writings,[1] and it is part of legal education to be familiar with comparative approaches. So while the rise of plea bargaining in Germany was not directly influenced by American practice, German academics and practitioners were generally aware of the nature and importance of plea bargaining in the United States.

The informal development of plea bargaining in Germany has, on the one hand, allowed plea bargaining to evolve flexibly in response to practical needs. On the other hand, it has produced tensions with

[1] *E.g.*, Karl F. Schumann, Der Handel mit Gerechtigkeit (1977); Thomas Weigend, Absprachen im ausländischen Strafverfahren (1990); Heinz J. Dielmann, *"Guilty Plea" und "Plea Bargaining" im amerikanischen Strafverfahren - Möglichkeiten für den deutschen Strafprozess?*, 1981 Goltdammer's Archiv für Strafrecht 558; Toni M. Massaro, *Das amerikanische Plea-Bargaining System: Staatsanwaltschaftliches Ermessen bei der Strafvefolgung*, 10 Strafverteidiger 457 (1989); Thomas Weigend, *Strafzumessung durch die Parteien: Das Verfahren des plea bargaining im amerikanischen Recht*, 94 Zeitschrift für die gesamte Strafrechtswissenschaft 200 (1982).

the preexisting legal framework. It is useful to examine how Germany addressed these tensions, particularly because the German criminal justice system has served as a model for a number of other civil-law countries around the world. The German experience may also offer broader lessons about the value of introducing a foreign legal practice through informal channels. Informal adoption may mean that the practice is more easily integrated into the receiving system since it has the support of legal practitioners. But the lack of legislative involvement may cause some important public concerns to be overlooked.

It is important to note at the outset that the guilty plea as such does not exist in Germany. A defendant may confess to his crime in open court, and this confession may be considered as evidence of his guilt and substantially shorten the trial. But the practice of waiving the trial altogether simply by pleading guilty or "no contest" does not exist. For this reason, the term "plea bargaining" is something of a misnomer as applied to Germany. Courts and practitioners ordinarily use two terms best translated as "understanding" (Verständigung) and "bargaining" (Absprachen). For the sake of consistency in this book, however, I will continue to use the term plea bargaining to describe the procedure by which defendants receive concessions in exchange for confessing to a crime and possibly undertaking other actions requested by the court or prosecution.

HISTORY OF PLEA BARGAINING IN GERMANY

As late as 1979, Germany could still be called a "land without plea bargaining."[2] During the next 30 years, however, several forms of bargaining grew rapidly in Germany. The changes were largely unnoticed at first but have become much more apparent and widely acknowledged since the late 1980s.

Plea bargaining in Germany was introduced by practitioners in response to an increase in the number of complex cases in the criminal justice system. Judges and prosecutors were looking to save time and resources as their caseloads grew. Defendants were looking for greater certainty and sentence reductions in exchange for their cooperation. Because no legislature had authorized it, the practice developed slowly and was initially limited to nonviolent crimes.

---

[2] John H. Langbein, *Land Without Plea Bargaining: How the Germans Do It*, 78 Mich. L. Rev. 204 (1979).

Over time, plea bargaining has become more accepted and more widely used. While a 1986 study found that plea bargaining occurred almost exclusively in white-collar and drug cases,[3] today it also happens frequently in sexual violence, organized crime, and corruption cases, and occasionally in homicide cases.[4] The German Federal Supreme Court and Constitutional Court have held that plea bargaining does not contravene fundamental constitutional and criminal procedure principles, and the legislature has just passed a law regulating the practice.[5] Still, many prosecutors and judges are reluctant to engage in plea bargaining in serious violent crime cases.

Until recently, the German Criminal Procedure Code had no specific provision for plea bargaining. Nonetheless, reforms to the Code in the 1970s provided some opportunities to resolve cases in a more consensual fashion. Several revisions to the Code gave prosecutors greater discretion to decline to file charges and to dismiss charges. In relaxing the principle of mandatory prosecution, these amendments paved the way for the introduction of bargaining. The following Section addresses how these amendments—and the practice that built upon them—generated tensions with other Code provisions, which are resistant to the consensual resolution of criminal cases by the parties.

CONFLICT BETWEEN PLEA BARGAINING AND THE INQUISITORIAL TRADITION

While plea bargaining has become increasingly common in Germany, many commentators believe it conflicts with several fundamental principles of German criminal procedure. In particular, scholars argue that plea bargaining is inconsistent with the principle of mandatory prosecution, the duty of the judge to investigate independently the facts of the case, the right to a public trial, the principle of orality (or the right to confront adverse witnesses), the presumption of innocence, and privilege against

[3] Raimund Hassemer & Gabriele Hippler, *Informelle Absprachen in der Praxis des deutschen Strafverfahrens*, 8 Strafverteidiger 360, 361 (1986).

[4] *E.g.*, Jenia Iontcheva Turner, *Judicial Participation in Plea Negotiations: A Comparative View*, 54 Am. J. Comp. L. 199, 217 (2006).

[5] Bundesministerium der Justiz, Pressemitteilungen, Bundestag verabschiedet Gesetzentwurf zur Verständigung in Strafverfahren, May 28, 2009, *at* http://www.bmj.bund.de.

self-incrimination.[6] It is notable that four of these six criticisms are similar to those often leveled against plea bargaining in the United States. The other two—the criticisms related to mandatory prosecution and the inquisitorial trial—arise from particular features of the German system.

To understand why the adoption of plea bargaining is seen as inimical to the values of the German system, it is helpful to review some of the central features of the inquisitorial procedural model.

In adversarial systems like those of the United States and England, it is the two parties, the defense and the prosecutor, that largely guide the criminal process. The prosecutor has broad charging discretion and decides which charges best fit the facts; the judge has limited influence on charging decisions. During the investigation, each of the parties gathers its own evidence. The defense cannot rely on the police and prosecution to gather exculpatory evidence or to disclose to it evidence material to the case. At trial, too, the two parties present their evidence, question witnesses, and select the jurors who will decide the case. The judge plays the role of a passive umpire. If the parties decide to omit certain evidence or dispense with certain charges, the judge will not intervene to correct them. At the end of trial, the court decides whether the prosecution has proven the accusation; judges and jurors are under no duty to seek out additional evidence on their own.[7] In this process, the truth is supposed to emerge as a result of the contest between the two parties, not as the product of an official inquiry led by the judge.

By contrast, in the inquisitorial (or "continental") model, which originated in continental Europe and is now used in many countries around the world, the judge plays a more active role in guiding the proceedings. The model is called inquisitorial precisely because of the emphasis on official judicial inquiry as a means of uncovering the truth. One of the key responsibilities of the court is to uncover the substantive truth of the case. To fulfill that responsibility, judges read the investigative file containing all the evidence gathered by the government. At trial, they conduct further investigation, by questioning witnesses, summoning experts, and requesting additional evidence as necessary.[8] If the parties try to dispense with certain facts, it is the judge's duty to correct them.

---

[6] *See* Antonio K. Esposito & Christoph J.M. Safferling, Development, *Report—Recent Case Law of the Bundesgerichtshof (Federal Court of Justice) in Strafsachen (Criminal Law)*, 9 German L.J. 683, 700 n.59 (2008).

[7] J.R. Spencer, *Introduction*, *in* European Criminal Procedures 1, 26 (Mireille Delmas-Marty & J.R. Spencer eds. 2002).

[8] Turner, *supra* note 4, at 215.

The court also has substantial control over the charges filed. When the charges do not adequately reflect the underlying events, judges can, after giving notice, convict the defendant on different charges. Judges also decide whether charges should be dismissed once the formal accusation has been filed, and their approval is often needed for a prosecutor to refrain from filing charges.[9] Further, the judge determines the verdict and sentence—a full jury is uncommon in continental systems. While jurors do sit on mixed juries alongside professional judges in many countries following the continental model, their influence on the verdict and sentencing is minimal.

The active role of judges and the emphasis on a thorough judicial inquiry in continental systems was long seen by commentators to conflict with the notion of a consensual settlement of criminal cases. As Thomas Weigend explains, this led some commentators to believe that inquisitorial systems like Germany would resist the adoption of plea bargaining:

> [T]he basic principles of German criminal procedure law seemed to create a firm bulwark against any invasion of plea bargaining. According to the inquisitorial principle (Amtsermittlungsgrundsatz) as embodied in the German Code of Criminal Procedure of 1877 (Strafprozessordnung), the court, upon receiving a formal accusation from the public prosecutor, is obliged at trial to conduct a full enquiry into the relevant facts of the case.
>
> The defendant does not plead but is invited (though not obliged) to make a statement in open court. Even if he comes forward with a confession at the beginning of the trial, that does not relieve the court of the duty to "discover the truth." According to paragraph 244 sec 2 *Strafprozessordnung*, the court is responsible for ascertaining that all evidence needed to discover the truth about the case is produced at trial. Hence, even when the defendant has confessed, the court may have to call witnesses and take other evidence in order to find out to what extent the defendant correctly and completely related the facts of the case.
>
> Nor is it for the parties to determine the kind of evidence that goes into the court's decision-making: It is the presiding judge who calls and interrogates witnesses and experts and also introduces documentary and real evidence. The court remains, moreover, unfettered by the legal "charges" cited in the accusatory instrument (*Anklageschrift*): The court's inquiry cannot go beyond the defendant's conduct as described in the *Anklageschrift*, but the court can determine that that conduct corresponds to crime definitions different from those suggested by the

[9] *Id.*

prosecution. How could anyone expect that plea bargaining might thrive in such adverse climate?[10]

Consider the following provisions of the German Criminal Procedure Code. In what way might they conflict with different forms of plea bargaining (e.g., charge bargaining, fact bargaining, and confession bargaining)?

German Criminal Procedure Code [*Strafprozessordnung, StPO*][11]

Section 155. Scope of the Investigation

(1) The investigation and decision shall extend only to the offense specified, and to the persons accused, in the charges.

(2) Within these limits, the courts shall be authorized and obliged to act independently; in particular, they shall not be bound by the parties' applications when applying a penal norm.

Section 156. No Withdrawal of the Indictment

The public charges may not be withdrawn after the opening of the main proceedings.

Section 170. Conclusion of the Investigation Proceedings

(1) If the investigations offer sufficient reason for preferring public charges, the public prosecution office shall prefer them by submitting a bill of indictment to the competent court. [. . .]

Section 238. Conduct of Hearing

(1) The presiding judge shall conduct the hearing, examine the defendant and take the evidence. [. . .]

---

[10] Thomas Weigend, *The Decay of the Inquisitorial Ideal: Plea Bargaining Invades German Criminal Procedure*, *in* John Jackson et al., Crime, Procedure and Evidence in a Comparative and International Context 39, 43-44 (2008).

[11] Ger. Crim. Proc. Code [*Strafprozessordnung*] [hereinafter StPO], *translated at* Oxford University, German Law Archive, http://www.iuscomp.org/gla/statutes/StPO.htm. The website states that the translation was provided by the German Federal Ministry of Justice.

Section 244. Taking of Evidence

[. . .] (2) In order to establish the truth, the court shall, proprio motu, extend the taking of evidence to all facts and means of proof relevant to the decision.

(3) An application to take evidence shall be rejected if the taking of such evidence is inadmissible. In all other cases, an application to take evidence may be rejected only if the taking of such evidence is superfluous because the matter is common knowledge, if the fact to be proved is irrelevant to the decision or has already been proved, if the evidence is wholly inappropriate or unobtainable, if the application is made to protract the proceedings, or if an important allegation which is intended to offer proof in exoneration of the defendant can be treated as if the alleged fact were true. [. . .]

Section 265. Change in Legal Reference

(1) The defendant may not be sentenced on the basis of a penal norm other than the one referred to in the charges admitted by the court without first having his attention specifically drawn to the change in the legal reference and without having been afforded an opportunity to defend himself. [. . .]

Section 266. Supplementary Charges

(1) If the public prosecutor at the main hearing adds new charges of further criminal offenses committed by the defendant, the court may, in an order, include them in the proceedings, if it has jurisdiction and the defendant consents thereto. [. . .]

LAW RELATED TO PLEA BARGAINING IN GERMANY

While the provisions excerpted above appear to set up obstacles to the introduction of plea bargaining, in the 1970s, the German legislature introduced amendments to the Criminal Procedure Code, which relaxed the principle of mandatory prosecution set out in Section 170 and instead provided for various ways in which the prosecution or the court could offer defendants more lenient treatment in exchange for cooperation.

As you read the following provisions of the German Criminal Procedure Code, consider how they might have paved the way for bargaining in criminal cases. In what types of cases might they allow a form of bargaining? What appear to be the roles of the prosecutor and the court in such bargaining?

German Criminal Procedure Code[12]

Section 153. Non-Prosecution of Petty Offenses

(1) If a less serious criminal offense is the subject of the proceedings, the public prosecution office may dispense with prosecution with the approval of the court competent for the opening of the main proceedings if the perpetrator's culpability is considered to be of a minor nature and there is no public interest in the prosecution. The approval of the court shall be not required in the case of a less serious criminal offense which is not subject to an increased minimum penalty and where the consequences ensuing from the offense are minimal.

(2) If charges have already been preferred, the court, with the consent of the public prosecution office and the indicted accused, may terminate the proceedings at any stage thereof under the conditions in subsection (1). [. . .]

Section 153a. Provisional Dispensing with Court Action; Provisional Termination of Proceedings

(1) In a case involving a less serious criminal offense, the public prosecution office may, with the consent of the court competent to order the opening of the main proceedings and with the consent of the accused, dispense with preferment of public charges and concurrently impose a condition upon the accused:

1. to make a certain contribution towards reparation for damage caused by the offense,
2. to pay a sum of money to a non-profit-making institution or to the Treasury,
3. to perform some other service of a non-profit-making nature,
4. to comply with duties to pay maintenance at a certain level, or
5. to participate in a seminar pursuant to section 2b subsection (2), second sentence, or section 4 subsection (8), fourth sentence, of the Road Traffic Act,

if such conditions and instructions are of such nature as to eliminate the public interest in criminal prosecution and if the degree of culpability does not present an obstacle. [. . .]

---

[12] *Id.*

(2) If the public charges have already been preferred, the court may, with the consent of the public prosecution office and of the indicted accused, provisionally terminate the proceedings up until the end of the main hearing in which the findings of fact can last be examined, and concurrently impose the conditions and instructions referred to in subsection (1), first sentence, on the indicted accused. Subsection (1), second to fifth sentences, shall apply mutatis mutandis. [. . .]

Section 153b. Dispensing with Court Action; Termination

(1) If the conditions exist under which the court may dispense with imposing a penalty, the public prosecution office may, with the consent of the court which would have jurisdiction over the main hearing, dispense with preferment of public charges.

(2) If charges have already been preferred the court may, with the consent of the public prosecution office and of the indicted accused, terminate proceedings prior to the beginning of the main hearing. [. . .]

Section 154. Insignificant Secondary Penalties

(1) The public prosecution office may dispense with prosecuting an offense:

1. if the penalty or the measure of reform and prevention in which the prosecution might result is not particularly significant in addition to a penalty or measure of reform and prevention which was imposed with binding effect upon the accused for another offense, or which he has to expect for another offense, or
2. beyond that, if a judgment is not to be expected for such offense within reasonable time, and if a penalty or measure of reform and prevention which was imposed with binding effect upon the accused, or which he has to expect for another offense, appears sufficient to have an influence on the perpetrator and to defend the legal order.

(2) If public charges have already been preferred, the court, upon the public prosecution office's application, may provisionally terminate the proceedings at any stage. [. . .]

Section 154a. Limitation of Prosecution

(1) If individual separable parts of an offense or some of several violations of law committed as a result of the same offense are not particularly significant

1. for the penalty or measure of reform and prevention to be expected, or
2. in addition to a penalty or measure of reform and prevention which has been imposed with binding effect upon the accused for another offense or which he has to expect for another offense, prosecution may be limited to the other parts of the offense or the other violations of law. Section 154 subsection 1, number 2, shall apply mutatis mutandis. The limitation shall be included in the records.

(2) After filing of the bill of indictment, the court, with the consent of the public prosecution office, may make this limitation at any stage of the proceedings.

(3) At any stage of the proceedings the court may reintroduce into the proceedings those parts of the offense or violations of law which were not considered. An application by the public prosecution office for reintroduction shall be granted. [. . .]

Until May 2009, the German legislature had not adopted rules that regulated bargaining directly. Despite the lack of authorization, bargaining was increasingly used by practitioners, so courts stepped in to provide guidance in particular cases. The current legal framework for plea bargaining has therefore largely been crafted by the judiciary. Three decisions are especially notable in this regard. They help provide an answer to the question asked earlier—how traditional German criminal procedure principles can be reconciled with plea bargaining.

In 1987, the Federal Constitutional Court (*Bundesverfassungsgericht* or *BVerfG*), the highest court with jurisdiction over constitutional questions, delivered the first landmark decision on plea bargaining.[13] The Court held that plea bargaining is not unconstitutional as long as it complies with certain recognized principles, including full investigation of the facts by the judge, a verdict based upon these facts and the law, compulsory prosecution, and proportionality between the punishment and the defendant's culpability.

In 1997, the Federal Supreme Court (*Bundesgerichtshof*, or *BGH*)[14] held that the Code of Criminal Procedure does not forbid agreements between the court and the parties as to the sentence to be imposed:[15]

---

[13] Kammerbeschluß vom 27. Januar 1987, NJW 1987, 2662, NStZ 1987, 419.

[14] The Federal Supreme Court is the highest court of appeals for criminal cases, unless a constitutional issue is involved, in which case the defendant can petition the Federal Constitutional Court.

[15] BGHSt 43, 195, Decision of August 28, 1997, *translated in* Stephen Thaman, Comparative Criminal Procedure 145-150 (2002).

> It is true, to be sure, that the German law of criminal procedure is designed in a way which is fundamentally inimical to settlements [. . .]; it prohibits the free disposition of the court and the procedural participants over the state's right to punish. [. . .]
>
> On the other hand the provisions of §153a StPO [Criminal Procedure Code], which make possible the conditional dismissal of the proceedings with the consent of the defendant and the public prosecutor, show that an agreement between the procedural participants—even as to the result and the termination of criminal proceedings—is not wholly alien to German criminal procedure. In addition there are other provisions which allow for the consent of the affected party to a certain legal consequence and are therefore linked as a rule with a prognosis as to the result of the trial. [. . .][16]

The Court emphasized that deals should be examined on a case-by-case basis for compliance with principles of procedural and substantive criminal law. For example, "fact bargaining" is not permitted under the law; judges remain obligated to ensure that parties are not seeking to present an agreed version of the facts that does not correspond to reality. Judges must examine the confession of the defendant for its credibility and, where necessary, gather further evidence to ascertain the truth. In addition, the defendant "must not be pressured to confess through threats of higher punishment or through promises of a benefit not provided by the law."[17] The results and the material content of bargaining discussions must be revealed during the main hearing and entered into the trial record. All parties, including the lay judges, must be included in the bargaining discussions. Finally, the court may not make a binding promise as to the specific sentence to be imposed, though it may set an upper limit that it will not exceed.

If each of these principles has been followed, the court will be bound by the agreement, unless "grave new circumstances present themselves after the deal, which were earlier unknown to the court and could influence the judgment."[18] If such circumstances arise, the court may deviate from the agreement after giving notice to the defendant. In the particular case before it, the Federal Supreme Court reversed the conviction because the trial court had not adhered to all of the relevant principles. In particular, the trial court had promised a firm sentence, rather than

---

[16] *Id.* at 145-146.

[17] *Id.* at 146.

[18] *Id.* at 149-150. The Court elaborated: "Such circumstances could, for instance, be that the act turns out to be a felony instead of a delict due to new facts or evidence [. . .] or that serious prior convictions of the defendant were unknown." *Id.* at 150.

a mere maximum limit, in exchange for the defendant's confession.[19] By binding itself to a particular result before the deliberations on the judgment, the trial court violated Sections 260(1)[20] and 261[21] of the Criminal Procedure Code.

The next major ruling on plea bargaining came in 2005, when the Grand Chamber of the Federal Supreme Court[22] intervened to resolve a split among several chambers of the same court on the permissibility of bargained-for appeals waivers. While reconfirming that plea bargaining is permissible under German law, the Grand Chamber imposed limits on the parties' ability to waive their rights to appeal as part of plea bargaining. In particular, the trial court may not participate in negotiations concerning appeals waivers. The court must also warn the defendant, in open court, that regardless of any bargain reached with the prosecution before trial, the defendant still has the right to appeal the final judgment; in other words, such bargains will not be enforced by the court. If after receiving this warning, the defendant nonetheless waives his right to appeal in court, the waiver will become effective.

Although the decision focused on the issue of appeals waivers, it was also important for reinforcing the acceptability of plea bargains in German criminal procedure and elaborating on the conditions for their validity.

German Federal Supreme Court Decision, March 3, 2005, BGH GSSt 1/04[23]

[. . .]

A

[. . .]

I. Two appeal proceedings are before the Third Criminal Chamber of the Federal Supreme Court. In both cases, the court must first decide

---

[19] *Id.* at 150.

[20] Section 260(1) reads: "The main hearing shall close with delivery of judgment following the deliberations."

[21] Section 261 reads: "The court shall decide on the result of the evidence taken according to its free conviction gained from the hearing as a whole."

[22] The Federal Supreme Court convening as a Grand Chamber is similar to a U.S. Appeals Court sitting *en banc*.

[23] I thank Professor Thomas Weigend, University of Cologne, for significant help and guidance on the translation of this decision.

on the validity of an appeals waiver. The Third Chamber has joined the two cases for consideration and decision.

1. In the case against J. (3 StR 415/02),[24] the issue revolves around an appeals waiver to which the parties "stipulated" as part of a bargain and which all sides formally declared after the verdict was rendered. The defendant now petitions the court to re-instate his right to appeal.

   The Regional Court of Duisburg found the defendant guilty on three counts of unlawfully distributing drugs in not insignificant amounts and sentenced him to four years and six months of imprisonment. Immediately after sentencing, the defendant waived his right to appeal. Five months later, in a petition dated 25 September 2002 and received by the court on 27 September 2002, the defendant filed an appeal and asked the court to restore him to the position he was in before his filing deadline had expired. In support of his petition, the defendant argues that the appeals waiver was part of a bargain concerning the judgment and was therefore invalid. The defendant claims that he did not become aware of this fact until September 20, 2002, the day his new defense attorney was granted access to his case file.

   The facts are as follows: After discussion of the facts and the law, followed by a one-hour adjournment, the following note was placed on the trial record: "After discussion of the facts and the law, the court promised a maximum imprisonment term of four years and nine months on the condition that the right to appeal be waived." At that point the representative of the prosecutor's office, as well as the defendant and his defense attorney, stated that they concurred with "such an agreement" and, respectively, "the promise of the court." After the charges were read, the defendant was informed that he was free to testify or to remain silent. He declared that he wished to testify. Afterwards, "the defendant confessed through his attorney that the charges were true." Furthermore, the defense attorney explained on behalf of his client that the defendant agreed to the "extrajudicial confiscation" of the seized narcotics and money. Thereupon, the court dispensed with the examination of the witnesses. After essentially concurring closing arguments from the prosecution and the defense, as well as the defendant's final words, the court pronounced the verdict and the sentence and ordered continuation of the defendant's detention. Immediately thereafter, the defendant, his defense

[24] Criminal judgments in Germany provide only the first letter of the defendant's name.

attorney, and the prosecutor waived their rights to appeal. Their declarations were read aloud and approved.

2. In the case against H. (3 StR 368/02), the appeals waiver itself was not part of the bargain. But the court noted that a waiver of legal remedies would be "desirable." In response to the court's question, the defendant and her defense attorney declared an appeals waiver after the verdict was pronounced. Notwithstanding the waiver, the defendant filed an appeal within the statutory period set forth in §341 StPO.

In a complex drug case involving multiple defendants, the regional court in Lüneburg found the defendant guilty on ten counts that included illegal importation of drugs and aiding and abetting the distribution of drugs in not insignificant amounts. The court sentenced the defendant to eight years and six months imprisonment. The defendant appealed this judgment on July 5, 2002, one day after the verdict was pronounced. The defendant is of the opinion that her appeal is admissible, even though she waived her right to appeal after the verdict was rendered. She argues that her appeals waiver is invalid.

The trial that gave rise to this appeal proceeded as follows: On the first day in court, the trial was temporarily adjourned in order to "give the parties (prosecution, defense, and court) the opportunity to explore a consensual settlement of the case." After one hour, the trial resumed. As to what happened then, the record of the proceedings states: "The presiding judge announced the contents of the conversation that was held during the trial break: The court suggests the following settlement of the case (appeals waiver desirable): In the event of a complete and credible confession from the defendant, the court would impose a sentence no higher than 8 years and 6 months. The trial was then once again adjourned to "allow the trial participants, in particular the defendants and their counsel, to discuss the court's suggestion." After 40 minutes, the trial resumed again. The trial participants, in particular the defendants and their counsel, stated: "We concur with the proposed trial settlement, including the suggested maximum sentence." Afterwards, counsel for the defendant announced that the charges against the defendant were true, and the defendant confirmed that the charges were correct.

At the next trial session, the verdict was rendered. Then the court instructed the defendants on their right to appeal and distributed relevant forms. While the other defendants did not waive their right to appeal, counsel for the defendant stated: "We waive our right to appeal." Upon the court's inquiry, the defendant stated, after a short conference with counsel, "I waive my right to appeal the verdict that was just pronounced." This statement was read into the record and approved. Immediately thereafter, the prosecutor also waived the right to appeal the verdict with respect to the defendant H.

II. The Third Criminal Chamber of the Federal Supreme Court regards the waiver of appeal in both cases as invalid. [. . .] According to the Chamber, an appeals waiver may not be agreed upon as part of a bargain, nor may the court initiate such an agreement. Because of the impermissibility of the way in which the trial court proceeded, the Chamber holds the defendants' appeals waivers to be invalid. [. . .][25]

IV. Thereupon the Third Chamber [. . .] submitted the following questions for decision to the Grand Chamber of the Federal Supreme Court [. . .]:

1. Is it permissible to agree, as part of a bargain, to waive the right to appeal?
2. Is it permissible for the court, in the context of a bargain, to initiate discussion of an appeals waiver by specifically bringing up or recommending such a waiver?
3. Is the defendant's appeals waiver valid if it was preceded by a bargain that impermissibly included a promise to waive the right to appeal, or if the court, without accepting an impermissible promise to waive the right to appeal, had only initiated discussion of such a waiver?

[. . .]

B

[. . .]

I.

To answer the questions presented to us, we must first decide upon the permissibility of judgment bargaining. It is true that the questions presented concern only the legality of appeals waivers that form part of a bargain. But these questions can be answered meaningfully only if bargaining itself is not illegal.

[25] [Here, the court notes the disagreement on the question of the permissibility of appeals waivers among different chambers of the Federal Supreme Court.—EDS.]

1. The Criminal Procedure Code does not recognize agreements about the outcome of a criminal trial as a method of resolving a case, nor does it recognize binding promises regarding the outcome of a trial. Yet despite the lack of legal regulation, a practice has developed within the criminal justice system, in which the participants not only discuss the status and prospects of the trial—which is not objectionable (see BVerfG – Kammer – NJW 1987, 2662)—but also, increasingly, make an agreement on the outcome of the trial, or attempt to reach such agreement. In a significant number of cases, the possibility of an appeals waiver is a component of such an agreement.
2. Over the last few years, the Federal Supreme Court has addressed on a number of occasions legal issues that have arisen out of this practice.
   a. At first, the Court had to examine, under different legal aspects, individual procedural issues typically associated with bargaining. Various judgments of the Federal Supreme Court dealt with possible judicial bias, undue influence on the will of a person under interrogation (§136a, Criminal Procedure Code), as well as violations of the fair trial principle, the right to be heard in court, and the right to present evidence. [. . .]
   b. In its decision BGHSt 43, 195, the Fourth Criminal Chamber of the Federal Supreme Court finally provided a general assessment of bargaining in the criminal process under the aspects of due process of law, the ideal of justice, and the need for a functioning system of criminal justice. The Chamber pronounced rules that, if adhered to by the trial court, would render bargaining (still) compatible with existing law.

      Accordingly, the following minimum requirements were laid down for a bargain to be permissible: There can be no bargain as to the verdict; the court must examine the confession for its credibility; all participants must be involved in the process; the results of the bargain must be made known and officially recorded; the court can promise only the upper limit of a sentence; the court may deviate from the promised limit only if significant new aggravating circumstances have developed; the intent to deviate must be communicated during trial; and finally, the sentence must be commensurate with the defendant's blameworthiness. It is unlawful to pressure the accused into a confession by threatening him with an inappropriately severe sentence or by promising him advantages not provided for by the law, to promise the accused a more lenient sentence in exchange for waiving his right to appeal [. . .], or to even make an appeals waiver part of the bargain.

c. In the meantime, each Criminal Chamber of the Federal Supreme Court has issued several opinions evaluating plea bargaining based on the minimum requirements of BGHSt 43, 195. [citations omitted]

3. The Grand Criminal Chamber (Große Senat für Strafsachen) holds that bargaining is in principle legal and compatible with the current Criminal Procedure Code. The Court has, however, reason to emphasize and to state more precisely the limitations on bargaining inherent in the Constitution and the Code of Criminal Procedure, as already set forth in BGHSt 43, 195.

a. Constitutional limitations on bargaining result especially from the principle of fair trial and the guilt principle.[26]

The defendant has the right to a fair trial based on the rule of law. [citations omitted] The way in which the court fulfils its duty to investigate the facts, the legal qualification of the offense, and the principles of sentencing cannot be left to arbitrariness or to the unfettered disposition of the parties and the court. Therefore, the court and the prosecutor are not allowed to engage in a settlement in the guise of a verdict or to barter with justice. Criminal proceedings may not be conducted, moreover, in a way that the accused becomes a mere object of the process. In order to maintain his rights, the accused must, within the framework provided by the Criminal Procedure Code, have the opportunity to influence the progress and the result of the trial, not only theoretically, but also practically. [citations omitted]

A central goal of a criminal process conducted under the rule of law is the ascertainment of the true facts as the necessary foundation for a just verdict. The examination of the facts by the trial court is governed by the requirement "to clarify the facts in the best possible manner"; this requirement is inherent in §244 of the Criminal Procedure Code and the Constitution. [citations omitted] The task of establishing the results of the process of taking evidence is, in principle, left to the deliberation of the court when determining the verdict, because the trial court must, in accordance with §261 of the Criminal Procedure

[26] [The guilt principle is the principle that criminal responsibility must be proportionate to personal culpability.—EDS.]

Code, derive the relevant factual findings from the totality of the trial. [citations omitted]

The punishment must be proportionate to the defendant's culpability. The principle that the punishment must be proportionate to culpability is of constitutional order. It is derived from Article 1, §1, and Article 2, §1 of the Basic Law, as well as from the principle of the rule of law. Section 46, para. 1 of the Criminal Code is an expression of this principle. [citations omitted] The sentence may not depart—not even downward—from its purpose to provide just punishment commensurate with culpability. The sentence must be proportionate to the level of personal culpability and to the degree of unlawfulness and dangerousness of the crime; it must also be consistent with sentences imposed in similar cases. [citations omitted]

b. Apart from the question concerning the legality of appeals waivers (see Part II), in consideration of the above-mentioned constitutional guidelines and their embodiment in the provisions of the current Criminal Procedure Code, the following minimum requirements for a permissible bargain must be met, as already laid out in the earlier decision of the Federal Supreme Court, BGHSt 43, 195:

The court may not hastily resort to a bargain without first fulfilling its duty to review the factual basis and especially the legal basis of the charges based on the case file. [citations omitted]

The reliability of any confession, which as a rule is part of a bargain, must be examined. The court must be convinced of its correctness. A self-incriminating confession that does not, in the case at hand, give rise to any particular doubt, must at least be so concrete that the court can determine whether the confession reflects the facts presented in the case file to such an extent that a further examination of the matter is not necessary. A mere formal confession without substance does not meet this standard. [citations omitted] For confessions "that implicate third parties" the Grand Chamber refers to BGHSt 48, 161.

The verdict cannot be part of a bargain, with the exception of the possibilities permitted in the interest of an efficient administration of justice by §§154 and 154a of the Criminal Procedure Code, which should not be applied in an unnecessarily restrictive fashion.

The difference between the sentence following a bargain and the sentence expected in the case of a contested trial may not be so large ("sentence gap") that it cannot be justified under applicable sentencing law and cannot be explained as a reasonable reduction of sentence because of the defendant's confession. This applies when the sentence suggested by the court in the absence of a bargain exceeds a justifiable limit and therefore results in intolerable pressure on the accused, but also when the sentence discount leads to a sentence below the level that could be considered proportionate to the defendant's guilt.

The court may, BGHSt 43, 195 (Headnote 2) notwithstanding, deviate from its sentencing promise not only because of new findings, but also—after giving due notice to the parties—if pertinent facts or legal issues that had existed during the bargaining process had been overlooked. [citations omitted] It would be indefensible for the court, while rendering a verdict, to bind itself to a significant mistake, in violation of §261 of the Criminal Procedure Code, only because the court had raised certain expectations on the part of the defendant in the course of bargaining; instead, the court must dispel any such expectations by giving appropriate notice.

4. The Grand Criminal Chamber is aware of the fact that the jurisprudence of the Federal Supreme Court, which generally allows bargains under the minimum requirements set out in the decision BGHSt 43, 195, has met with criticism in the literature. Apart from doubts as to whether the goal to set up a framework for bargaining has been achieved, and whether that goal is indeed even attainable [. . .], the Federal Supreme Court has been accused of exceeding its legal authority to develop the law by introducing an institutionalized bargaining procedure. This concern is not shared by the Grand Criminal Chamber.
   a. It is true that the Criminal Procedure Code does not contain provisions on bargaining. In fact, the Criminal Procedure Code is in principle adverse to bargaining. It is also true that the recognition of binding agreements as to the sentence is difficult to reconcile with §261 of the Criminal Procedure Code, even when such agreements are only as to the maximum length of the sentence, as required by BGHSt 43, 195. It should also not be overlooked that bargains, more than proceedings conducted in strict accordance with the Criminal Procedure Code, run the risk of falling short of the requirement that the court fully investigate the facts of the case (§244 para. 2 Criminal Procedure Code).

      Finally, bargaining—which is in essence the submission of a confession in exchange for a binding promise of a sentence—in many ways needs further development and guidelines beyond those provided by the BGHSt 43, 195 decision. It is necessary to determine, in particular, who is to be bound by the promise of a sentence: only the trial court which has made the promise, or the appellate court as well, or perhaps even the court to which the case is remanded after a successful appeal. It is further indispensable to determine whether and under what conditions a sentence promise can lose its binding force (see above 3(b)). Especially considering that an agreement is no longer binding if new facts are discovered or even if elements relevant to the sentence had been overlooked, one must ask whether—and if so, under what conditions—a confession given pursuant to an agreement can still be used as evidence after the court's sentencing promise has lost its binding force, and what considerations may apply when the court determines the evidentiary value of such confession. There must also be regulation as to whether the court's promise is binding even when necessary participants had not been involved or heard during the negotiations—in particular, when the prosecutor was not involved in the bargaining or was unable to agree with the results. The question of the binding nature of an agreement also arises when the result of negotiations before trial has not been discussed at trial and entered into the trial record, in violation of the guidelines in BGHSt 43, 195. With respect to the appeals process, questions arise beyond those presented in this case concerning appellate waivers. It is also necessary to decide whether and to what extent certain appeals claims—for example, those concerning the court's duty of establishing the facts—are excluded, given the special circumstances of negotiations, for example, the self-contradictory conduct on the part of the appellant.[27]

b. Dealing with these questions—and others which may arise depending on the response given to those mentioned—is necessary, but difficult, because the Criminal Procedure Code does not recognize a consensual process leading to a verdict and sentence and therefore provides no standards for struc-

---

[27] The "self-contradictory conduct" to which the Court refers is the following: The defendant agrees to a reduced sentence in exchange for a confession and thus implicitly waives a full-scale investigation of the case. He then brings an appeal charging that the court did not fulfill its duty to fully investigate the case. That is why the Court suggests that this claim should be excluded as a basis for appeal. Email from Thomas Weigend to author, May 19, 2008.

turing such a process. Therefore, the introduction of negotiation proceedings into the strictly formalized criminal process through judicial decisions is pushing against the limits set by the Basic Law, which has limited the judiciary's power to develop the law by the way in which it has allocated the tasks of the legislature and the judiciary. But these limits have not been overstepped:

aa. The Basic Law rejects a narrow legal positivism, as can be seen from Article 20, Section 3, which provides that judges are bound by "law and justice." The responsibility of judges is not merely to recognize and enunciate legislative decisions. In principle, judges are not prevented from engaging in "creative jurisprudence," which contains elements of personal choice. In particular, the highest courts have claimed this authority from the very beginning, with the endorsement of the Constitutional Court. [citation omitted] As the Constitutional Court has specifically pointed out, the Grand Chamber, to which §132 sec. 4 of the Code of Court Organisation (GVG) assigns the particular duty to develop the law, is especially entitled to this authority.

The judge has a right to a "more liberal application of legal norms" [. . .] when the written norm, if strictly applied, would no longer fulfill its intended purpose. The interpretation of a legal norm cannot be forever tied to the meaning it had at the time when the norm was established. One must consider the reasonable function the law could fulfill at the time of implementation. "The norm always exists in a context of social relationships and sociopolitical views, which the norm is meant to operate on; under certain circumstances, the contents of the norm can and must change as these views and relationships change." (BVerfGE 34, p. 288) [. . .]

bb. When these standards are applied, the preconditions exist for a judicial development of the Criminal Procedure Code. Especially in light of the undeniable need for a functioning criminal justice system, courts can permit bargaining that fulfills the above-mentioned minimal requirements.

The principle of the rule of law, the state's duty to protect the safety of its citizens and their trust in the effective functioning of public institutions, and not least the requirement of treating equally all persons accused in criminal proceedings all compel the relevant public entities, and especially the institutions of criminal justice, to ensure that the public claim to enforcing the criminal law is asserted to the greatest extent possible, taking all potential criminal cases into account. Public institutions must not forego this claim arbitrarily or for invalid reasons generally, partially or in particular cases. The rule of law can be realized only if it is certain that criminals are prosecuted, judged, and justly sentenced in accordance with applicable law. [citation omitted]

Under the current legal and practical conditions of criminal justice, the criminal justice system would no longer be able cope with the above-mentioned demands without judicial authorization of negotiations. Especially in light of the meager resources of the judicial system (see the resolution of the conference the State Ministries of Justice and the Federal Ministry of Justice on 17/18 June 2004: "The State Ministries of Justice and the Federal Ministry of Justice again take notice that the criminal justice system is working at the limit of its capacity."), the criminal justice system could no longer function effectively if the courts were generally forbidden from negotiating with the parties the contents of the judgment to be handed down. Insofar as bargains meet the stated minimum requirements, they make it possible overall to accommodate the sometimes conflicting demands of a properly functioning criminal justice system.

This is especially true with regard to the principle of speedy justice, which is an element of the principle of the rule of law, as well as with regard to the principle of efficient procedure. Both of these principles can determine to what extent the court must strive to investigate the facts of the case. The gravity of the crime and the significance and relevance of further evidence-gathering are to be balanced against the disadvantage of delaying the process. [citation omitted] The Criminal Procedure Code—like any other procedure code—takes account of the interest in efficient proceedings, especially where there is a risk of undue delay. [citations omitted] For example, §154 sec. 1 no. 2 of the Criminal Procedure Code expressly permits a partial dismissal of charges "if a judgment on this act cannot be expected within a reasonable time." Under the same conditions, prosecution can be dropped with respect to certain separable elements of an offense or to several instances of a series of violations (§154a sec. 1 2nd sent. of the Criminal Procedure Code); this limitation of the criminal prosecution also allows for a charge reduction [*Reduzierung des Schuldspruchs*]. [citation omitted] The court may also refrain from imposing forfeiture under §§430, 442 of the Criminal Procedure Code if the necessary proceedings would require "an unreasonable effort." In addition, a trial delay may lead to a sentence below the level that would be commensurate with the defendant's guilt, even if the delay has been caused by the court's overburdened docket. [citations omitted]

The development of criminal procedure law connected to the judicial authorization of negotiations is defensible on constitutional grounds because the right to a fair trial also protects witnesses, specifically victim-witnesses, from becoming a mere object of a trial conducted under the rule of law. [citation omitted] In the legislature's view, the role of a social judicial system is not only the investigation of the crime and the determination of guilt or innocence of the accused in a just trial, but also the protection of the victim's interests (compare the reasoning of the Federal Government in the proposal of the Victim's Rights Reform Law of 24 June 2004, BGB1 I 1354, BT-Drucks. 15.2536). A concern for witnesses and victims can be a reason for refraining from the further investigation of facts (especially by applying §§154, 154a of the Criminal Procedure Code), even if this means forsaking a potential finding of increased culpability of the defendant. [. . .]

cc. The Grand Criminal Chamber would refrain from developing the law by authorizing bargaining (within the established narrow limits) to respond to the changed conditions and to safeguard the effectiveness of the criminal justice system, were a relevant law to be expected from the legislature. [citation omitted] But despite an urgent need for regulation, there is no concrete prospect of legislative action.

II.

On the basis of its finding that bargains are permissible when the stated requirements are met, the Grand Criminal Chamber holds, in response to the first and second questions presented, that it is impermissible for the court to negotiate an appeals waiver with the other participants before the verdict has been handed down (accord, BGHSt 43, 195). Beyond that, it is impermissible for the court to participate in any form in an appeals waiver.

It is beyond argument that the extreme case in which the sentence length is tied to a promise to waive the right to appeal violates the principle that sentencing must be proportionate with the offender's guilt. [citation omitted] Furthermore, negotiations may not take place concurrently with the trial proceedings, as a freestanding, informal process; they must not be conducted under a cloak of unaccountability, and their contents must be subject to review by the appellate court. [citation omitted] As the referring Chamber has correctly stated, there is no legitimate interest that would justify the authorization of an appeals waiver negotiated as part of a bargain. In addition, allowing such waivers may produce severe risks not only for the legal culture but also for the effective protection of essential interests in a criminal procedure conducted according to the rule of law.

In bargained cases, too, there must be an effective opportunity for obtaining review of the trial court's decision by the appellate court. Yet if the trial court becomes involved, in the course of negotiations, in an agreement to waive appeals rights, or if it goes so far as to encourage such a waiver, the court demonstrates that it does not wish its decision to be subjected to further judicial review. This harms the dignity of the court and hurts its authority. But above all, such a procedure raises serious concerns that when a trial court expects that its decision is not subject to review, it may not fulfill as conscientiously its duties to examine carefully the facts of the case, to apply the relevant substantive criminal law to the facts, and to assess a commensurate sentence.

On these grounds, the court cannot be permitted to play a role in negotiations that include an appeals waiver. The parties entitled to appeal remain at liberty, even before the verdict, but without the participation of the court, to have discussions as to the decision to appeal. But the court must not actively participate in discussions that involve, beyond an agreement on the verdict and sentence, the possibility of an appeals waiver; the court must neither raise the issue nor endorse or demand an appeals waiver. The court must, in the context of negotiations and before the verdict, refrain from any comment that could objectively be understood as indicating that the court would be glad to receive an appeals waiver, or that a waiver could be advantageous to the defendant.

The Grand Criminal Chamber understands that the parties will rarely need to ask for appellate review after the conclusion of a bargain that has been negotiated under fair conditions. It is nevertheless essential to retain the possibility of reviewing every judgment within the limits of appellate procedure, and thereby to make it possible to assess whether bargained judgments are conducted within the limits of permissible bargaining. [. . .]

Notes and Questions:

1. According to the German Federal Supreme Court, how can German-style plea bargaining be reconciled with traditional inquisitorial principles of criminal procedure? Do you believe that the Court adequately addresses the tension between these principles and plea bargaining?
2. How has the Federal Supreme Court balanced the principles of fair trial, "which include that the court may not act contrary to its own earlier explanations upon which a party has relied,"[28] and the principle that punishment must be proportionate to guilt and must take into consideration all the relevant facts and law? Do you believe that the balance the Court struck is just? How does the Court's approach compare to that of American courts?
3. The Court poses several difficult questions, without offering concrete answers to them. How would you respond to two of these questions?

    a. Which courts should be bound by the trial court's promise concerning a maximum sentence: only the trial court that has made the promise, or also the appellate court and/or the court to which the case is remanded after a successful appeal?
    b. Should a court be able to use a confession given pursuant to a bargain as evidence after the bargain has fallen apart? If so, under what conditions? What considerations may apply when the court determines the evidentiary value of such a confession?

4. Should defendants be allowed to waive the right to appeal the verdict as part of a plea bargain? Why or why not? How did the Grand Chamber of the Federal Supreme Court answer this question? What do you think about the merits of this approach? How does it compare to the approach of American courts?
5. What does the court's duty to confirm the credibility of the confession (or to confirm the factual basis of the bargain) entail?

---

[28] BGH 43, 195, *translated in* Thaman, *supra* note 15, at 149.

6. In what cases may a large sentencing discount put intolerable pressure on the accused and thus violate the principles laid out by the Federal Supreme Court? In interviews with this author, several German judges have stated that a typical sentencing discount for a plea bargain is around 30 percent. Is that a reasonable discount, or might it be too coercive in certain circumstances? What about cases where the defendant would be offered probation as part of a plea bargain, but would face prison time if convicted after a contested trial? Given the absence of sentencing guidelines in Germany, how does the court make a prediction about what the sentence would be in the absence of a plea bargain? Might plea bargaining have a "ratcheting up" effect, whereby courts could be tempted to inflate the predicted sentences in the absence of a plea bargain in order to induce a defendant to cooperate?
7. The Federal Supreme Court states that "[c]riminal proceedings may not be conducted . . . in a way that the accused becomes a mere object of the process." In the same opinion, however, the court notes that "in light of the meager resources of the judicial system . . . , the criminal justice system could no longer function effectively if the courts were generally forbidden from negotiating with the parties the contents of the judgment to be handed down." Does the defendant in fact become "an object of the process" for the sake of ensuring the effective functioning of the criminal justice system? Could plea bargaining be justified on non-utilitarian grounds?
8. Based on the court judgments and Criminal Procedure Code provisions excerpted above, what are the requirements for validity of a negotiated judgment in Germany? After identifying these requirements, consider the following account of German plea bargaining practice. Does plea bargaining in practice comply with the requirements established by the courts and the Code? What type of regulation might reduce the discrepancies between the law and practice of plea bargaining?

Jenia Iontcheva Turner, *Judicial Participation in Plea Negotiations: A Comparative View*

54 AM. J. COMP. L. 199, 220-222 (2006)

Because negotiations occur off-the-record in Germany, public scrutiny of the process is largely limited to the participation of lay judges in the final sentence deliberations. But even their role is rather minimal.

Once the protocol is read out in public and the defendant confesses to the crime as agreed, the professional judges retire back to a conference with their two lay colleagues. Usually, it is during this conference that the lay judges first hear about the plea discussions. They rarely play a role in the negotiations because they are not empanelled until the main proceedings begin. Moreover, unlike the professional judges, they are not allowed to review the case file. They have to rely on the professional judges' representation of the facts to make their decision, so they are easily swayed by the judges' opinion. While some professional judges are more solicitous of the laypersons' opinions on the plea negotiations and the result reached, others simply tell them the outcome and ask for their consent. For all of these reasons, lay judges influence the verdict and sentence in negotiated cases only in the most exceptional circumstances.

The transparency of the process is further reduced because judgments after a plea bargain are likely to be much shorter than in a case that has been fully tried. This is especially true where the defendant has waived the right to appeal the judgment. In most cases, such a waiver is an implicit part of the plea bargain. It is rarely stated expressly, however, because the case law forbids judges to discuss appellate waivers in connection with a plea deal. The parties can discuss such waivers in an informal manner, without the court's involvement. While this informal agreement has no binding force, the attorneys, who are usually repeat players in the local criminal justice system, have no interest in upsetting the deal by filing an appeal. Waivers therefore regularly accompany plea bargains.

Case law further provides that judges cannot promise to impose a specific sentence during the negotiations and can only state a cap beyond which they would not go. The rationale behind this prohibition is that judges should be able to adjust the sentence in light of additional facts that might be revealed at trial. In reality, the cap itself may be a signal about the expected sentence, or the judge may informally note in the negotiations what the expected sentence would be.

In 2006, the Federal Ministry of Justice drafted a proposal for amending the Code of Criminal Procedure to regulate plea bargains expressly. A number of changes were proposed, but perhaps the most significant were the additions to Article 257. In May 2009, the German legislature adopted the draft proposal largely unchanged. Since the law was passed as this book was going into production, I have identified in footnotes only the few material changes in the final version of the legislation.[29]

Federal Ministry of Justice, Draft Proposal to Amend the Code of Criminal Procedure (excerpt)[30]

§257b

During the main proceeding, the court can discuss the status of the case with a view toward expediting the proceedings.

§257c

(1) In appropriate cases, during the main hearing [*Hauptverhandlung*], the court may reach an understanding with the parties about the future proceedings in the case, as well as about the outcome of the case.

(2) An understanding of this kind could encompass only such legal matters that pertain to the verdict and related decisions, measures related to the trial proceedings, and the conduct of the parties during the proceedings. With the consent of the accused, the court can, after freely evaluating all the evidence in the case, as well as considering general sentencing principles, indicate the maximum and minimum sentence to be expected. Neither an appeals waiver nor correctional and detention conditions could form part of the understanding.[31]

(3) The parties have the opportunity to present their positions. A formal agreement is reached if neither the accused nor the prosecution object.

(4) The court may reject the agreement (Para.3, second sentence) only when its evaluation of the evidence or the law changes during the remaining proceedings or further conduct by the accused

---

[29] Some of the subsections have been divided and have been renumbered, but I have not identified these changes, as they are not material. For the final version of the law in German, see Beschlussempfehlung und Bericht des Rechtausschusses, May 20, 2009, *at* http://www.bmj.bund.de/files/-/3689/Beschlussempfehlung_Bericht_Verstaendigung_Strafverfahren.pdf.

[30] Referentenentwurf eines Gesetzes zur Regelung der Verständigung im Strafverfahren, May 18, 2006, *at* http://www.bmj.bund.de/files/-/1234/RefE%20Verständigung.pdf (author's own translation).

[31] The last sentence of the final version omits "appeals waiver" and reads: "Neither the verdict of guilt nor correctional or detention conditions could form part of the understanding." But a subsequent provision, Section 302, of the final legislation, clearly precludes the parties from agreeing to waive appellate remedies as part of a bargain.

contradicts the basis on which the court made its sentence prediction. Such a rejection does not as a matter of principle conflict with the use of the accused's statements. The court must promptly inform the parties of its rejection of the agreement.[32]

(5) The court must inform the accused about the preconditions and consequences of a rejection of the agreement. If the accused is not so informed, the statements of the accused can be used only with the accused's consent.[33]

Notes and Questions:

1. Is the final legislation an improvement over the guidelines on bargaining offered by the courts? Is it an improvement over the draft proposal? If so, in what way?
2. If you were in charge of proposing a plea bargaining provision to be added to the German Criminal Procedure Code, how would you draft it?
3. Sections 4 and 5 of Article 257c of the draft legislation reflected case law on rejection of plea agreements and withdrawal of confessions. Under it, a court could deviate from a plea agreement if "grave new circumstances present themselves after the deal, which were earlier unknown to the court and could influence the judgment." But the court had to give notice to the defendant and allow him to readjust his defense. The defendant could withdraw his confession in response, but most courts had held that the confession could be used as evidence against him in future proceedings. This meant that the defendant was likely to be convicted if the original confession appeared to be credible, but also that his sentence was likely to be lower in consideration of the confession. Under the final version of the legislation, a court can reject an agreement only "when legally or factually significant circumstances were overlooked or presented themselves for the first time, and the court concludes for this reason that the predicted sentence is no longer proportionate to guilt." Importantly, the court cannot

[32] The provision now states that: "The court may reject the agreement only when legally or factually significant circumstances were overlooked or presented themselves for the first time, and the court concludes for this reason that the predicted sentence is no longer proportionate to guilt. The court may also reject the agreement when further conduct by the accused contradicts the basis on which the court made its sentence prediction. The court may not use the defendant's confession in future proceedings. The court must promptly inform the parties of its rejection of the agreement."

[33] The provision now reads that: "The court must inform the accused about the preconditions and consequences of a rejection of the agreement."

use the defendant's confession in future proceedings. This is a significant departure from previous law on plea bargaining and makes the process fairer to defendants.

Under both earlier case law and the new legislation, absent "grave new circumstances," both the court and the prosecutor will be held to their promises under a plea agreement, but such promises must be entered on the record to be enforceable.[34] For a discussion of the law on withdrawal and breach, see Lutz Meyer-Gossner, *Der gescheiterte Deal*, 12 Strafverteidiger Forum 401 (2003). Compare this law to the provisions on withdrawal and breach in the United States. In your opinion, which system addresses withdrawal and breach more fairly or more effectively, and why?

4. Consider the following evaluation of the draft proposal. Do you agree with it?

Thomas Weigend, *The Decay of the Inquisitorial Ideal: Plea Bargaining Invades German Criminal Procedure, in* John Jackson et al., Crime, Procedure and Evidence in a Comparative and International Context 39, 54-55 (2008)

Although the German legislature has not so far amended the Code of Criminal Procedure to legitimise "plea bargaining," there exist several drafts for statutory regulation of the practice. In 2006, the Federal Ministry of Justice made public a draft that would integrate "understandings" (*Verständigungen*) between the court and the parties into the Code of Criminal Procedure. The Ministry Draft follows, with small variations, the rules set up by the Federal Court of Appeals [Federal Supreme Court]. It aims at legalizing the present practice while at the same time professing adherence to the "traditional principles of German criminal procedure."

The Ministry Draft would insert into the Code of Criminal Procedure a new paragraph 257c. According to that new provision, the court "can" during trial[35] enter into an "understanding" with the parties. With the defendant's consent, the court can define maximum and minimum

[34] BGH 1 StR 420/03, Urteil vom 16. Dezember 2004.

[35] [Footnote in original] The Draft does not contain rules as to negotiations before (rather than during) trial except for a general authorisation for the prosecutor and the court to discuss the state of the proceedings with the parties (paras 160a, 202a Ministry Draft). . . .

limits for the sentence that it will impose conditional on parties' "procedural conduct" or their "actions with respect to the proceedings" (*verfahrensbezogene Maßnahmen*). By these vague terms, the Ministry Draft refers to a confession made by the defendant in open court, but also to other procedural activities, such as waiving motions for taking additional evidence or (on the part of the prosecution) dismissing unrelated charges against the defendant. If none of the parties objects, the provisional proposal becomes binding upon the court. Yet the court can withdraw from the "understanding" if the parties fail to fulfil the court's expectations with respect to their "procedural conduct" or if the court arrives at a different evaluation of the factual or legal situation (paragraph 257c sec 4 Ministry Draft). If the sentence is within the limits previously announced by the court, the judgment can be appealed only on limited grounds.

The Ministry Draft, although proclaiming adherence to "traditional principles," provides a blank cheque to the courts and does very little to regulate the new practice. Several features of the Ministry Draft point into the direction of unrestricted judicial discretion: For one, the defendant is accorded no right to an offer of an "understanding" by the court—it is left to the court's discretion whether to enter into negotiations with the parties, what sentence range to offer and what conditions to impose. There is no explicit obligation on the court to take evidence even when the defendant's confession is obviously incomplete.

Nor does the Ministry Draft oblige judges to keep their word after they have ostensibly committed themselves to an "understanding"; instead, it shifts the risk of any unexpected turn of the events to the defendant. Not only can judges impose a more severe sentence when they find the defendant's confession to be less extensive than they had anticipated; they can also deviate from the "understanding" if, for whatever reason, they determine that the facts[36] or the law (!) are different from what they had thought. This would create only a limited risk for the defendant if he were able to withdraw his confession in case the court reneges on the deal. In the German system, however, a confession is not a procedural declaration but a factual statement—once made it cannot easily be undone. The Ministry Draft in fact declares any statement the defendant has made in court to be admissible against him even when

[36] [Footnote in original] "New facts" can of course derive from the defendant's confession. This means that the defendant must be extremely careful not to say too little (which could be interpreted as an insufficient "procedural conduct") or too much (which might provide the court with "new facts" on which to base a more severe sentence).

the "understanding" has failed, provided that the defendant had been informed of that possibility (paragraph 257c sec 5 Ministry Draft).[37]

In short, the Ministry Draft creates a judge's paradise: The court can make use of its broad sentencing authority to pressurise the defendant into co-operation whenever (and if) the court wants; and the court still has free rein even after the defendant has irretrievably incriminated himself by making a confession in open court.

Nor does the Ministry Draft meaningfully circumscribe the contents of bargained-for judgments. The Draft emphasises that "understandings" can only refer to sanctions, not to the offence of which the defendant is to be convicted (paragraph 257c sec 2 Ministry Draft). But there are no substantive guidelines as to how much weight the sentencing court can (or must) give to the defendant's confession, and the court does not have to indicate that weight in the judgment. The court's judgment is not based on evidence taken at the trial, and it is not based on spelled-out considerations of substantive justice—all that legitimises the court's pronouncement of the verdict and sentence is the consent of the parties. This marks a radical deviation from basic tenets of German criminal procedure, a shift from a judgment based on truth and justice to a judgment based on the defendant's submission. His submission is in turn brought about by the threat of harsher punishment if he refuses to confess.

PRACTICE OF PLEA BARGAINING IN GERMANY[38]

PARTICIPANTS

In contrast with the United States, plea bargaining in Germany usually involves not only the defense attorney and the prosecutor, but also the court. In some minor cases, the defense may negotiate solely with the prosecutor about the filing of charges, and then simply seek approval of the bargain by the court. But in more serious cases, plea bargaining always involves the court.

Such bargaining is most commonly initiated by the defense attorney, though judges may also start the discussions. The discussions in more serious cases typically occur in the judge's chambers or in a courthouse conference room and include the defense attorney, the prosecutor, and at least one judge. In the *Landgericht*, a felony court composed of two

---

[37] Note that the final version changes that provision so that if the bargain is rejected, the defendant's confession can no longer be used against him in future proceedings.

[38] This Section is based in large part on Turner, *supra* note 4, at 217-220.

or three professional and two lay judges,[39] the negotiations could involve either just the presiding judge, or the presiding judge and the judge responsible for drafting the court's judgment, or sometimes all three professional judges. The lay judges are usually absent from the initial negotiations, as they are not yet empanelled at that point.[40] The defendant is also not present, but the defense attorney is expected to consult with him or her before and after the plea discussions. While victims generally play a greater role in German criminal procedure than they do in the United States,[41] they have no influence over the negotiations and are not consulted before an agreement is reached.

TIMING

In less serious cases, where the prosecution has discretion to decline to file charges, negotiations typically occur before the charges are filed. But in other cases, negotiations occur after the charges are filed and formal proceedings have begun in court.

SUBJECT MATTER

No statutory provisions limit plea bargaining to particular offenses. While in its early days, plea bargaining was limited primarily to white-collar crime and drug trafficking cases, today it occurs in a wide range of cases. Still, practitioners remain reluctant to negotiate about violent offenses such as assault and homicide. Plea bargaining is often used in rape cases, however, on the theory that it can spare the victim the trauma of testifying in court.

As in the United States, negotiations may concern the charges, the sentence, or both. But German prosecutors' discretion to bargain is narrower than that of their American counterparts. The German Criminal Procedure Code limits the extent to which prosecutors can decline to file charges. Felony charges must be filed if there is an adequate evidentiary

[39] More serious cases are tried in *Landgericht*, or district court, before a mixed panel of two or three professional and two lay judges. Misdemeanors are tried in *Amtsgericht*, or county court—either by a single professional judge, or, if the case concerns a more serious offense (including some crimes that would be considered felonies in the United States), by a mixed court consisting of one professional and two lay judges. Richard S. Frase & Thomas Weigend, *German Criminal Justice as a Guide to American Law Reform: Similar Problems, Better Solutions?*, 18 B.C. Int'l & Comp. L. Rev. 317, 321 (1995).

[40] Although the Federal Supreme Court has held that the lay judges must be involved in the negotiations, this rarely occurs in practice. Turner, *supra* note 4, at 220.

[41] *See* William T. Pizzi & Walter Perron, *Crime Victims in German Courtrooms: A Comparative Perspective on American Problems*, 32 Stan. J. Int'l L. 37 (1996).

basis to do so.[42] Once the trial begins, the prosecution cannot withdraw the indictment or reduce the charges; only the court may do so.[43] In addition to having significant control over the charges, judges have very broad discretion in the area of sentencing. Prosecutors therefore cannot credibly represent that the court will accept a particular charge or sentence bargain. That is one of the main reasons why negotiations in Germany involve judges to a much greater degree than in the United States.

In less serious cases, German prosecutors have greater discretion to refrain from filing charges.[44] It is in these cases that they are likely to engage in bargaining without directly involving the court. Most common is bargaining under Section 153a of the Criminal Procedure Code, which allows prosecutors to decline to file charges on certain conditions—for example, when the defendant pays restitution or makes a contribution to a charity.[45] Although Section 153a applies to crimes carrying a minimum sentence of less than one year in prison, most assault and theft cases, as well as a number of white-collar crimes, fall into that category. In practice, the parties sometimes agree to a dismissal under Section 153a even for more serious crimes. This bargaining occurs without any active involvement by the judge. The prosecutor obtains the judge's approval only after the parties have negotiated and reached an agreement on their own.

Charge bargaining with the court occurs when evidence on some counts proves less convincing than anticipated by the prosecution, or when the case is very complex and contains a number of repetitive offenses. In the latter case, the court may dismiss a number of charges so as not to waste time in reviewing each individual count of the accusation.[46] When charges are dismissed purely for administrative efficiency, the defendant's sentence may not be reduced, or may be reduced only slightly. On the other hand, when charges are dismissed because some

---

[42] StPO, *supra* note 11, §170(1).

[43] *Id.* §§156, 154II (court may do so upon application by the prosecution), 153II (court may do so with the consent of the prosecution and the defense).

[44] *Id.* §§153(1), 153a. Although court consent is required for terminations under §153a and terminations of more serious cases under §153, in practice, approval is rarely withheld.

[45] *Id.* §153(a)(1). Other conditions include paying compensation to the victim, performing charitable works, or undertaking specific support obligations. Prosecutors decline to file charges under Section 153a in about 7 percent of cases. Statistisches Bundesamt, Fachserie 10, Reihe 2, Gerichte und Staatsanwaltschaften 140 (2001).

[46] StPO, *supra* note 11, §154.

counts cannot be proven, the defendant usually receives a reduced sentence.[47]

The court is even more closely involved in sentence bargaining. Although no statutory provision authorizes it, sentence bargaining has become common in Germany because it appears to offer distinct advantages to all involved. In particular, in return for a reduced sentence and perhaps better detention conditions, the defendant can offer several benefits to the court and prosecution.

First, the defendant may provide a confession made on the record in court. The defendant's confession is often rather summary, but it is valuable to the court and prosecution because it largely obviates the need for further evidence gathering and saves time. In complicated white-collar crime cases or in organized crime cases with international dimensions, a confession may reduce the length of trial from weeks or months to hours. In sexual violence cases, it can also spare a victim the trauma of testifying. In drug-related or money-laundering prosecutions, the defendant may also offer his cooperation with other investigations, in return for a promise by the prosecutor to recommend a more lenient sentence to the court. (In these cases, prosecutorial recommendations carry greater weight because specific statutory provisions direct judges to consider cooperation with the prosecution as a mitigating sentencing factor.[48] This practice is discussed at greater length in the section on Cooperation Agreements below.)

While there is no set sentencing discount for confessing and cooperating with the court and prosecution, according to judges and practitioners interviewed by this author, the average discount appears to be around 30 percent of the projected sentence after a contested trial.[49] But in cases that may result in punishment of up to two years of imprisonment after a contested trial, the defendant is frequently offered probation and a suspended sentence, which is a significantly more valuable discount.

Critics have argued that there is no objective way to measure the bargaining discount. Judges often inform the defendants of both the

---

[47] Interview # 15, Landgericht Judge, Leipzig, *cited in* Turner, *supra* note 4, at 219 n.105 (giving as an example a case where the defendant was indicted on 1,080 counts of drug-dealing: "A large part of the indictment could not be proven because of the lack of credibility of some of the witnesses who were drug addicts. . . . The defense said that the defendant would confess to a number of the charges—about 400, and also would give information about the origin and transportation of the drugs; the prosecution agreed that on these conditions, it was prepared to drop the other counts under Section 154, and then we agreed relatively easily on a sentence of six years.").

[48] Controlled Substance Law [*Betäubungsmittelgesetz*] [hereinafter BtMG] §31; Ger. Crim. Code [*Strafgesetzbuch*] [hereinafter StGB] §261(10).

[49] Turner, *supra* note 4, at 235.

sentence after a contested trial and the sentence after a confession. Since the same judges who set the discount have vast discretion to determine the sentence after a contested trial, they may be inflating that potential sentence in some cases to make the bargained-for sentence appear more attractive to the defendant.

To understand this critique, it is important to examine the sentencing authority of German judges. The law requires judges to provide reasons for the sentences they impose, but otherwise sets few limits. The German Criminal Code provides a maximum and, more rarely, a minimum sentence for each offense. At times, it also indicates distinct sentencing ranges for less serious or more serious instances of the offense. The Code includes certain aggravating sentencing factors as offense elements—for example, selling or trafficking a "not insignificant amount" of drugs, acting as a member of a criminal gang, or committing a crime by use of weapons.[50] Other factors considered at sentencing include the motive and state of mind of the perpetrator, prior criminal history, and whether the perpetrator has tried to reconcile with the victim or has provided restitution.[51]

What weight should be attached to each of these factors is not clear, however. Judges have considerable discretion in deciding how much each factor will count at sentencing. As long as the trial court addresses the relevant factors in a reasoned opinion, the appellate courts are unlikely to intervene. At the same time, following the principle that the sentence must be proportionate to the defendant's guilt, the Federal Supreme Court has recently become more active in reversing sentences that it finds unduly severe or lenient. As plea bargaining has spread in Germany, appellate courts have become particularly concerned that negotiated sentences might be disproportionate to defendants' culpability. The Federal Supreme Court has repeatedly emphasized that sentences must be neither too lenient as a result of a plea bargain, nor too severe where plea negotiations have failed.

Waiving Rights. In exchange for a sentencing discount, the defense may also agree to refrain from filing further motions—a concession that saves the court valuable time. As part of the bargain, the defendant also waives his right to remain silent by confessing. Further, until recently, the defendant and the prosecutor could agree to waive their rights to

---

[50] *E.g.*, BtMG, *supra* note 48, §29(a)(2) (more than an insignificant amount of drugs); StGB, *supra* note 48, §244(1) (armed theft); §244(2) (theft as a member of a gang).

[51] StGB, *supra* note 48, §46.

appeal, but case law imposed limits on such bargains, and recent legislation specifically prohibited them.[52]

Other waivers inherent in American plea bargaining do not occur in Germany. For example, while plea bargaining shortens the trial, it does not eliminate it altogether; formally, therefore, the defendant is not waiving his right to trial. Similarly, in a formal sense, the defendant retains the right to confront witnesses at trial, but the practical effect of exercising that right would be negligible in light of the defendant's own confession.

Ad Hoc Plea Bargaining. "Ad hoc" plea bargaining in Germany is not formally approved by the courts or the Code, but it occurs occasionally. This refers to a situation in which defendants accept, as part of a bargain, punishment that the court would not be authorized to impose after a contested trial—for example, paying back taxes or paying money to a charitable organization (other than in conditional dismissals authorized by §153a).[53] Courts and prosecutors rarely suggest such bargains, and the Federal Supreme Court has refused to uphold them.[54] The recent legislation on bargaining also expressly prohibits bargaining about correctional or detention conditions and limits bargaining to "legal matters that pertain to the verdict and related decisions, measures related to the trial proceedings, and the conduct of the parties during the proceedings."

Cooperation Agreements. Several statutory provisions provide specifically for sentencing reductions in return for defendants' cooperation with the government. These are called *Kronzeugen* ("crown witness") provisions[55] and have been included in legislation related to drug trafficking, money laundering, and terrorism crimes.[56] As of August

---

[52] Appeals waivers were commonly negotiated before these recent prohibitions because they allowed the court to write a shorter judgment and protected the bargain from challenges. Writing a full judgment is a very time-consuming task for German courts. StPO, *supra* note 11, §267. I am grateful to Thomas Weigend for calling this provision to my attention.

[53] BGH Decision of Feb. 19, 2004, 4 StR 371/03 (BGHSt 49, 84).

[54] *Id.*

[55] The term "crown witness" was borrowed from Britain and dates back to at least the eighteenth century when it was used to describe informants who would testify for the Crown against accomplices in return for a more lenient disposition of their own case. Peter J.P. Tak, *Deals with Criminals: Supergrasses, Crown Witnesses, and Pentiti*, 5 Eur. J. Crime Crim. L. & Crim. Just. 2, 2-3 (1997).

[56] StGB, *supra* note 48, §129 (terrorism); §261 (money laundering); BtMG, *supra* note 48, §31 (drug-related offenses).

2008, the German Parliament was considering a general crown witness provision that would authorize sentencing reductions for cooperation with the government in any criminal case. The law would also regulate the practice in greater detail.[57] (As this book was going into production, at the end of May 2009, the German legislature passed the law.)[58]

Under the existing regime, the crown witness laws provide that when a defendant reveals information that could help prevent the commission of a serious crime or assist in the investigation of a crime already committed (including his own crime),[59] he or she may receive a sentencing concession and may, in exceptional cases, be exempt from punishment. Because the crown-witness provisions are offense-specific, both the crime committed by the defendant as well as the crime prevented or about which the defendant provides information must belong to the class of offenses specified—drug trafficking, money laundering, and terrorism cases.[60] But in practice, as part of plea bargaining, courts often mitigate sentences in exchange for cooperation even where no specific statutory provision exists—for example, in white-collar criminal cases.[61] The court may treat the defendant's act as a less serious instance of the charged offense, thus lowering the applicable sentencing range,[62] or it may simply reduce the sentence within the broad range afforded to it by statute.

One complication in German cooperation agreements relates to the timing of the performance. The defendant may agree to cooperate either before or after he is charged, and either before or after his sentencing. If he cooperates with the prosecution before his own sentencing, he cannot be assured of what discount, if any, he would receive from the court.

---

[57] Gesetzentwurf der Bundesregierung, Entwurf eines Gesetzes zur Änderung des Strafgesetzbuches, Strafzumessung bei Aufklärungs- und Präventionshilfe, *at* http://dip21.bundestag.de/dip21/btd/16/062/1606268.pdf [hereinafter Gesetzentwurf der Bundesregierung].

[58] Bundesministerium der Justiz, Pressemitteilung, Bundestag verabschiedet „Kronzeugen"-Regelung, May 28, 2009, *at* http://www.bmj.de.

[59] The provisions state that the offender would receive the concession in exchange for information that may help in the investigation of his own crime and the prevention of crimes by others, but in practice, it has been used similarly in cases where the offender provides information that helps in the investigation of others.

[60] Hans-Jörg Albrecht, Country Report on Germany, *at* http://www.wodc.nl/images/Werkdocument%201%20Germany_tcm44-59194.pdf. The new law abandons this requirement. *See supra* note 58.

[61] 2006 Hearings on a Draft Crown Witness Law Before the German Parliament, Testimony by Florian Jessberger, Institut für Kriminalwissenschaften, Humbold-Universität, Berlin, *at* http://webarchiv.bundestag.de/archive/2006/1206/ausschuesse/archiv15/a06/Unterlagen_oeffentliche_Anhoerungen/Aax_-_Kronzeugenregelung/5_Protokoll.pdf [hereinafter Jessberger Testimony].

[62] StGB, *supra* note 48, §46(2).

Some defense attorneys have argued that the defendant may end up worse off after cooperating. After cooperating, some defendants may find that they have confessed to a broader set of actions than the police and prosecutor would have been able to prove on their own. In these cases, even if the court mitigates the sentence in exchange for cooperation, a defendant may still be sentenced to more prison time than he would have been had he refused to cooperate.[63]

Prosecutors have also complained about the difficulty of enforcing cooperation agreements. In Germany, trial and sentencing are part of a unitary proceeding, and there is no gap between the plea hearing or trial and the sentencing. In the United States, the gap between trial and sentencing gives prosecutors time to obtain testimony from cooperating defendants in other ongoing cases. By contrast, a German defendant may receive his sentencing discount before he has testified for the government in other cases. If he changes his story during the subsequent testimony, the prosecution has no means of enforcing the cooperation agreement. Unlike in the United States, there is no provision for awarding a sentencing discount to a cooperating defendant within a year after his sentencing. The German Parliament considered a provision allowing the government to open new proceedings against a defendant when, at a later trial against other defendants, he testifies contrary to his earlier testimony in his own case. But such a provision was denounced as being contrary to fair trial principles.[64]

As a practical matter, prosecutors have attempted to ensure that defendants cooperate by trying them jointly with other defendants against whom they are expected to testify. If joint trials are not possible, prosecutors may at least seek written statements from defendants that may be used in future trials even if the defendants become uncooperative.

In addition to the concern that "crown witnesses" may change their stories after receiving a sentencing discount, the procedures for cooperation agreements have been criticized on other grounds.[65] A broad

[63] Rechtsanwälte Breidenbach & Popovic, Kronzeuge, *at* http://www.kanzlei-breidenbach.de/Kronzeuge-31-BtMG.51.0.html.

[64] Jessberger Testimony, *supra* note 60. The current proposal provides for criminal sanctions for a person who falsely raises suspicion about other crimes in order to receive a sentencing discount. Gesetzentwurf der Bundesregierung, *supra* note 57.

[65] For a review of expert opinions on the advantages and disadvantages of "crown witness" provisions, see 2006 Hearings on a Draft Crown Witness Law Before the German Parliament, *at* http://webarchiv.bundestag.de/archive/2006/1206/ausschuesse/archiv15/a06/Unterlagen_oeffentliche_Anhoerungen/Aax_-_Kronzeugenregelung/5_Protokoll.pdf; *see also* Tak, *supra* note 55, at 12.

objection to cooperation agreements is that they lead to unwarranted inconsistency in sentencing. Because defendants are not guaranteed a specific sentence in return for their cooperation, cooperation agreements are also said to create unpredictability and unfairness for defendants. Finally, as in the United States, commentators and defense attorneys have criticized cooperation agreements for their potential to result in the conviction of innocent persons.[66] Since defendants are offered an incentive to testify against others, there is a risk that they may seek to inculpate innocent persons.

Notes and Questions:

1. In what respects is the German approach to plea bargaining significantly different from the practice in U.S. federal courts? Address the issues of who participates in negotiations, what subjects plea bargaining can cover, and what restrictions are placed on the practice.
2. Is the German practice of negotiating for a shorter trial in exchange for a reduced sentence a relevant point of comparison to U.S. plea bargaining? In Germany, a trial—albeit a very truncated one—occurs even after sentence negotiations. Therefore, the court hears some evidence related to the charges and this makes it more likely that the "deal" will rest on a factual basis. Given this central difference between German and American practice, in what ways is comparison relevant or useful?
3. Are there aspects of German plea bargaining that you would like to see imported to the American criminal justice system? Why? What conflicts might arise with existing American rules of criminal procedure?
4. Place yourself in the position of each of the two parties in the criminal process and evaluate the German system of plea bargaining. If you were a prosecutor, would you rather plea bargain in the United States or in Germany? If you were a defendant, would you rather be subject to the rules of plea bargaining in the United States or in Germany?
5. As discussed above, German judges actively participate in plea negotiations. Consider the advantages and disadvantages of this approach. Would you recommend that American judges become more involved in the plea bargaining process? If judges were to become more involved, would there be a greater threat of coercion

---

[66] Tak, *supra* note 55, at 4, 12 (also citing other authorities).

of the defendant (particularly if the same judge who is involved in plea bargaining would also preside over a trial and impose the sentence when the bargain fails)? Could a judge who has taken part in plea bargaining remain unbiased at trial, in cases in which the bargain falls through? What additional measures or regulations would be necessary to minimize the risks of coercion and bias?

6. Why are German courts resistant to "ad hoc" plea bargains? In what way might such bargains conflict more seriously with inquisitorial principles?
7. Some German defense attorneys warn their clients that, by cooperating, they may reveal a broader set of self-incriminating actions than the police and prosecutor would be able to prove on their own. When that happens, even if the court mitigates the sentence in exchange for cooperation, a defendant may still be punished more harshly than if he refuses to cooperate. Is the same concern likely to be present for American defendants who cooperate with the government? Why or why not?

EVALUATING THE GERMAN PLEA BARGAINING REGIME

What are the advantages and disadvantages of the German model of plea bargaining? Consider the following assessments.

Jenia Iontcheva Turner, *Judicial Participation in Plea Negotiations: A Comparative View*

54 Am. J. Comp. L. 199, 223-237 (2006)

C. Assessing the German Model: Advantages and Disadvantages

[. . .] 1. The Benefits of Certainty

The first advantage of the German model of judicial supervision is that it offers the parties greater certainty about plea bargaining outcomes than a system in which the judge passively verifies the plea after the fact.

As noted earlier, German judges have wide sentencing discretion, and even seasoned attorneys have a difficult time predicting the sentence in a particular case. [. . .] During plea negotiations, judges are actively involved, openly discussing the merits of the case and the range of acceptable dispositions. [. . .]

2. Accuracy and Fairness

[. . .] [P]lea bargaining may undermine the judge's duty to investigate the "truth of the matter." It shortens significantly the actual trial and sentencing proceedings, so the judge has less opportunity to verify independently the factual basis for the defendant's admission of guilt. [. . .]

The rise of plea bargaining has undoubtedly shifted some emphasis from truth-seeking to efficiency in German criminal practice. The concessions of truth-seeking to efficiency are much discussed in German legal scholarship and were raised by some of the interviewees. For example, some defense attorneys intentionally file multiple evidence-gathering motions, or threaten to summon witnesses living abroad, which might prolong the proceedings substantially. Some judges would grant the defendant sentencing concessions in exchange for the defense ceasing the evidence-gathering motions. These judges are offering a discount that has nothing to do with the blameworthiness of the defendant. The sentence is lower not because the defendant is less culpable, but because the court is too busy to address all the motions filed by an aggressive defense attorney.

Another concession to efficiency is the shortening of the process by which the facts of the case are established. Although judges are supposed to verify themselves the factual basis of the case, when a case is plea bargained, they are more likely to accept "quick confessions" in which the defendant admits simply that the charges as laid out by the prosecution are correct. Such a quick confession may fail to illuminate the details of the case. A plea bargain based on a "confession" of this kind may produce a worse outcome for the defendant than a full trial, especially where the defense attorney and the judge make an inaccurate assessment of the few facts uncovered early in the proceedings. Truth-seeking may also be jeopardized where judges agree to dismiss a number of provable "collateral" charges in exchange for a confession to the "main" charges and a quicker resolution of the case. The majority of judges interviewed admitted that they are most likely to plea bargain where the case is more legally or factually complex and the evidentiary record more unwieldy. [. . .]

Still, judges have not abandoned their commitment to truth-seeking. Both the German Constitutional Court and the German Federal Supreme Court have repeatedly held that the duty to seek the truth requires judges to probe into the veracity of defendant's confessions resulting from a plea bargain. Trial judges themselves, as well as other lawyers, perceive the judges' role in plea bargaining at least in part as official investigators of the truth. As one defense attorney—otherwise skeptical of the fairness of plea bargaining—explained, judges play a central role in plea negotiations, leading the discussions and focused on uncovering the truth. Judges themselves deny sacrificing accuracy for efficiency and emphasize their role in imposing a just sentence. When they speak about "quick confessions," it is often regarding cases they have heard or read about in appellate case law, but rarely regarding their own cases. Those who acknowledge ending evidence-gathering early note that they do so only when the written record before them clearly establishes the defendant's guilt. They insist that they carefully review the file compiled by the police and even after a confession, ask clarifying questions to confirm the facts in the record. Where the file reveals ambiguities in the evidence, judges affirm that they would follow up with additional questions or where that is not enough, with further evidence-gathering. Some would conduct several days of proceedings before they conclude what an appropriate disposition might be.

When it comes to negotiations of charge dismissals, judges assert that such dismissals do not impair the accuracy of sentencing. In some cases, the court dismisses charges because the defense has shown that they are based on weak evidence. Even where that is not the case, the judge has vast sentencing discretion where numerous offenses have been charged, so the dismissal of "collateral" charges does not have a significant influence on the ultimate sentence. One judge gave the example of charge dismissals in a mass fraud case, where it would be impractical to call witnesses to confirm each instance of fraud. The dismissal of charges for 30 or even 60 instances of fraud out of 200 would not, on its own, have an influence on the sentence. Even if some of the facts were not entirely clarified during the trial, the sentence may still reflect the defendant's blameworthiness. [. . .]

Other features of the German plea bargaining process also suggest that judges remain oriented toward truth-seeking. Unlike their American counterparts, German judges cannot accept a "plea of guilty" where a defendant protests his innocence. A sentence discount can be offered only where the defendant confesses guilt and thus at least minimally assists in the search for truth. German defendants cannot "plead" to hypothetical crimes, or to real crimes they could not have committed. And the practice of "fact bargaining"—whereby the parties misrepresent facts in order to ensure a particular sentence negotiated between them—seems to occur rarely, if at all, in Germany. As a Hamburg prosecutor explained, "It is wrong to bargain about the evidence . . . . It is one thing for a plea bargain to leave a question open, for example, whether a crime was committed by a gang, but it is another to make it part of the bargain that the conclusion would be that it was not committed by a gang." The rarity of fact bargaining in Germany is probably due to the absence of sentencing guidelines and the greater limits on charge bargaining. Because the court and the parties in Germany are not constrained by narrow sentencing ranges, they need not alter the facts to achieve a particular sentence.

In comparison to their American counterparts, German judges are also provided with better tools to fulfill their duty of investigating the evidence. To begin, the evidence on file at the time of charging is often more complete than the evidence that American prosecutors have in their possession when they plea bargain. German prosecutors begin plea bargaining only after the police have completed their investigation. Moreover, German police and prosecutors have a duty to investigate and gather exculpatory, as well as inculpatory evidence. Other factors being equal, the earlier, fuller investigation of the facts in Germany means not only that the prosecution will be less likely to bring innocent defendants to the negotiating table, but also that it will be less likely to give unwarranted sentence reductions to defendants who have committed serious crimes. By contrast, in the United States, "[u]nder the pressure of a heavy, time-consuming caseload, the prosecutor may easily be seduced at an early stage of the proceedings, before such facts are more fully developed, by the offer of a quick guilty plea in exchange for a light sentence, only to discover too late that the offense, or the offender, was far more serious than originally thought."

The scope of discovery afforded to the defense is also greater in Germany. The German system requires the prosecutor to disclose fully its evidence, and the requirement applies at all stages of the investigation. This is in stark contrast to U.S. practice at the federal level, where pre-plea discovery is much more limited. Broader and earlier disclosure by the prosecution, as practiced in Germany, ensures that the court hears more informed arguments by the defense during plea discussions and can better evaluate the accuracy and fairness of a proposed plea bargain.

The judge herself has access to the entire file before she meets with the parties for plea discussions. This access to the record allows judges to step in where lawyers may be failing in their representation. Some judges see this supervisory role as flowing naturally from the duty to ensure that the plea reflects the true facts. As a Berlin judge observed:

> The court does have a supervisory function, to verify the evidence. The tendency with prosecutors is that they have investigated the case, they

> have delivered the charges . . . and have done everything they had to do so that they think: "I would not have brought charges if I were not convinced that the accused was the perpetrator." But this is not necessarily true; there are also cases where the evidence presents itself quite differently. And that is the task of the court, of course also of the defense attorney, but in the first place of the court, to find out, what the evidence really is.

The same judge also opined that it is "important for the court to support a little bit the defense attorney or the prosecutor who is unable to represent her position adequately." Other judges explained that they are most likely to take a lead in the negotiations where they see an inexperienced or incompetent defense attorney. They see their role as looking out for the interests of the defendant, but also as ensuring that the sentence reflects the gravity of the crime. In pursuing these goals, the judge may intervene by advising a defendant directly (though not too emphatically) about the benefits of a confession where the lawyer fails to do so, or may suggest a sentence higher or lower than the one offered by the prosecution. [. . .]

3. Judicial Supervision and Coercion

If some commentators are concerned that judges in Germany do not supervise the plea carefully enough, others worry that a dominant judge might prejudge the case and coerce a defendant into entering a plea. Concerned about the coercive potential of active judicial participation in plea bargaining, the Federal Supreme Court has held that the defendant cannot be pressured to enter a plea bargain through threats of a higher sentence or through unlawful promises. There are both substantive and procedural aspects of the case law against judicial coercion.

On the procedural side, the Federal Supreme Court has held that the substance of the plea bargain must be announced in open court, on the record, and with all parties present. This rule minimizes the possibility of judicial coercion, but it is not followed scrupulously in practice. As mentioned earlier, the common practice is for the parties, together with the judge, to meet in private and engage in preliminary plea negotiations. These negotiations rarely include the lay judges. The defendant is also usually absent, although his counsel is there to represent his interests. Although the defense attorney can insist that the substance of the plea negotiations be entered on the record, attorneys rarely do so, lest they upset the plea bargain or strain relations with the court. The record commonly includes only the result of the negotiations—typically, the sentence that the defendant may expect in return for a confession. The open-court announcement of the result would not mention potentially unlawful promises or threats that might have influenced the defense to accept the bargain. It offers neither a meaningful guarantee of transparency nor an effective safeguard against judicial coercion.

A substantive safeguard against judicial coercion is the rule that a judge may be disqualified from a case for bias. Removal for bias can occur if the judge fails to include a relevant party in the negotiations, or if she makes remarks that might coerce the defendant into confessing. It may sometimes be hard to distinguish whether the judge is simply informing the defendant of the likely outcome of trial in the absence of a confession or pressuring the defendant to make a confession. The standard is whether a reasonable defendant would conclude that the judge has predetermined the outcome of the case. Under that standard, remarks by the judge suggesting that the evidence is stacked against the defendant and that a confession would mean a lighter sentence, especially when couched in reproachful language, may be grounds for removal. A judge may also be disqualified if he expresses a clear opinion on how the case should be resolved before reviewing all of the evidence. The case law on judicial bias deters at least some judges from being too assertive in plea negotiations or committing to a particular sentence.

Even where a defendant fails to file a motion to disqualify an overbearing judge for bias, he may raise the question of judicial coercion on appeal. If he shows that the judge used threats of a higher sentence or unlawful promises to procure a plea bargain, the judgment would be reversed. The availability of appellate remedies is therefore a critical procedural safeguard against judicial coercion. But as mentioned earlier, recent case law has sanctioned appeals waivers, as long as the court has not been complicit in obtaining them. In any event, formal limits on appellate waivers have not been observed closely in practice. The repeat interaction between judges, prosecutors, and defense attorneys in a particular district means that judges could refuse to bargain in the future with those attorneys who regularly seek appellate review of plea bargains with the court.

While these protections against judicial overreaching are often circumvented in practice, several structural safeguards help minimize the overall coerciveness of German plea bargaining. First, plea negotiations still occur in fewer cases in Germany than in the United States. While the percentage of cases plea bargained varies greatly by locality and by type of case, the average national figure is estimated to fall somewhere between 30 and 50 percent. The rate is significantly lower than in the United States, where over 90 percent of convictions are by guilty plea. The common presumption in Germany, at least at present, is that the case will go to trial and not that it will be plea-bargained. This presumption may reduce the likelihood that judges will press for a plea bargain, or that defendants will quickly accept one.

Another reason for the lower level of coerciveness of German plea bargaining is the relative mildness of the expected post-trial sentence and the smaller discounts given to defendants who confess guilt. German sentences expected after trial are significantly lower than American post-trial sentences. The highest statutory sentence is 15 years, except in cases of murder, where life imprisonment is mandatory. The vast majority of criminal cases are resolved through fines. Moreover, plea bargaining is rarely used to dispose of violent crime cases. For that reason, in many of the cases that are resolved through bargaining, the expected sentence is likely to be fairly low.

The reward that German defendants are likely to receive for confessing and cooperating is also likely to be somewhat lower than that given to American defendants. While in U.S. federal court, the average discount for pleading guilty could be as high as two-thirds off the sentence expected after trial, in Germany, an admission of guilt is commonly rewarded with a one-fourth to one-third reduction in the expected sentence. Accordingly, the difference between the bargained-for and post-trial sentences is at most five years; more often, it is mere months. Where trial courts go beyond this accepted sentencing discount, appellate courts may step in. Although German appellate courts rarely intervene in sentencing matters, they are more likely to do so in cases where the differential between a bargained-for sentence and the sentence considered proportional to the offense is deemed too great. At the same time, appeals of an excessive plea discount are rare because defendants have no interest in contesting a lenient sentence, and prosecutors avoid challenging bargains to which they have already agreed.

There is an important exception to the generally low sentencing discounts offered in Germany. Defendants receive a substantial plea discount when the execution of their sentence is suspended, which can occur when the imprisonment imposed does not exceed two years. As part of a plea bargain in less serious cases, the court often reduces the time to which the defendant is sentenced to two years or less, suspends execution of the sentence, and grants probation. Here, the discount is worth a lot more than the reduction in the sentence itself—it spares the defendant from spending any time behind bars. Still, when it comes to sentences served, low plea discounts combine with mild sentences to reduce somewhat the coerciveness of plea bargaining.

Other features of the German process, however, leave room for judicial coercion and raise more serious concerns. As noted earlier, appellate waivers are a common feature of plea agreements—whether as a formal or informal matter. Even where the parties exercise their right to appeal, the lack of a record of the substance of plea discussions also means that appellate courts cannot adequately police judicial behavior. As one practitioner has suggested, German defense attorneys have not made good use of all the procedural protections against coercion available under the Federal Supreme Court's case law.

The case law itself is not always sensitive to dangers of coercion. For example, it provides that statements by the defendant offered to support the plea bargain may be considered by the court at a subsequent trial if the bargain falls through. Once the defendant has made some incriminating statements pursuant to a plea bargain, he or she has no good exit strategy if the bargain falls through.

There are two structural features of German procedure which further increase the risk of coercion. The first is the common practice of German judges to initiate plea discussions, and the second is the participation of the judge involved in the negotiations in the trial of the defendant where the negotiations fail. Where the judge initiates the plea discussions, a defendant may feel additional pressure to confess—both because of the inherent authority of the court and because the same judge or judges who are involved in the plea negotiations would decide the defendant's guilt or innocence and sentence if a bargain falls through. [. . .]

Notes and Questions:

1. Do you agree that the German model of judicial involvement in plea bargaining is more likely to produce accurate and fair outcomes than the traditional American model of plea bargaining? What specific features of German plea bargaining tend to enhance accuracy and fairness? Do you believe that any of these features could be usefully adopted by American jurisdictions? Why or why not?
2. In what ways have German courts tried to minimize the risks of bias and coercion that accompany judicial involvement in plea negotiations? Do you believe that these safeguards are likely to be effective? Are there additional measures that German courts

should adopt to reduce the possibility that judicial bias or coercion would influence case outcomes?

Markus Dirk Dubber, *American Plea Bargains, German Lay Judges, and the Crisis of Criminal Procedure*

49 Stan. L. Rev. 547, 604-605 (1997)

Based on an account of the traditional German criminal process as an inquisitorial proceeding dominated by a powerful judge whose sole aim is to obtain a confession from the defendant, some German commentators have welcomed plea bargaining. According to this account, the German defendant's role in the proceedings is entirely passive, and is limited to responding to the interrogation by the presiding judge who knows the case file prepared by the prosecution that contains all facts relevant to the resolution of the case. The defendant develops no evidence on her own; she merely motions the court to do the investigating for her. She may request that the court call certain witnesses and appoint certain experts, but she never takes the active role of developing a case and presenting it to the court. [. . .]

Against the background of this image of the German criminal process, some German commentators regard plea bargaining as an opportunity for the defendant to take a more active role in the process. In this view, plea bargaining strengthens the defendant's position by permitting her to shape the proceedings that will settle her fate. Plea bargaining appears as a process that permits the resolution of disputes in the course of a rational discourse among equals. With an occasional nod in the direction of modern discourse and process theories, it is said that the participation of the defendant in the dialogic process both improves the quality of its resolution and legitimizes it. In this light, plea bargaining appears as the paradigm of a new rational approach to criminal procedure that seeks to replicate the rational "seminar atmosphere" of certain German white collar trials.[67]

---

[67] [Footnote in original] Klaus Lüderssen, Abschaffen des Strafens? 17, 18 (1995). Langbein, from this standpoint, has it exactly backwards. It is not plea bargaining, but the current German judge-dominated criminal process that resembles the medieval inquisitorial process. *See* Werner Schmidt-Hieber, Verständigung im Strafverfahren 9-13 (1986); Joachim Herrmann, *Bargaining Justice—A Bargain for German Criminal Justice?*, 53 U. Pitt. L. Rev. 755, 775 (1992) (arguing that "[t]raditional unilateral decisionmaking has, to some extent, been replaced by a cooperation of prosecutors, judges, defense counsel and

Professor [Klaus] Lüderssen has gone one step further: he sees the rise of plea bargaining as an important indication of an actual paradigm shift. He calls for the abandonment of traditional substantive and procedural criminal law and advocates the resolution of what are now criminal cases in private tort actions. According to Lüderssen, plea bargaining serves as a model for the rational, dialogic resolution of disputes between victim and offender. Lüderssen views this dialogic resolution as the only way to legitimize the imposition and infliction of sanctions in our modern society of autonomous persons.[68]

Thomas Weigend, *The Decay of the Inquisitorial Ideal: Plea Bargaining Invades German Criminal Procedure, in* John Jackson et al., Crime, Procedure and Evidence in a Comparative and International Context 39, 59-64 (2008)

[. . .] As a matter of procedural theory, the outcome of the bargaining process (that is the verdict and sentence) can be "correct" only if it reflects the "true" seriousness of the crime the defendant has culpably committed and the need (if any) to impose crime-preventive measures on him. The fact that both the prosecution and the defense are (for different reasons) "happy" with the result of their negotiations does not mean that that outcome fulfils the requirements of criminal "justice." On the contrary, it is more likely than not that the bargained-for sentence fails adequately to reflect the defendant's guilt because it is either too lenient (when the defence has managed to extract unwarranted concessions) or too severe (when the defendant has submitted to a compromise judgment in light of an adverse evidentiary situation).

Those who draw a parallel between the virtue of compromise in civil and criminal matters overlook the crucial difference between those two areas of law: In a typical civil case, any outcome that subjectively satisfies both parties is a "correct" outcome because it is only their individual (and in most cases financial) dispute that is to be resolved. In criminal matters, by contrast, the accusing "party" (in most cases: the public prosecutor) does not bring suit to vindicate his personal interest but that of society at large. Society's interest in criminal matters is twofold. First, crimes are events that cause public concern sufficient to trigger

---

the accused," who now "feels authorized to participate in the process of defining guilt and punishment").

[68] [Footnote in original] *See* Klaus Lüderssen, *supra* note 66, at 323.

an official enquiry, and the purpose of that enquiry is to authoritatively determine what happened and who is responsible for any harm that occurred. Secondly, society is interested in having social peace restored by imposing adequate sanctions as well as in having future harm averted by minimizing the risk emanating from dangerous persons.

None of these purposes can be achieved by the mere fact that two or three individuals have arrived at a compromise (for example, that the suspect should make a payment or spend some time in detention). The public interest aroused by a suspected crime requires an independent determination of what happened, why it happened and what the appropriate consequences should be; and the public interest in restoring peace requires a sanction that "truly" reflects the harm that the offender has culpably caused. The public is rightfully incensed when it learns that a suspected offender, who may or may not have committed a grieveous wrong, had his attorney strike a deal for him—a deal under which the suspect may pay a sum of money or receive a suspended jail sentence on the basis of just a formal acceptance of the indictment. In some countries, the public may have learned to accept this special kind of "justice" because the state claims to be unable to afford to bring all suspects to trial, but that nevertheless remains an uneasy compromise between the requirements of justice and fiscal necessity.

Whatever practical compromise may have invaded the administration of justice, "consent" theories are insufficient to legitimise criminal convictions and sentences. Such legitimacy can be had only when an ostensibly honest attempt has been made to bring out the truth—be it through an "inquisitorial" judicial investigation, be it through a trial mechanism that relies on adversarial parties to challenge each other's versions of "the truth."

But isn't the quest for "truth," suggested here as the "true" meaning of the criminal process, an elusive chase for a multi-coloured butterfly that can never be caught? Can we ever know what "really" happened and, if so, can we find out by using the crude methods of a judicial enquiry mostly relying on witness testimony, or by conducting a public trial with all its contingencies and formalities? That is a philosopher's question, and I will not even try to answer it (though I suspect that the answer has to be negative). The simple and practical reply to the doubts about the chances of ever "finding the truth" is that of Sisyphus—we must make our best effort even if we cannot succeed. Nothing less is required when the state claims the power of inflicting punishment on one of its citizens.

That does not mean that every case requires a full trial with evidence being presented on every fact that might conceivably be relevant. No criminal justice system demands "full proof" with respect to uncontested issues. Even in systems that adhere to the inquisitorial model, the fact-finder takes certain matters for granted and concentrates his efforts on those issues that the defense and the prosecution present in a different light. One of the (informal) purposes of the pre-trial investigation in inquisitorial systems is a preliminary assessment of the evidence and the definition of issues that will have to be proved (or contested) at the trial. The same effect is reached in the adversarial process by letting the parties define the conflict: There will not be any evidence offered or taken on facts the parties have agreed on.

Most procedural systems have ways of dealing with uncontested cases without a trial. In Germany, for example, the majority of criminal cases not rejected or diverted by the prosecutor are resolved by a "penal order" procedure,[69] that is a criminal judgment drafted by the prosecutor and signed by the judge after a summary *ex parte* examination of the facts presented by the prosecutor. The defendant need not be asked in advance for his consent to the issuance of a penal order; but when he receives a penal order he can file an objection and will then automatically be granted a trial. In Italy, there exists the option for the defendant to submit to a single judge's decision based on the file of the pre-trial investigation.[70] The judge can hear additional evidence if he deems it necessary to reach a decision. The defendant is rewarded for his waiver of a full trial by a sentence reduction by one third.

Such simplified, abbreviated procedures are unobjectionable when used for totally or largely uncontested cases. Their outcome is not based on a "consent principle" but on pre-trial proceedings, ideally with full participation rights of the defence, that both parties and the decision-making judge agree to have sufficiently determined the relevant facts. Such abbreviated trials need not be limited to petty offenses but have a large potential field of application. They may blend into special short-track trials for confession cases as envisaged by Damaška in the context of

---

[69] [Footnote in original] Paras. 407-412 *Strafprozessordnung*. Penal orders are mostly used to impose fines. The maximum punishment that can be imposed by penal order is a prison term of one year, suspended.

[70] [Footnote in original] *Giudizio abbreviato*, arts. 438-443 Codice di Procedura Penale. A similar procedure exists in Polish law; see art. 335 Kodeks postępowania karnego.

international criminal justice.[71] Such mini-trials involving a re-affirmance of the basic facts of the case have great theoretical appeal as a middle ground between a full-scale trial and a merely formal assent of the parties to the court's decision. Whether they also thrive in practice will depend on a variety of factors, most prominently the incentives given to parties for choosing the middle ground over trial or informal negotiations.

[Weigend next addresses the question of how—if at all—the triumphant advance of negotiated judgments in Continental Europe could be reconciled with inquisitorial theory.] [. . .]

There are two possible answers to that query. Optimists could argue that the ancient hierarchical model of state has everywhere made room for a more "democratic," coordinate organization of authority, with an ensuing shift from court-imposed judgments to party-controlled proceedings. [. . .]

[Plea bargaining could be associated with party empowerment] only if "bargaining" indeed occured on an equal level, between equally strong parties and with an open end. None of these conditions applies when the prosecutor or the court dominate "negotiations" through their sanctioning authority, and the defendant's sole choice is between accepting the sentence offered to him and forgoing trial, or running the high risk of a much more severe punishment. [. . .]

We are left, then, with the pessimist interpretation of recent developments. The advance of plea bargaining in Germany and elsewhere does not signify a more equitable allocation of power in the criminal process but a deplorable dilution of the inquisitorial ideal. That ideal had protected the defendant against abuse and unjust sanctioning through the barrier of truth-finding: Only if conscientious and independent officials are convinced, on the basis of a comprehensive and serious inquisition of the relevant facts, that the defendant is guilty can he be subjected to criminal punishment proportional to his proven guilt.

When truth-finding is replaced by mechanisms designed to coerce the defendant into giving his "consent" to a proposed judgment, this may in individual instances lead to the same or even a more lenient sanction than would have been imposed after an "old style" trial—but the principle that had protected defendants against being overwhelmed by a powerful state system fails to operate, and the defendant is left to fend for himself in a fight that lacks rules other than the law of the marketplace. Many judges and prosecutors, to be sure, will refrain from abusing

---

[71] [Footnote in original] Damaška, *Negotiated justice* (n. 1) at 1037-1038.

their power and will endeavour to treat defendants fairly. But that is not the point. The problem is that the practice of negotiating for justice does not have a basis in law (even if a savings clause should be inserted into the Code of Criminal Procedure) or in procedural principle. Its basis is expediency only—and that, I am afraid, is not a proper foundation of a system of criminal justice.

Notes and Questions:

1. Compare the views of Klaus Lüderssen, as described by Markus Dubber, and those of Thomas Weigend. Lüderssen believes that plea bargaining enhances party autonomy and "serves as a model for the rational, dialogic resolution of disputes between victim and offender." By contrast, Weigend rejects the view of plea bargaining as empowering defendants and argues that prosecutors and courts dominate plea negotiations, "and the defendant's sole choice is between accepting the sentence offered to him and forgoing trial, or running the high risk of a much more severe punishment." In your opinion, which view is more persuasive with respect to the German system of plea bargaining?
2. Reconsider Judge Easterbrook's defense of plea bargaining. Easterbrook argues that all sides—the defense, the prosecution, and the public—are better off as a result of plea bargaining. In particular, plea bargaining frees up prosecutorial resources, which means that a greater number of crimes are prosecuted, serving the public interest of enforcing the criminal law. How does Thomas Weigend respond to the argument that plea bargaining benefits all sides and should therefore be welcomed?
3. Weigend argues that efficiency in the criminal justice system can be achieved through resource-saving procedures that are fairer than plea bargaining. As an example, Weigend refers to the "penal order" procedure (*Strafbefehlsverfahren*). Germany uses penal orders to process certain minor, but high-volume cases, where the evidence appears beyond doubt, and the accused consents. The maximum offense that may be imposed by penal order is one-year imprisonment, suspended; most penal orders result in the imposition of a fine. The prosecutor and the defense do not negotiate the sentence. Instead, the prosecutor files an application for a penal order that lays out the facts of the crime and the charges and specifies the punishment to be imposed. The defendant may accept it, in which case the court will typically grant the prosecutor's motion, or he may object to it within two weeks

and automatically receive an ordinary trial. Penal orders take the pressure off the prosecution of more serious crimes. Because of its efficiency, this procedure has also been adopted by a number of other European countries. Could the United States also adopt this practice? In what cases would it be most useful and most likely to work? How does the penal order procedure compare to plea or confession bargaining?

4. Weigend remains pessimistic about the possibility of reconciling inquisitorial principles with plea bargaining. What features of plea bargaining does he find most objectionable? Do you agree?

COMPARING PLEA BARGAINING IN THE UNITED STATES AND GERMANY

Plea Bargaining Feature	Germany ("Understandings"/ Bargains)	United States [most jurisdictions]
Legislative Authorization	Yes (since May 2009, after bargaining had occurred informally for many years).	Yes.
Typical Participants	Judge, defense attorney, prosecutor.	Prosecutor and defense attorney during negotiations; judge involved at guilty plea hearing.
Timing	Typically after charges are filed, but some occur before charges are filed.	At any time in the process, but earlier guilty pleas are rewarded with greater concessions.
Subject Matter	Defendant does not plead guilty, but confesses; sentence bargaining; charge bargaining is rare; bargaining rarely used for serious violent crimes cases.	Both charge and sentence bargaining; no limit on the types of cases in which bargaining is used.
Discovery/Disclosure	Defense has the right to inspect complete case file before negotiations (at the conclusion of the investigation).	Limited pre-plea discovery; under the Constitution, prosecutor must disclose evidence that is materially exculpatory and relates to factual innocence; many jurisdictions' Rules often require additional disclosure.
Cooperation Agreements	Yes, although often difficult to enforce.	Yes.
Waiver of Rights	Cannot negotiate an appeals waiver; cannot waive trial entirely	Few limits on bargaining for waivers of rights; cannot waive right to effective assistance of counsel

Conditions for Validity of Guilty Plea/Confession and Plea Agreement	Confession must be voluntary and supported by the facts; the result of negotiations must be entered on the record; all trial participants must be involved in the negotiations; the court may not promise a specific sentence, but may set an upper sentencing limit; the sentence must be proportionate to guilt.	Guilty plea must be knowing, voluntary, and factually based.
Withdrawal and Breach	The court may reject the bargain when "legally or factually significant circumstances were overlooked or presented themselves for the first time, and the court concludes for this reason that the predicted sentence is no longer proportionate to guilt. The court may also reject the agreement when further conduct by the accused contradicts the basis on which the court made its sentence prediction. The court may not use the defendant's confession in future proceedings. The court must promptly inform the parties of its rejection of the agreement." Absent significant new circumstances, both the court and the prosecutor will be held to their promises under a plea agreement, but such promises must be entered on the record to be enforceable.	After the court has accepted the guilty plea, the defendant may withdraw the plea if the court has rejected the plea agreement between the parties, or if the defendant shows a "fair and just reason." After sentencing, the defendant may not withdraw the guilty plea unless he can show that withdrawal must be permitted to avoid "manifest injustice." Either side may seek rescission of the plea agreement or specific performance as a remedy for breach of the agreement by the other party.

HYPOTHETICALS

Plea Bargaining in a Drug Trafficking Case in Germany

Hans Bauer

Hans Bauer and Michael Schmitt worked as partners to import 15 grams of methamphetamine hydrochloride (a.k.a. "ice") into Germany from the Netherlands each month during a four-month period in 2004. Bauer, who had contacts with manufacturers of the drug in the Netherlands, got 60 percent of the profit. Schmitt got 40 percent of the profit, in exchange for driving with Bauer to the Netherlands, bringing back the drugs, and then helping to arrange for their distribution in Germany.

Hans Bauer had been convicted of forcible rape in 1988 and of possessing an "insignificant amount" of cocaine in 2000. In 2005, he was arrested for his role in the importation of drugs from the Netherlands and their subsequent distribution in Germany. Originally, Bauer was charged under Section 30a(1) of the Narcotics Act with importing and distributing a "not insignificant amount" of methamphetamine hydrochloride as a member of a criminal gang. The prosecution alleged that Bauer had imported methamphetamine hydrochloride from the Netherlands into Germany on at least four occasions, importing and distributing a minimum of 60 grams of the drug. The prosecution suspected that he worked with at least three other people to distribute the drug, and it charged all of them with drug trafficking offenses in separate proceedings. The prosecution claimed that the four had worked together with the intent to jointly commit drug-related crimes.

Bauer's defense attorney argued that Bauer was improperly charged as a member of a gang, because the group of four that imported drugs into Germany had worked together only occasionally and were not a cohesive group created specifically for the purpose of trafficking in drugs. In addition, Bauer's defense attorney requested that the court appoint an expert to review the purity of the drugs seized, arguing that the methamphetamine content in the drugs was so low that it did not meet the threshold of a "not insignificant amount." Although the court did not believe that the defense arguments were strong,[72] it wanted to avoid protracted proceedings and a possible appeal on the questions raised by the defense, so it agreed to negotiate with the defense. The prosecution wanted to get Bauer's coop-

[72] The BGH held (but not until 2008) that a "not insignificant amount" of methamphetamine hydrochloride is less than 6.2 grams. BGH 2 StR 86/08, Urteil vom 3. Dezember 2008. I thank Till Gut for bringing this case to my attention.

eration in other cases, so it was also willing to negotiate about the charges and the sentence.

After negotiations, Bauer entered into an agreement with the prosecution and the court, under which he promised to admit his guilt in open court and provide information that would lead to the arrest of other persons who sold drugs. In return, the prosecution and the court would treat the case as a "less serious case" under Section 30a(3) of the Narcotics Act, which prescribes a minimum sentence of six months and a maximum sentence of five years (Section 30a(1), by contrast, carries a mandatory statutory minimum of five years); the court also agreed to mitigate his punishment under Section 31 for assisting the government in other investigations. As a result of these concessions by the court and the prosecution, Bauer would be sentenced to three years of imprisonment. The judgment in Bauer's case was to be entered the day after the negotiations ended.

Michael Schmitt

Michael Schmitt, Hans Bauer's partner, did not have prior criminal history. But he did not cooperate with the prosecution or negotiate with the prosecution and the court. After a three-day trial, he was convicted of importing and distributing a not insignificant amount of methamphetamine hydrochloride as a member of a criminal gang. Under the statute, Schmitt was subject to a mandatory minimum sentence of five years. Because Schmitt failed to cooperate and provide information about his own case or other cases, he received six years of imprisonment.

Brigitte Mann

Brigitte Mann was Michael Schmitt's girlfriend, and she was also involved in the drug distribution, but short of being a member of the criminal gang. She was not involved in the importation of drugs and had taken part in drug deals with Schmitt and Bauer only occasionally, in large part because of her relationship to Schmitt. She had acted as a drug courier within Germany and delivered 15 grams of methamphetamine hydrochloride to buyers. She identified several of the buyers herself and earned a commission based on the amount she sold. She was charged with distributing a not insignificant amount of methamphetamine hydrochloride in violation of Section 29a(1)(2) of the Narcotics Act. She also had a prior drug possession conviction. If she had been convicted on the above charge, she would be facing a sentence of between 1 and 15 years of imprisonment.

But after negotiations between the defense, the prosecution and the court, the court agreed to treat Brigitte Mann's act as a less serious instance of the offense under Section 29a(2) and to give her a sentence of between three months and five years. In turn, she would cooperate with the government in providing information in her own case and other drug cases and testify in two trials against other drug traffickers. The defense also pointed out that Brigitte Mann was addicted to drugs and argued that she committed the crime in order to support her habit. The defense therefore asked the court to impose at most a one-year suspended sentence with probation and noted that Mann would commit to enroll in therapy to treat her addiction. Although the prosecution objected and argued that Mann had not committed the crime merely to support her addiction, the court agreed that if Mann confessed to her crime, cooperated with the government in other cases, and enrolled in therapy, the court would impose at most a two-year suspended sentence with probation. Mann did confess at her own trial. At the trial, the prosecution also interrogated her about the role of Michael Schmitt in the drug distribution scheme, and Mann provided detailed testimony on that point. The court then imposed a two-year suspended sentence with probation and instructed Mann to undergo therapy as part of her probation.[73]

After she was sentenced, under the agreement with the court and the prosecution, Mann was to testify in the trial of Michael Schmitt about Schmitt's role in the drug distribution ring. But once she was on the stand, she claimed that she did not know exactly what role Schmitt played and that she only knew that he had traveled to the Netherlands with Hans Bauer on one occasion. The prosecution called one of the judges from Mann's trial to testify about what Mann had said at her own trial. Despite the judge's testimony, the prosecution was concerned that Mann's retreat from her earlier testimony may hurt the value of that testimony in Schmitt's trial.

Helena Hauser

Helena Hauser was also a drug courier working with Bauer, Schmitt, and Mann. Like Brigitte Mann, she identified buyers within Germany and received a commission based on the amount of drugs she sold.

During her interrogation by the police, Hauser gave some information both about her involvement in the distribution of drugs and about the operation of the drug distribution ring more generally. Like Brigitte Mann, Hauser was charged with distributing a not insignificant amount of methamphetamine hydrochloride in violation of Section 29a(1)(2) of the Narcotics Act and faced a minimum sentence of one year. In the pretrial discussions with the court and the defense, the prosecution argued that

[73] *See* StGB, *supra* note 48, §56c(3)(1).

Hauser had not cooperated fully with the authorities and that her information had not provided any new leads in the investigation. The prosecution did not think that she should receive a sentencing reduction for her cooperation. But the court pointed out that Hauser could receive a sentence reduction under Section 31 even if she had not cooperated fully with the government and that, in any event, it was within the court's discretion to decide whether she had cooperated fully and whether she should receive a sentencing discount. In the end, the parties reached an agreement under which Hauser would receive no more than one year of imprisonment if she confessed at trial and testified in detail about the operation of the drug distribution ring.

Once the main hearing resumed, the court announced on the record the result of the pretrial discussions and the commitments exchanged. As agreed upon during the pretrial discussions, Hauser confessed about her role in the drug distribution ring. In the course of her testimony, it became clear that Hauser had been involved not only in the distribution of the drugs, but also in the importation of drugs. (She had driven Hans Bauer and some of the drugs back from the Netherlands on at least one occasion, and she was rewarded with a portion of the drugs in return for her services.) In light of this new evidence, the court decided that Hauser should be charged under Section 30(1)(4), which specifically prohibits the importation of a "not insignificant amount" of drugs and requires a minimum sentence of two years. The court warned Hauser that she might be convicted under Section 30(1)(4) given her new admissions and stated that the proceedings could be suspended if she needed more time to defend herself on the new charges. After discussing this with her attorney, Hauser decided not to ask for a suspension. The court therefore continued with the proceedings and eventually sentenced Hauser to two years and three months.

Notes and Questions:

1. Compare the culpability of the defendants and the bargains they reached with the prosecutor. Are the disparities among the sentences that each of the four defendants received fair and justified? Do you believe that any of the sentencing discounts were too large and therefore potentially coercive?
2. Was the court justified in reclassifying the charges against Hans Bauer, based on the defense's arguments that Hans Bauer was not a member of a criminal gang and that the amount of drugs he imported and sold was insignificant? Is it relevant that the court considered these arguments weak? Given that the court treated Bauer's case as a "less serious case," is it fair that Bauer's partner,

Michael Schmitt, who was involved in the same enterprise, did not have his case treated as a "less serious case"? Is the judgment against Bauer consistent with the obligation of judges to investigate the facts fully and independently?

3. Once Brigitte Mann had been sentenced, there appeared to be little that the prosecution or the court could do to enforce the agreement among them as to her cooperation in other cases. To support the case against Schmitt, the prosecution had to rely on Mann's statements from her own trial. The prosecution could have charged Mann with perjury for her testimony during Schmitt's trial,[74] but it would have been difficult to prove that Mann had lied during Schmitt's trial. In particular, the prosecution would have had difficulty showing that Mann's lack of memory at Schmitt's trial was intentionally false. In addition, false statements during her own trial are not punishable, so if confronted with her earlier statements, Mann could simply say that she was lying then. Because of this difficulty of proof, German prosecutors bring perjury prosecutions only very rarely, in cases of blatant lies.[75] The German legislature is now considering legislation to regulate better such cooperation agreements. Do you think that the legislation should allow the court to order defendants like Mann to abide by their agreements and testify consistently with their previous statements? Should it allow the reopening of proceedings and the readjustment of sentences of such defendants? Is there any other mechanism that could protect the prosecution against defendants who fail to honor their commitments?
4. Can Helena Hauser enforce the court's promise to sentence her to no more than one year of imprisonment? Is the court allowed to renege on its promise in light of the new facts? How would this situation be resolved in a U.S. federal court?

Plea Bargaining in a Homicide Case in Germany

Peter Weber and Johann Retter were acquaintances who lived in Munich. After an altercation, Peter stabbed Johann and killed him. Peter was charged with manslaughter under Section 212 of the Criminal Code.[76]

---

[74] *Id.* §153 ("Whoever as a witness or expert gives false unsworn testimony before a court or other agency competent to examine witnesses and experts under oath shall be punished with imprisonment from three months to five years.").

[75] I thank Thomas Weigend for his comments on the law and practice of perjury prosecutions in Germany.

[76] Peter was charged under Section 212 of the Criminal Code, which pertains to manslaughter: "(1) Whoever kills a human being without being a murderer, shall be punished for

During pretrial, the defense attorney requested a meeting with the court and the prosecutor to discuss the situation. At the meeting, the defense attorney pointed out that Peter had been provoked by Johann who had come to his home, insulted him and his girlfriend, and hit him several times. Johann was known to be violent, and Peter stabbed him out of fear that Johann would otherwise hurt Peter and his girlfriend. The presiding judge and the prosecutor had some doubts about this version of the events and about the strength of the self-defense claim. But on the other hand, there was at least some evidence that the killing might have been in self-defense, and the prosecution's evidence that it was manslaughter was not solid. Other than Peter and his girlfriend, there was only one person who overheard the incident—one of Peter's neighbors. The neighbor claimed he heard nothing to suggest insults or attacks by Johann. But the neighbor was a drug addict, had had numerous brushes with the law himself, and had also had disputes with Peter in the past. The credibility of his testimony was therefore doubtful.

The presiding judge and the prosecutor agreed that if Peter confessed to killing Johann in response to an insult, he would be convicted of a "less serious case of manslaughter" under Section 213 of the Criminal Code. Section 213 applies "[i]f the person committing manslaughter was provoked to rage by maltreatment inflicted on him or a relative or a serious insult by the person killed and was thereby immediately torn to commit the act, or in the event of an otherwise less serious case." The punishment under Section 213 is between one and ten years (compared to the possibility of a sentence between five years and life imprisonment under Section 212). The presiding judge made a commitment not to impose a sentence longer than four years.

But the presiding judge also had to discuss this agreement with the other two professional judges and the two lay judges on the court. These judges rejected the agreement. One of the professional judges argued that there should never be bargaining about serious violent crime cases, and the other pointed out that the proposed solution does not help the discovery of the true facts of the case. The lay judges agreed with the concerns raised by the professional judges and also worried that Peter's sentence would be too lenient. Consequently, the presiding judge informed the defense and the prosecution that the bargain was not approved by the court and that they would have to proceed to trial. At trial, after admitting that he killed

---

manslaughter with imprisonment for not less than five years. (2) In especially serious cases imprisonment for life shall be imposed."

Johann, but arguing that he did so in self-defense, Peter was convicted and sentenced to six years. He has now appealed the verdict.

Notes and Questions:

1. Should the remaining judges of the court have agreed to the deal struck by the presiding judge, the prosecutor, and the defense attorney? Were these judges correct that plea bargaining in violent crime cases is less acceptable than in other cases? Were they correct to insist that bargaining should not occur when there are factual doubts about the guilt of the defendant?
2. Could Peter successfully argue on appeal that the agreement between him, the prosecutor, and the presiding judge ought to be enforced? What legal right might he argue has been violated by the failure to abide by the agreement?

CHAPTER

3 Introducing Plea Bargaining as Part of Comprehensive Legal Reform

Russia and Bulgaria

INTRODUCTION

Criminal procedure is not an area in which one would necessarily expect a global convergence of rules. No gains of trade are likely to occur from such convergence, as might be the case in various areas of business law. Nor is there a serious collective action problem that could be solved by harmonizing criminal procedure. While transnational crimes such as money laundering, human trafficking, and terrorism may benefit from cross-border cooperation among law enforcement agencies, action against such crimes typically does not require comprehensive harmonization of criminal laws and procedures. Accordingly, few international treaties address questions of criminal law and procedure, and those that do generally deal with laws related to specific transnational crimes or with questions that arise when nationals of one country commit crimes in a different country. Moreover, criminal procedure is often seen as an area of the law that is too central to national sovereignty to be frequently and significantly influenced by the practices of other countries.

Despite the lack of obvious incentives for harmonization, convergence does appear to be occurring at least in some areas. The recent diffusion of plea bargaining across the world is a case in point. Plea bargaining now exists on six continents and continues to be on a global march. A partial explanation for the phenomenon may be found in rising crime rates, increasing complexity of cases, and more extensive protection of defendants' rights in many countries, all of which place additional burdens on criminal justice systems. But these factors are unlikely to be the whole story. As this chapter suggests, the convergence may also be attributable in part to informal cross-national exchanges among lawyers, judges, and other policy makers.

The best example of proliferation of plea bargaining by way of reform efforts may be found in Europe, particularly Eastern Europe. Since the collapse of the Iron Curtain, countries from Eastern Europe and the former Soviet Bloc have been reforming their criminal justice systems to ensure that they conform to modern notions of a fair trial and individual rights. At the same time, rising crime rates have led to demands on these countries to process criminal cases more efficiently.

Reform of criminal procedure in Eastern Europe has occurred in the context of broader harmonization of criminal laws in Europe, under the auspices of the European Union (EU)[1] and the Council of Europe (Council).[2] The Council has led toward harmonization by pressing countries to implement the decisions of the European Court of Human Rights (ECHR). The ECHR ensures that states observe the European Convention on Human Rights, including its provision on the right to a fair and speedy trial.[3] Both the Council and the EU have also issued nonbinding, but highly influential, recommendations on criminal procedure issues.[4]

The EU and the Council of Europe have also spearheaded reform initiatives in Eastern Europe as part of a larger effort to address transnational crime. For example, "Octopus," a program of the Council and the European Commission[5] designed to combat corruption and organized crime, has assisted 18 Eastern European countries in bringing laws, institutions, and practices in line with EU and ECHR law.[6] A key recommendation of such reform programs has been that these coun-

---

[1] The European Union is a political and economic partnership of 27 European countries, and it has the power to legislate in a number of areas, including the common market, monetary union, international trade, and the environment. Since September 11, EU legislators have increasingly taken joint action on criminal law matters.

[2] The Council of Europe is an organization with 47 member states, which "seeks to develop throughout Europe common and democratic principles based on the European Convention on Human Rights and other reference texts on the protection of individuals." Council of Europe, About the Council of Europe, *at* http://www.coe.int/T/e/Com/about_coe.

[3] Council of Europe, Convention for the Protection of Human Rights and Fundamental Freedoms art. 6, Nov. 4, 1950, Europ. T.S. No. 5, 213 U.N.T.S. 221 [hereinafter European Convention on Human Rights].

[4] For an overview of the EU influence on harmonization of European criminal law and procedure, see, for example, J.R. Spencer, *Introduction*, *in* European Criminal Procedures 1, 50-65 (Mireille Delmas-Marty & J.R. Spencer eds. 2002).

[5] The European Commission is an institution of the EU that is independent of national governments and acts in the interests of the EU as a whole. One of its key tasks is to implement and monitor the administration of EU laws and policies.

[6] Octopus Programme Against Corruption and Organised Crime, About Octopus, *at* http://www.coe.int/t/e/legal_affairs/legal_co-operation/combating_economic_crime/3_technical_cooperation/OCTOPUS.

tries should find ways to expedite criminal proceedings.[7] Candidacy for membership in the European Union placed significant pressure on many countries to implement the reform recommendations.

At the same time, the U.S. Department of Justice, through its Office for Prosecutorial Development Assistance and Training (OPDAT), has promoted criminal procedure reform along adversarial lines in Eastern Europe. As part of its law-reform efforts, OPDAT has urged Eastern European countries to adopt tools used in the United States to combat organized crime more effectively. These include undercover investigations, witness protection, testimonial immunity, and plea bargaining.[8]

In response to these various influences, a number of Eastern European and former Soviet states have turned to plea bargaining as a way to resolve cases more speedily. At the time of this writing, at least the following countries from the region have explicitly adopted a form of plea bargaining: Bosnia and Herzegovina, Bulgaria, Croatia, Estonia, Georgia, Hungary, Latvia, Lithuania, Macedonia, Moldova, Poland, Russia, Serbia, Slovakia, and Slovenia. At least across Eastern Europe, then, plea bargaining appears to be on a triumphal march.[9]

This chapter reviews the adoption of plea bargaining in two Eastern European countries: Russia and Bulgaria.[10] Plea bargaining has taken a

---

[7] *E.g.*, OCTOPUS, Final Recommendations and Guidelines for Action Addressed to the Government of Latvia, Feb. 13, 1998, *at* http://www.coe.int/t/f/affaires_juridiques/coop%E9ration_juridique/combattre_la_criminalit%E9_%E9conomique/3_coop%E9ration_technique/octopus/1996-1998/Octopus(1998)04%20-%20Latvia.asp [hereinafter OCTOPUS, Latvia Recommendations]; European Commission, Bulgaria: 2005 Comprehensive Monitoring Report, COM (2005) 534 final, Oct. 25, 2005 [hereinafter European Commission Report]; Council of Europe, Committee of Ministers, Recommendation No. R (86) 12 of the Committee of Ministers to Member States, Concerning Measures to Prevent and Reduce the Excessive Workload in the Courts (Adopted by the Committee of Ministers on 16 September 1986 at the 399th meeting of the Ministers' Deputies) [hereinafter Recommendation No. R (86)]; EU-Bulgaria Joint Parliamentary Committee, Final Statement, 22nd mtg., Brussels, Sept. 14, 2006, *at* http://www.parliament.bg/?page=news&lng=en&SType=show&id=999. The Council of Europe has also recommended that benefits be extended to defendants who admit the facts of the case and cooperate with law-enforcement agencies. Recommendation R. 87 (1987) and Explanatory Memorandum (1987) 333, *cited in* Mirjan Damaška, *Negotiated Justice in International Criminal Courts*, 2 J. Int'l Crim. Just. 1018 (2004).

[8] Department of Justice, Office of Overseas Prosecutorial Development, Assistance and Training, DOJ/OPDAT Central and Eastern Europe (CEE) Programs, *at* http://www.usdoj.gov/criminal/opdat/cntrl-east-europe/OPDAT_CEE.html.

[9] *See* Thomas Weigend, *Die Reform des Strafverfahrens: Europäische und deutsche Tendenzen und Probleme*, 104 Zeitschrift für die Gesamte Strafrechtswissenschaft 486, 493 (1992).

[10] The author is originally from Bulgaria, so her knowledge of the language and the legal system of Bulgaria was an important reason for selecting the country as one of the two case studies in this chapter.

somewhat different form in these two countries, but a number of similarities exist. In particular, both Russia and Bulgaria have largely rejected the American model of plea bargaining and have instead adopted a more inquisitorial approach to the practice. Reflecting this inquisitorial approach, neither Russia nor Bulgaria allows charge or fact bargaining. Both provide a greater role for victims in the process, and both require a defendant who pleads guilty to be represented by defense counsel. Finally, both prohibit the use of plea bargaining in serious violent crimes. These features are also common in other Eastern European countries, suggesting a broader trend.[11]

After examining the extent to which Russia and Bulgaria have combined inquisitorial and adversarial elements in adopting plea bargaining, the chapter evaluates whether this mix of elements has served them well. The chapter points to evidence that initial misgivings about plea bargaining have been overcome and that the practice has now been widely accepted by practitioners. Still, commentators continue to raise questions about the potential abuses of plea bargaining. The Russian and Bulgarian systems both suffer from corruption. The problem is especially serious in Russia, which vests prosecutors with vast powers, yet has a weak defense bar.[12] This raises serious questions as to whether plea bargaining is likely to produce fair outcomes in Russia and Bulgaria, as well as in other Eastern European countries that are still struggling to establish robust legal systems.[13]

---

[11] *See* Katarzyna Girdwoy, *Agreements in Polish Criminal Procedure*, 12 Ius Gentium 37 (2006); Julia Peters et al., *Negotiated Case-Ending Settlements: Ways of Speeding up the (Court) Process*, 14 Eur. J. Crim. Pol'y Res. 145, 151 (2008) (discussing Croatia, Hungary, and Poland); Erika Róth, *The Prosecution Service Function within the Hungarian Criminal Justice System*, 14 Eur. J. Crim. Pol'y Res. 289 (2008); Stephen C. Thaman, *Plea Bargaining, Negotiating Confessions, and Consensual Resolution of Criminal Cases*, *in* General Reports of the XVIIth Congress of the International Academy of Comparative Law 951 (K. Boele Woelki & S. Van Erp eds., 2007); Ksenija Turković, *The Prosecution Service Function within the Croatian Criminal Justice System*, 14 Eur. J. Crim. Pol'y Res. 263 (2008).

[12] Police often interfere with defense rights, and many defense attorneys are too pliable, corrupt, or not sufficiently competent to respond to such pressure. *E.g.*, William Burnham & Jeffrey Kahn, *Russia's Criminal Procedure Code Five Years Out*, 33 Rev. Cent. & E. Eur. L. 1, 33, 42-45 (2008). In addition, the low pay for defense attorneys results in lack of preparation and poor performance at trials. *Id.* at 73-74.

[13] *See, e.g.*, Stephen C. Thaman, *The Two Faces of Justice in the Post-Soviet Legal Sphere: Adversarial Procedure, Jury Trial, Plea-Bargaining and the Inquisitorial Legacy*, *in* Crime, Procedure and Evidence in a Comparative and International Context 99, 111 (Maximo Langer & Peter Tillers eds., 2008) (quoting J.D. Reichelt, *A Hobson's Experiment: Plea Bargaining in the Republic of Georgia*, 11 J. E. Eur. L. 159, 185 (2004) (referring to plea bargaining in Georgia as an "institutionalized form of bribery")).

In conclusion, the experience of Russia and Bulgaria highlights how criminal procedures can converge throughout a region as part of concerted law-reform efforts. At the same time, it demonstrates the difficulties with transplanting legal ideas from systems with very different traditions and calls for greater attention to context in law-reform efforts.

RUSSIA

HISTORY OF PLEA BARGAINING IN RUSSIA

Like other countries emerging from a communist past, beginning in the 1990s, Russia undertook comprehensive legal reform, including reform of its criminal justice system. The 1993 Russian Constitution introduced in its Article 123(3) "the principle of adversariness and equality of the parties,"[14] a stark departure from Russia's inquisitorial tradition. Reforms culminated in the adoption of a new Criminal Procedure Code in 2001. The Code was influenced in part by provisions of the European Convention of Human Rights, to which Russia acceded in 1996, and in part by American rule-of-law initiatives, which promoted the introduction of adversarial principles in criminal procedure.[15] More broadly, the reforms aimed at liberalizing criminal procedure as a way of showing Russia's break with its totalitarian past.[16]

At the same time that Russia tried to liberalize its criminal procedure, its criminal justice system was under pressure to be more efficient. Crime rates were rising sharply, overburdening the courts,[17] and the reforms themselves were likely to make the criminal process more costly. In particular, the introduction of jury trials, a more robust right to counsel, and the general shift toward adversarial proceedings were expected to increase the cost of processing cases. To address the existing and anticipated burdens, drafters of the new Criminal Procedure Code considered introducing plea bargaining. They enlisted the help

---

[14] Russ. Const. art. 123 (3), *translated in* Stanislaw Pomorski, *Modern Russian Criminal Procedure: The Adversarial Principle and Guilty Plea*, 17 Crim. L. F. 129, 129 (2006).

[15] Matthew J. Spence, *The Complexity of Success: The U.S. Role in Russian Rule of Law Reform*, 60 Carnegie Papers 13 (2005), *available at* http:// www.carnegieendowment.org/files/CP60.spence.FINAL.pdf.

[16] Pomorski, *supra* note 14, at 129.

[17] *Id.* at 136; Jason Bush, *What's Behind Russia's Crime Wave?*, Bus. Week, Oct. 19, 2006.

of American lawyers in the process, and some have argued that U.S. involvement was critical to the adoption of plea bargaining.[18]

While American lawyers did influence the drafting process,[19] ultimately, Russian legislators did not adopt American-style plea bargaining. The American model was perceived as not well suited to Russia's inquisitorial tradition and particularly to the principle of mandatory prosecution, the requirement that a conviction rest on evidence beyond the accused's confession, and the duty of the court to examine the evidence independently.[20] For these reasons, Russian legislators opted for a more inquisitorial form of plea bargaining, modeled largely on the Italian *patteggiamento*.[21] They initially limited plea bargaining to only minor crimes carrying a maximum sentence of up to five years (now the limit is ten years).[22] They called the procedure a "special trial," rather than a "guilty plea" procedure. They provided that the defendant would not be pleading guilty, but "acceding to the charges";[23] this means that, at least formally, the court would determine guilt in light of the evidence presented and that charge bargains would not be allowed.[24] Finally, they

---

[18] Spence, *supra* note 15, at 3-4, 12; Stephen Thaman, *The Nullification of the Russian Jury: Lessons for Jury-Inspired Reform in Eurasia and Beyond*, 40 Cornell Int'l L.J. 355, 367 (2007).

[19] The requirements for a valid accession to the charges in Russia are similar to those for a valid guilty plea in the United States—that it be voluntary, informed, and factually based. Like in the United States, the judge has to provide reasons for accepting the defendant's accession. Finally, appeals of judgments following a plea agreement are very limited, as they are in the United States. *See* Thaman, *supra* note 18, at 368.

[20] Burnham & Kahn, *supra* note 12, at 88.

[21] Like Russia, Italy had adopted a comprehensive criminal procedure reform that introduced a number of adversarial features, including plea bargaining, but had adapted these to an underlying inquisitorial model. The Italian process is formally called "application of punishment upon request of the parties," but is commonly known as *patteggiamento*, or bargaining. It was introduced in 1988. *See* Thaman, *supra* note 11.

[22] The Italian procedure is similarly limited to less serious crimes. *See, e.g.*, Luca Marafioti, *Italian Criminal Procedure: A System Caught Between Two Traditions*, *in* Crime, Procedure and Evidence in a Comparative and International Context 81, 89 (Maximo Langer & Peter Tillers eds., 2008).

[23] Similarly, the Italian procedure is called "application of punishment upon the request of the parties." *Id.*

[24] Burnham & Kahn, *supra* note 12, at 88. The court has a similar responsibility to review the evidence in Italy, and Italy similarly prohibits charge bargaining. *See, e.g.*, William T. Pizzi & Mariangela Montagna, *The Battle to Establish an Adversarial Trial System in Italy*, 25 Mich. J. Int'l L. 429, 438, 443-444 (2004).

set a minimum discount for admitting guilt—one-third of the statutory maximum for the crime charged.[25]

LAW AND PRACTICE OF PLEA BARGAINING IN RUSSIA

Articles 314-317 of the Russian Criminal Procedure Code lay out the provisions for the "special trial procedure."[26] Article 314 states that the procedure begins with a motion by the defendant—a motion to accede to the charges, waive ordinary trial procedures, and accept punishment. The defendant may make the motion at the preliminary hearing or whenever he becomes acquainted with the materials in the case (i.e., at the conclusion of the investigation, when the defendant and his attorney have the right to inspect the complete case file compiled by investigators).[27]

The Code says nothing about negotiations between prosecution and defense before the defendant files a motion. Yet it is likely that such negotiations will occur, given that both the prosecutor and the victim must consent to the motion in order for the court to accept it.[28] The concessions that the parties are likely to exchange include prosecutorial promises to recommend a lenient sentence and the defendant's promises to admit guilt and to cooperate with the prosecution in other cases.[29] The victim may also be involved and ask for restitution or apology.[30]

Charge bargaining is unlikely to occur because of the principle of mandatory prosecution and the lack of broad prosecutorial charging discretion. As Stanislaw Pomorski explains, however, certain "low visibility" charge bargains may still occur despite the formal ban on such practices.[31] For example, Article 14 §2 of the Russian Criminal Code allows the prosecutor not to file charges when the crime is insignificant or not "socially dangerous." Article 77 allows the prosecutor not to file charges

---

[25] Russ. Crim. Proc. Code §316 (7) (2001, with amendments through 2005), translation *available at* http://www.legislationline.org/upload/legislations/9a/eb/3a4a5e98a67c25d4fe5eb5170513.htm. By contrast, the Italian procedure limits the discount to no more than one-third of the "normal sentence." Marafioti, *supra* note 22, at 89 & n.34.

[26] Russ. Crim. Proc. Code, *supra* note 25.

[27] Burnham & Kahn, *supra* note 12.

[28] Russ. Crim. Proc. Code, *supra* note 25, §314 (1); Pomorski, *supra* note 14, at 139-140.

[29] Pomorski, *supra* note 14.

[30] *Id.*

[31] *Id.*

against a "person who has committed a crime for the first time of a minor or average gravity . . . if it is established that as a consequence of a change of situation this person or the act committed by him ceased to be socially dangerous."[32] Such provisions grant some discretion to prosecutors and may therefore facilitate a limited form of charge bargaining.[33]

The parties' negotiations about the sentence are not binding on the court. The court has the ultimate sentencing authority, but the Code specifically provides that the defendant's sentence under the special trial procedure "may not exceed two-thirds of the maximum term or the extent of the strictest punishment envisaged for the committed crime."[34] Of course, a prosecutorial recommendation for a discount of more than one-third is likely to be followed by the court, so this is likely to encourage negotiations between the parties about the sentencing recommendation.

The court also has an important role in ensuring that the defendant's motion follows the Code's requirements. First, the court must ensure that the defendant understands the consequences of the motion and has filed the motion voluntarily.[35] Second, the court must confirm that the evidence supports the charges against the accused.[36] In doing so, the court must rely solely on the investigative file.[37] Ironically, this provision harks back to Russia's older, pre-2001 inquisitorial process, in which judges relied almost exclusively on the evidence in the investigative file to reach a verdict. The court may, however, go beyond the investigative file and hear witnesses to examine circumstances related to sentencing.[38]

While the requirements above are similar to the requirements for a guilty plea in the United States, the Russian "motion to accede to the charges" must meet two additional requirements that go beyond American prerequisites for a valid guilty plea. First, a Russian defendant must file the motion only after consulting with defense counsel. Counsel must also be present at the hearing to review the motion, and this right can-

---

[32] *Id.*

[33] Similar provisions have given rise to a limited form of charge bargaining in Germany, even though Germany, like Russia, follows the principle of mandatory prosecution and prohibits charge bargains. *See supra* Chapter 2.

[34] Russ. Crim. Proc. Code, *supra* note 25, §316 (7).

[35] *Id.* §314(2).

[36] *Id.* §316(7).

[37] *Id.* §316(5).

[38] *Id.*

not be waived, unlike in the United States.[39] Second, victims are entitled to participate in the hearing on the motion, and during the hearing, the court must "clarify the victim's attitude to the defendant's position."[40] As mentioned earlier, victims can also veto the court's acceptance of the motion.

If a Russian court finds that the defendant's petition for a special trial procedure is not voluntary, informed, factually based, or supported by the prosecution and the victim, then the court will set the case for trial under the ordinary procedures.[41] If defense counsel is not present at the hearing on the petition, the court must appoint counsel for the accused.[42]

The Code is silent on the consequences of either the defendant's withdrawal of his "accession to the charges" or a breach by either party of the related agreement. If the special trial procedure is to maintain its effectiveness, it is likely that courts will develop a way of enforcing the parties' promises. But like in other inquisitorial countries, it is not clear whether the defendant can take back statements made during the negotiations or while acceding to charges in open court. It is possible that such statements will be admissible at a later trial if the agreement falls through.

The special trial procedure has been subject to review in the Russian Constitutional Court and the Russian Supreme Court, and so far, it has survived scrutiny in both courts. The Russian Constitutional Court upheld the constitutionality of the procedure in a 2006 ruling.[43] The petitioner, a defendant who had been convicted under the special trial procedure, claimed that the procedure violated his right to participate actively in his own defense, the right to have the facts of his case independently investigated by a judge, and the right to appeal factual, as well as legal, errors. The Court held that the special trial procedure did not deprive defendant of these rights, but instead gave him the option to choose a different process for resolving his case, one that may be more beneficial to him. The Court emphasized, however, that for the special procedure to be constitutional, the defendant's choice must be made voluntarily

---

[39] *Compare id.* §315(1), *with* Iowa v. Tovar, 541 U.S. 77 (2004).

[40] Russ. Crim. Proc. Code, *supra* note 25, §316(4).

[41] *Id.* §314(3) & (4); §316(6).

[42] *Id.* §315(1).

[43] Opredelenie Konstitutsionnogo Suda RF No. 417-O, Oct. 17, 2006, *at* http://www.lawrussia.ru/texts/legal_319/doc319a997x911.htm.

and with full understanding of the character and consequences of the procedure.[44]

In 2004 and 2006, the Russian Supreme Court also pronounced on the subject of the special trial procedure and set additional restrictions.[45] The Court held that a defendant may not accede selectively to only some of the charges against him; he must either accept the special procedure for all counts of the accusation, or proceed to the ordinary procedure. Nor can the defendant benefit from the special trial procedure if he has failed to satisfy fully a civil suit for damages arising from the offense charged. In the case of a joint trial of several defendants, if the trial cannot be severed, all defendants must choose the special trial procedure, or the case will proceed to ordinary trial.[46] Finally, if one of the defendants is a juvenile, and his case may not be severed from the rest, all defendants must proceed to a regular trial.[47] The imposition of these additional restrictions appears to signal the Court's continued unease with the special trial procedure.[48]

RECEPTION OF PLEA BARGAINING IN RUSSIA

Like the Russian Supreme Court, a number of commentators have expressed concerns with Russia's foray into plea bargaining. One eminent Russian academic argued that plea agreements are "alien to Russian mentality" and "an immoral, reprehensible, dishonest phenomenon"; they "demean[] the government, suggesting its helplessness, its inability to solve crimes" and they "demean the investigator, the prosecutor, and the judge since they will have to bargain with the criminal."[49] Other commentators have also decried bargains as producing unwarranted lenient treatment for criminals, which could damage the legitimacy of the criminal justice system.[50]

---

[44] *Id.*

[45] Pomorski, *supra* note 14, at 137.

[46] *Id.*

[47] Decree No. 60 of the Plenary Session of the Supreme Court of the Russian Federation, Dec. 5, 2006 at §7, Rossiyskaya Gazeta, *at* http://www.rg.ru/2006/12/20/poriadok-dok.html.

[48] Pomorski, *supra* note 14, at 137 (citing Decree No. 1 of the Plenary Session of the Supreme Court of the Russian Federation, Mar. 5, 2004 at §28, *Bulleten' Verkhovnogo Suda Rossiisskoi Federatsii*, No. 5 (2004)).

[49] I. Petrukhin, *Sdelki o priznanii viny chuzhdy rossiskomu mentalitetu*, 5 Rossiskaia Iustitsiia 35 (2001), *cited and translated in* Pomorski, *supra* note 14, at 135.

[50] Irina Dline & Olga Schwartz, *The Jury Is Still Out on the Future of Jury Trials in Russia*, 11 E. Eur. Const. Rev. (Winter/Spring 2002), *at* http://www3.law.nyu.edu/eecr/vol11num1_2/features/dline.html.

Yet others are concerned with the potential abuses of the new procedure, calling it a "dangerous phenomenon" that ignores the terrible misuses of false confessions during totalitarian times.[51] According to this group of commentators, the special procedure is also worrisome in that it gives too much power to prosecutors and trial judges, leading to potential arbitrariness in its application. Given the weakness of the Russian defense bar, some commentators are further concerned that prosecutors may dominate the process and that "plea bargaining could be used by an overly powerful Russian government to force innocent people to admit guilt for crimes they did not commit."[52] Although trial judges supervise the process, the very limited right to appeal from the special trial procedure means that arbitrary decisions made by trial judges might remain unchecked.[53]

Given the pervasive corruption of the Russian legal system,[54] these are valid concerns. Because of its informality and lack of transparency, plea bargaining may be especially prone to abuse in corrupt systems such as Russia, regardless of the formal protections provided under the Code.

Notes and Questions:

1. Both the Russian Supreme Court and a number of commentators have expressed serious concerns about the fairness and potential abuses of the special trial procedure. Yet despite such criticism, the procedure has been increasingly used by practitioners and sanctioned by courts.[55] The following statistics on the use of the

---

[51] Pomorski, *supra* note 14, at 136 (citing authorities); Dline & Schwartz, *supra* note 50.

[52] Leonard Orland, Essay and Translation, *A Russian Legal Revolution: The 2002 Criminal Procedure Code*, 18 Conn. J. Int'l L. 133 (2002).

[53] Thaman, *supra* note 18, at 368 (quoting a former Russian Moscow City Court judge, Sergey Pashin, for his concern that "the conveyor belt to work over people into the condition of camp dust is especially effective in the summer when it is impossible to breathe in the pretrial detention centers and tuberculosis and consumption flourish. Then the detainee admits anything in order to be quickly punished and to go to the penal colony where it is easier to live.").

[54] Tom Blass, *Combating Corruption and Political Influence in Russia's Court System* 31, 31-34, *in* Transparency International, Global Corruption Report 2007; *see also* Marck Franchetti, *Traffic Incident Gives Insight into Russia's Corrupt Legal System*, Sunday Times, June 29, 2008, *at* http://www.timesonline.co.uk/tol/news/world/europe/article4231219.ece.

[55] Even some academic commentators have called for extending the practice to more serious crimes, suggesting that academic opposition to plea bargaining has lessened as well.

special procedure in Russia were reported by William Burnham and Jeffrey Kahn:

> For 2006, in the Justice of the Peace courts, 108,000 were decided using guilty pleas, which constituted 22.4% of all decided cases, up from 72,000 and 17.1% in 2005, and this up from only 20,000 cases and 12% in 2003. In the district courts in 2006, special procedures disposed of 213,800 criminal cases or 37.5% of the total number of decided cases, up from 168,100 or 30% in 2005. The largest portion of such cases consisted of theft (42.2%), robbery (30.5%), and unlawful activity with drugs (40.6%). In the subject-level courts, only about 2% of decided cases were disposed of on this basis, though the number of guilty pleas in that court is increasing as well. The low number of guilty plea cases in the subject-level courts is attributable to the fact that a high percentage of cases in this court involve maximum sentences of over 10 years, thus making them ineligible for guilty pleas.[56]

Why are judges and lawyers increasingly relying on the special trial procedure, despite the potential problems identified by commentators? In what ways might the procedure serve the interests of lawyers and judges even when it might not be in the interest of the defendants and victims in their cases or of the public at large?

2. Despite significant involvement by American advisors in the drafting of the Russian Criminal Procedure Code, Russian legislators largely rejected the American model of plea bargaining. What might account for this? Do you believe that the ultimate model chosen by Russia is a better fit for its system?
3. Given the corruption of the Russian legal system and its weak implementation of defense rights, were legislators wise to limit the application of plea bargaining to less serious offenses? Under the circumstances, should legislators have refrained altogether from adopting plea bargaining?
4. In Italy, the country that served as a model for the Russian special trial procedure, prosecutors who refuse to accept a defendant's request to plea bargain must explain and justify their reasons for doing so, and defendants may renew their application for a reduced sentence before the court. Judges must similarly provide

---

L.P. Izhnina, Osobiy poryadok sudebnogo zasedaniya po UPK RF: problem teorii i praktiki na primere Nizhegorodskoy oblasti, *at* http://iuaj.net/lib/konf-MASP/iznina.htm.

[56] *Russia's Criminal Procedure Code Five Years Out*, *supra* note 12, at 90-91.

reasons for accepting or rejecting sentence agreements between the parties. Should Russian legislators have imposed a similar requirement for reason-giving as part of introducing the special trial procedure? What are the advantages and disadvantages of such a requirement?

BULGARIA

HISTORY OF PLEA BARGAINING IN BULGARIA

Like its other Eastern European counterparts, Bulgaria's criminal justice system has been in transition since the fall of communism in 1989. The rapidly changing political environment has pulled the criminal justice system in different directions. On the one hand, reforms have been shaped by a greater concern for civil liberties and calls for more effective oversight of the government's actions in the criminal process. Bulgaria's accession to the European Convention on Human Rights in 1992 also required concrete legislative changes to ensure compliance with the Convention's provisions on fair trial rights and freedom from arbitrary detentions.

At the same time, rising crime rates have led to demands for more "law and order," and the accession to the European Union in 2007 increased the pressure on Bulgarian legislators to take more effective measures against corruption, money laundering, and organized crime. The EU's recommendations concerning the criminal justice system called for greater efficiency in processing criminal cases, shorter investigations, and the strengthening of prosecutorial powers over investigative and charging decisions. As part of its EU accession strategy, the Bulgarian Parliament adopted a new Criminal Procedure Code in October 2005, which incorporated EU suggestions for reform and entered into force in April 2006.[57] The new Code and its provisions on plea bargaining were also consistent with the Council of Europe's recommendations to reduce

[57] EU-Bulgaria Joint Parliamentary Committee, Final Statement, 22nd mtg., Brussels, Sept. 14, 2006, *at* http://www.parliament.bg/?page=news&lng=en&SType=show&id=999 (noting "the entry in force on 29 April 2006 of the new Penal Procedure Code, the results achieved so far for fast and efficient procedures and of the progress accomplished in the area of legal aid and witness protection; [and] expect[ing] the changes introduced to ensure efficiency of the investigation and to make the system in general more efficient and transparent by eliminating overlapping of functions").

excessive judicial workload[58] and with the right to a trial "within a reasonable time" under the European Convention on Human Rights.[59]

While criminal procedure reform was strongly encouraged by the European Union and formed part of Bulgaria's strategy for accession to the EU, the provisions on plea bargaining were also influenced by exchanges between Bulgarian lawyers, judges, and policy makers and American advisors, including lawyers from the Department of Justice and the American Bar Association's Central and Eastern Europe Legal Initiative (ABA-CEELI). In these interactions, American advisors promoted plea bargaining and advised Bulgarian lawyers and judges about the way plea bargaining operates in the United States.

Plea bargaining was first introduced in Bulgaria in January 2000 through amendments to the 1975 Bulgarian Criminal Procedure Code. This legislation, however, permitted plea bargaining only for relatively minor crimes, such as theft and traffic offenses.[60] In that respect, Bulgaria continued to reflect what was then the generally skeptical continental attitude toward plea bargaining. The Bulgarian provisions on plea bargaining did not copy a particular foreign model,[61] but their features reflect the influence of the Italian and German models of plea bargaining, and to a lesser degree, the American model.

Despite its initial limited scope, plea bargaining proved quite popular among practitioners once it was introduced. Its application was extended in 2001 and again in the new 2006 Criminal Procedure Code. This was again part of a larger effort to speed up proceedings and reduce case backlog, largely in response to criticism by EU and American observers about the long delays in Bulgarian investigations and trials.[62] The 2006 Code provides that plea bargaining can be used for the resolution of most cases, including assault, manslaughter, drug trafficking, and finan-

---

[58] Recommendation No. R (86), *supra* note 7.

[59] European Convention on Human Rights art. 6 (1), *supra* note 3.

[60] American Bar Association Central European and Eurasian Law Initiative, Draft Report on Plea Bargaining Roundtable Discussion, July 27, 2001, Plovdiv, Bulgaria (on file with author) [hereinafter CEELI Draft Report].

[61] Telephone Interview with Judge Ekaterina Trendafilova, International Criminal Court, Jan. 21, 2006. At the time of the interview, Judge Trendafilova was a professor of criminal justice at Sofia University Law School. Judge Trendafilova had also chaired the working group that helped draft amendments to the Bulgarian Criminal Procedure Code.

[62] European Commission Report, *supra* note 7; U.S. Department of State, Bulgaria, Country Reports on Human Rights Practices—2004, Feb. 28, 2005, *at* http://www.state.gov/g/drl/rls/hrrpt/2004 [hereinafter 2004 State Dep't Report].

cial crimes. Plea bargaining is still not permitted in certain very serious criminal cases, such as murder or international crimes.[63]

As of this writing, it is not clear yet how many cases are resolved by plea bargaining under the new framework. Data from 2000, when plea bargaining was first introduced and was still limited to minor cases, show that 36.6 percent of all criminal cases were resolved by a plea agreement.[64] In 2004, 38.6 percent of criminal cases were resolved by plea agreement, and 41 percent of convicted persons pleaded guilty.[65] The percentage of plea agreements in 2004 varied significantly by category of crime, with the highest numbers of agreements entered in cases of document fraud (69 percent), disturbance of the peace and public order (56 percent), economic crimes (55 percent), crimes against the judicial system (51 percent), assault (49 percent), and property crimes (45 percent).[66] It is likely that the 2006 Code, which extends the application of plea agreements to more serious crimes, has led to a significant increase in plea bargaining, particularly because practitioners and judges have become much more comfortable with the practice since 2000.

LAW AND PRACTICE OF PLEA BARGAINING IN BULGARIA

Articles 381 to 384 of the Bulgarian Criminal Procedure Code govern plea agreements. The law provides for two types of plea agreements: (1) Article 384 agreements, which can be made after formal charges are filed with the court, but before the completion of the judicial inquiry ("trial agreements"), and (2) Article 381 agreements, which can be made after the police have completed their investigation and transferred the case to the prosecutor ("pretrial agreements").

Plea negotiations in Bulgaria are conducted between the defense attorney and the prosecutor. Neither the defendant nor the court participates. For that reason, if the prosecutor asks for plea negotiations and the defendant is unrepresented, the court is required to appoint counsel

---

[63] Bulg. Crim. Proc. Code §381.2, *translated at* http://www.legislationline.org/documents/section/criminal-codes.

[64] Center for the Study of Democracy, Judicial Anti-Corruption Program 48 (2003), *available at* http://unpan1.un.org/intradoc/groups/public/documents/UNTC/UNPAN012391.pdf; *see also* Gergana Marinova, *Bulgarian Criminal Procedure: The New Philosophy and Issues of Approximation*, 31 Rev. Cent. & E. Eur. L. 45, 76 (2006) (citing statistics suggesting that the procedure is used in about 30 percent of all criminal cases).

[65] National Statistical Institute, Crimes and Convicted Persons: Data from 2004 tbls. 7, 12 (2005), *at* http://www.nsi.bg.

[66] *Id.* tbl. 12.

before negotiations can proceed.[67] Typically, defense attorneys initiate plea negotiations.[68] Because most defendants do not obtain counsel until after the charges are filed with the court, negotiations usually begin only at that point.[69] As a result, most plea agreements are concluded under Article 384, which governs trial agreements.[70] But defendants who can afford counsel and hire one earlier in the process prefer to begin negotiations before formal charges are filed with the court, because they can typically get a better deal at that stage.[71] Unlike in the United States and consistent with the inquisitorial tradition, as soon as the investigation is completed (and thus before negotiations begin), the defense is entitled to inspect the entire investigative file.[72]

Plea agreements must be in writing to be valid.[73] They usually entail the exchange of a promise by the defendant to admit guilt and pay reparations for a promise by the prosecutor to recommend a lenient sentence.[74] A single judge of the court of first instance must approve the plea agreement, under criteria discussed later in this Section. Once it is approved, the plea agreement has the force of an ordinary judgment, but it may not be appealed in the ordinary course; by entering into a plea agreement, therefore, the defendant effectively waives his right to appeal.[75]

---

[67] Bulg. Crim. Proc. Code, *supra* note 63, §384.2; Normativna uredba, Prekratyavane na nakazatelnoto proizvodstvo sus sporazumenie [Regulation on the disposition of criminal cases through a plea agreement] (on file with author) (undated, but pertaining to pre-2006 provisions on plea agreements).

[68] CEELI Draft Report, *supra* note 60.

[69] *Id.*

[70] Bulg. Crim. Proc. Code, *supra* note 63, §384 (providing for agreements after the judicial inquiry begins); CEELI Draft Report, *supra* note 60, at 2. Another reason for the greater use of trial agreements under Article 384 is that the prosecutor has a better understanding of the case once the trial begins and has had a chance to evaluate the case based on interactions with the defense. *Id.* at 5.

[71] Alexander Petrov, *Sporazumenieto chesto e otkaz ot pravosudie [A Plea Agreement Is Often a Denial of Justice]*, Sega, Feb. 19, 2008, *at* http://www.segabg.com/online/article.asp?issueid=2891§ionid=31&id=0001301.

[72] Laszlo Darotsi & Todor Kolarov, Institutat na sporazumenieto za prekratyavane na nakazatelnoto proizvodstvo, CEELI Report (1999) (on file with author); Marinova, *supra* note 64, at 66-67.

[73] *E.g.*, Marinova, *supra* note 64, at 76.

[74] The parties may also bargain about the execution of the sentence, the suspension of privileges, and so on. Petur Raymundov, Osobeni Nakazatelni Proizvodstva: Sporazumenieto [Special Criminal Proceedings: Plea Agreement] 304 (2005).

[75] *Id.* at 346-351 (explaining that although ordinary appellate remedies are unavailable, extraordinary remedies may be available, for example, if the parties allege serious procedural violations).

At least as of 2000, prosecutors were not relying on plea bargaining to obtain additional information about other crimes or other defendants.[76] Traditionally, Bulgarian prosecutors have not taken an active role at the investigative stage, and this has led to minimal or no interaction between witnesses and prosecutors before trial; the lack of interaction may partially explain why prosecutors have failed to take advantage of plea agreements to obtain witness cooperation.[77] Cooperation agreements would also be more difficult to enforce, as in other inquisitorial systems, because of the unitary proceeding for accepting the guilty plea and imposing the sentence (which leaves prosecutors no time to ensure that a defendant complies with his cooperation agreement before he receives a sentencing discount).[78] Finally, the limited number of cases in which plea bargaining was allowed under the old Code may be another reason for the relative lack of cooperation agreements. Notably, the old Code did not provide for plea bargaining in complex drug cases and other serious felonies. It is yet to be seen whether prosecutors will begin making greater use of plea bargaining under the new Code to resolve group crimes such as drug trafficking and organized crime.

Charge bargaining also does not seem to occur in Bulgaria.[79] Bulgarian prosecutors are still formally bound by the principle of mandatory prosecution and do not have the discretion to charge a crime less serious than the facts would warrant. Current practice appears to conform to the letter of the law in this respect.

The court's primary role in the process is to review the plea agreement presented by the parties. At the plea hearing, the court must ask the defendant whether he understands the charges, whether he admits guilt, whether he understands the consequences of the plea agreement, whether he is prepared to accept those consequences, and whether he has signed the agreement of his own free will.[80] In practice, defendants themselves give a formulaic statement—prepared by their attorney—

---

[76] Darotsi & Kolarov, *supra* note 72, at 4.

[77] *E.g.*, American Bar Association, Prosecutorial Reform Index for Bulgaria 31-32 (2006), *at* http://www.abanet.org/rol/publications/bulgaria-pri-2006.pdf [hereinafter Prosecutorial Reform Index].

[78] A similar reluctance to use plea bargaining to obtain cooperation from defendants has been observed in other European countries as well, in large part because of difficulty in enforcing cooperation agreements. *See, e.g.*, Organization on Security and Cooperation in Europe, Plea Agreements in Bosnia and Herzegovina: Practices Before the Courts and Their Compliance with International Human Rights Standards 1, 20-22 (2d ed. 2006).

[79] E-mail from Ivaylo Rodopski, District Court Judge, Sofia County, to author, Jan. 26, 2006; *see also* Marinova, *supra* note 64, at 75.

[80] Bulg. Crim. Proc. Code, *supra* note 63, §382(4).

that addresses all of these points.[81] Judges rarely conduct any inquiry of the defendant to ensure that there is factual basis for the agreement. If the judge accepts the agreement, he or she does not need to write a fully reasoned judgment.[82] Most decisions therefore simply reiterate the terms of the plea agreement.[83]

The court may suggest changes to the agreement and, if so, it must discuss these with the prosecution and the defense.[84] Changes are typically proposed when the court views the negotiated sentence as too low. The negotiations may resume if the court has suggested modifications to the agreement, and a new agreement may then be concluded. If the parties and the court continue to have serious disagreements, and the court concludes that the plea agreement does not adequately consider the public and the victim's interests, the court may reject the agreement as "contrary to law or morals" and send the case to trial under the ordinary procedure.[85] Pretrial agreements under Article 381 are rarely rejected as "contrary to the law or morals."[86] However, judicial oversight of trial agreements under Article 384 appears to be more vigilant.[87] This is in part because Article 384 gives judges more leeway to reject agreements,[88] but also because, by the time that the case has been filed with the court, judges are more familiar with the case.[89]

---

81 *E.g.*, Case of M.V.S., Protocol of the Proceedings 24B, Kostinbrod District Court (Rayonen sud), Nov. 19, 2008 (accepting an Article 381 plea agreement in a DWI case) (on file with author); Case of P.B.P., Protocol of the Proceedings 22B, Kostinbrod District Court (Rayonen sud), Nov. 6, 2008 (same) (on file with author); Case of C.N.J., Protocol of the Proceedings, Radnevo District Court (Rayonen sud), Nov. 20, 2008 (accepting an Article 384 plea agreement in a DWI case) (on file with author).

82 There is some disagreement whether the court has to provide any reasoning at all when it accepts a plea agreement. At least some judges think they need not provide reasons for accepting a plea agreement. On the other hand, some commentators maintain that such reasons must be outlined to show that the agreement has a valid factual basis.

83 *See supra* note 81.

84 Bulg. Crim. Proc. Code, *supra* note 63, §382(6).

85 *Id.* §38 (7).

86 Darotsi & Kolarov, *supra* note 72, at 2 (noting that judges reject such agreements as contrary to law and morals in less than 5 percent of cases).

87 *See id.*

88 Whereas Section 384(1), which governs trial agreements, provides that the "court *may* approve" the agreement, Section 382(7), which pertains to pretrial agreements, reads that the court "shall approve the agreement where it is not contrary to the law or the morals." *See id.* In practice, courts use the standard of "contrary to the law or the morals" for all plea agreements. *See supra* note 81.

89 CEELI Draft Report, *supra* note 60, at 3.

If the court rejects the agreement, any self-incriminating statements that the defendant makes during the plea colloquy are deemed to have no probative value in future trials.[90] In this regard, Bulgaria seems to have departed from inquisitorial models of plea bargaining and to have aligned itself with the American approach to guilty plea withdrawals.

Unlike American plea bargaining, the Bulgarian procedure on plea agreements, at least on paper, appears to show greater consideration for victims' interests. Before reviewing the role of victims in plea agreements in Bulgaria, it is important to note their role in criminal proceedings more generally. Under the Bulgarian Criminal Procedure Code, victims are entitled to participate as private accessory prosecutors alongside the public prosecutor in criminal cases. In this role, they can inspect the investigative file, file pleadings, ask questions of witnesses, and appeal the judgment.[91] In addition, victims can join a civil claim to the criminal proceeding and ask for damages for material or nonmaterial (moral) injuries.[92] Victims typically exercise this right, because the joinder of civil claims to the criminal case is much easier and cheaper than instituting a separate civil case.[93]

The plea agreement procedure attempts to safeguard some of these broader victims' rights. First, the Criminal Procedure Code provides that when the crime has caused material damages, the court may not approve a plea agreement until the defendant has returned the stolen property or has paid restitution to the victim.[94] In addition, if the parties reach a plea agreement during pretrial proceedings, the court must notify the victim of the agreement and of the right to file a civil claim for nonmaterial damages.[95] More significantly, victims who become parties to a case—that is, participate as private prosecutors or civil claimants—must consent to an agreement reached during trial proceedings before a court can approve the agreement.[96] Some observers view this provision as an impediment to the smooth functioning of plea bargaining.[97] Others, however, report that victims rarely participate and that even when they

---

[90] Bulg. Crim. Proc. Code, *supra* note 63, §382(8).

[91] *Id.* §§76-79. For a brief overview of victims' rights in Bulgarian criminal procedure, *see* Prosecutorial Reform Index, *supra* note 77, at 28-29.

[92] *Id.* §84.

[93] Marinova, *supra* note 64, at 60.

[94] Bulg. Crim. Proc. Code, *supra* note 63, §381(3).

[95] *Id.* §382(10).

[96] *Id.* §384(3).

[97] CEELI Draft Report, *supra* note 60, at 4.

do, their objections rarely result in a veto of the agreement.[98] A more systematic study of this question is needed to understand whether the provision for a victim veto right has a real effect in practice.

Despite the provisions for victim participation and mandatory restitution of material damages, plea agreements can still compromise important victims' rights. In particular, victims play no role in *pretrial* plea agreements. Such agreements can be approved without the victim's agreement, as long as the defendant has compensated all material damages. This means that victims have to bring a separate civil case to obtain "nonmaterial damages," which include health expenses and pain and suffering damages and can be quite significant. The costs and the delays associated with such a civil proceeding prevent many victims from pursuing their claims. In this way, pretrial plea agreements undermine the rights of victims both by precluding victims' participation in the criminal case and by hampering the recovery of nonmaterial damages.[99]

Finally, as in the United States, the law fails to provide a set sentencing discount for guilty pleas. In fact, a common complaint among practitioners is that there are no guidelines on the sentencing consequences of plea agreements.[100] An amendment to the Criminal Procedure Code did offer some guidance by allowing courts to sentence below the statutory minimum when a case is resolved through a plea agreement.[101] This amendment aimed to encourage more defendants to enter into plea agreements. But it still leaves significant discretion to the court and has been criticized for allowing courts to impose unduly lenient sentences and to treat similarly situated defendants unequally.[102]

RECEPTION OF PLEA BARGAINING IN BULGARIA

When plea bargaining was first introduced in Bulgaria in 2000, it was seen by some as "heresy" and contrary to the continental legal tradition.[103] Among practitioners, prosecutors were the most skeptical about it in the early months of its operations. But perceptions have changed as plea bargaining has become a common practice among prosecutors,

---

[98] E-mail from S. Dimitrova, Bulgarian Attorney, to author, Jan. 16, 2006.

[99] *See* Raymundov, *supra* note 74, at 362-363.

[100] CEELI Draft Report, *supra* note 60.

[101] Bulg. Crim. Proc. Code, *supra* note 63, §381(4).

[102] Raymundov, *supra* note 74, at 360; Petrov, *supra* note 71.

[103] *See* CEELI Draft Report, *supra* note 60, at 1.

defense attorneys, and courts.[104] The 2006 extension of plea bargaining to more serious crimes was encouraged by a number of attorneys and academic commentators.[105]

It is not yet clear to what extent the introduction of plea bargaining has fulfilled its promise of increasing the efficiency of the Bulgarian criminal justice system. It seems to be functioning smoothly in practice and is seen by many practitioners and academic commentators as an important element in the effort to streamline proceedings and reduce the caseload of Bulgarian courts. While some foreign observers have commented on the insignificant reduction in caseloads resulting from plea bargaining,[106] this is probably attributable to the novelty and limited application of plea bargaining until the recent amendments of the Criminal Procedure Code.

A more serious problem is the potential for abuse of the practice. Observers have criticized the lack of internal supervision of prosecutors' performance in plea negotiations, particularly at the pretrial stage.[107] Some commentators have argued that this results in agreements that propose unduly lenient sentences and treat similarly situated defendants differently.[108] There is also a widespread popular concern that the prosecution service lacks transparency and accountability.[109] In addition, plea bargaining is reportedly seen by many Bulgarians as a practice that benefits only the wealthy, who can "buy their way out of charges."[110] The lack of transparency of plea negotiations renders the practice especially prone to abuse by corrupt judges, prosecutors, and defense attorneys. Criticisms of plea bargaining are therefore unlikely to subside until

---

[104] *See id.*

[105] *Id.* at 5.

[106] 2004 State Dep't Report, *supra* note 62.

[107] CEELI Draft Report, *supra* note 60, at 3.

[108] *Id.*; Raymundov, *supra* note 74, at 360; Alexander Alexandrov, *Neobyavenata amnistiya [The Undeclared Amnesty]*, Sega, Sept. 12, 2006, *at* http://www.segabg.com/online/article.asp?issueid=2412§ionid=31&id=0001501; Petrov, *supra* note 71.

[109] European Commission Report, *supra* note 7 ("Last but not least, no steps were taken in the reporting period to modernise the prosecution service, although there remains a need to make it more transparent and accountable."); Prosecutorial Reform Index, *supra* note 77, at 20 (reporting a study in which 57.1 percent of respondents believed that nearly all, or most, prosecutors are corrupt).

[110] 2004 State Dep't Report, *supra* note 62; *see also* Marinova, *supra* note 64, at 76 (noting that most people do not know about the introduction of plea bargaining, but that when they hear about it, "they generally view it as something quite undesirable, as a way for criminals to avoid justice and punishment"); *see also* Petrov, *supra* note 71.

the criminal justice system as a whole is seen as less corrupt and more effective.

Notes and Questions:

1. Bulgarian courts appear to have great discretion to reject plea agreements. They may reject any agreement that they believe is "contrary to the law or the morals." What might be the effect of such broad judicial discretion to reject plea agreements? Are judges in the United States similarly free to reject plea agreements? Should they be given greater discretion in this respect, or should their discretion to reject agreements be reduced?
2. The Bulgarian system of plea bargaining provides two main ways in which victims' interests can be safeguarded: (1) the defendant must pay restitution before the court approves a plea agreement; and (2) the victim who has joined the case as a private prosecutor or civil claimant must consent to a "trial agreement" under Article 384. Does this approach adequately safeguard victims' interests in plea bargaining? Does it overprotect them? Should other countries like the United States and Germany consider adopting a similar model?
3. In your opinion, are there provisions in the Bulgarian Criminal Procedure Code that are more likely to produce fair and accurate guilty pleas than the typical guilty plea in American courts?
4. Corruption remains a serious problem in the Bulgarian legal system.[111] Given this fact, should plea bargaining have been extended to some more serious crimes under the 2006 Code? Should the Code have provided greater guidance on sentencing discounts for a guilty plea? Are there other provisions that Bulgaria could adopt to ensure that plea bargaining is fair and legitimate?

DIFFUSION OF PLEA BARGAINING IN EASTERN EUROPE

The rapid diffusion of plea bargaining throughout Eastern Europe suggests that criminal procedures may converge across borders even in

---

[111] *E.g.*, Transparency International, Press Release, *Bulgaria and Romania Must Produce Concrete and Irreversible Anti-Corruption Results*, Feb. 12, 2009, *at* http://www.transparency.org/news_room/corruption_news/ti_in_the_news/2008; *EU Warns Bulgaria and Romania on Corruption*, Spiegel Online, June 27, 2007, *at* http://www.spiegel.de/international/europe/0,1518,491087,00.html.

the absence of formal treaties. The convergence in this case occurred largely through informal exchanges between government officials, lawyers, and policy makers across borders, typically in the context of law-reform projects or in the process of acceding to the European Union. Advisors from the U.S. Department of Justice, the American Bar Association, the European Union, the Council of Europe, and U.S. and European embassies were often involved in these efforts.

These foreign advisors worked with their Eastern European counterparts in several arenas to promote the adoption of more efficient criminal procedures such as plea bargaining. Sometimes, they were directly involved in the legislative stages of law reform, offering drafting assistance for amendments to Criminal Procedure Codes. Matthew Spence documents the critical role that American advisors played in the drafting of the Russian provisions on plea bargaining:

> Drafting assistance did . . . make a difference at the stage of second-order implementing legislation, once Russian political coalitions had aligned to create a space for U.S. influence. Plea bargaining was the most significant provision that made it into the code only after U.S. involvement. The introduction of this provision illustrates how U.S. assistance helped Russian reformers overcome specific practical and political obstacles that might have derailed the legislation. . . . Russian drafters had not seriously considered [plea bargaining] before the American suggestion, and its introduction was a heated political fight. Although jury trials without plea bargaining would have overwhelmed Russia's already over-extended court system, many Russians felt that confessions before trial in plea bargaining smacked too much of the forced confessions of Stalin's show trials. U.S. experts helped explain the concept, offered ideas about how to make it happen, and eased fears about the confessions' Stalinist overtones.[112]

While drafting assistance during the legislative process was undoubtedly critical in a number of countries, much of the foreign assistance focused on implementation. Foreign advisors helped inform lawyers and judges about plea bargaining, increase public acceptance of the practice, and train lawyers and judges how to use it in concrete cases.[113]

---

[112] Spence, *supra* note 15.

[113] *See, e.g.*, DOJ/OPDAT, Recent Achievements, *at* http://www.usdoj.gov/criminal/opdat/recent-achieve/rachieve.html; Günther Müller, Germany, Report on Special Procedures and Mechanisms to Expedite Criminal Proceedings: A Comparative Analysis, EU

Although European and American advisors generally agreed that Eastern European countries had to speed up their criminal proceedings, they often parted ways on the details of implementing this recommendation. While the United States heavily promoted its own model of plea bargaining, some European advisors rejected it as inconsistent with European criminal procedure traditions. For example, when OCTOPUS, a joint project of the Commission of the European Communities and the Council of Europe to combat corruption and organized crime in Eastern Europe, issued recommendations to Latvia in 1998, it noted the need for expediting criminal proceedings, but observed that:

> discussions in Europe have indicated that the American concept of plea-bargaining, wherein the defence counsel and the prosecutor in effect agree to the charges and on the defendant's plea, is ill-suited to the fundamental principles of European criminal procedure. For example German and Italian practice is based on close supervision by the judge of any such discussions.[114]

As the examples of Russia and Bulgaria showed, competing models of criminal procedure were influencing Eastern European countries as they deliberated how to speed up their criminal proceedings. The choice of model was influenced in part by each country's practical needs and underlying legal values. Typically, Eastern European legislators adopted models closer to those used by other major inquisitorial systems, such as the Italian and German systems. As Stephen Thaman observes, the Italian "*patteggiamento* became one of the main models for guilty plea mechanisms which have been introduced in Europe [and] the former Soviet Republics."[115] But the degree of influence on the drafting process by foreign advisors also mattered, according to Thaman: "[A] more wide-open negotiation of guilty pleas has been adopted in some countries [such as Estonia, Latvia, Lithuania, Moldova and Georgia] based on the classic American model and often as the result of American influence in the legislative process in those countries."[116]

The Eastern European experience suggests that countries are likely to adopt a particular model of plea bargaining based in part on the fit

---

Twinning Programme on Criminal Procedure Reform, Workshop, Sofia, Apr. 18-20, 2006 (on file with author), *at* http://www.mjeli.government.bg/Npk/news.aspx?cc=en&.

[114] OCTOPUS, Latvia Recommendations, *supra* note 7.

[115] Thaman, *supra* note 11, at 973-974.

[116] *Id.*

of the model with the country's legal tradition and in part on the influence of foreign advisors. Difficulties may arise, however, when a country chooses a model because of foreign political influence and without due regard to the model's likely fit with the adopting legal system. A practice that may work fairly well in an established adversarial system may flounder when implemented in a system with an inquisitorial tradition and a weak regard for defense rights.

This does not mean, however, that countries undertaking law reforms should not consider foreign models. Careful borrowing from abroad can be very helpful to law reformers. When done with appropriate attention to context, it allows legislators to learn from the experience of jurisdictions that have faced similar problems. More generally, convergence through law reform may often be preferable to convergence under a treaty mandate, particularly in politically sensitive areas like criminal law and procedure. It leaves national legislators greater control over the process and thus greater flexibility in adapting foreign models to their own legal system's needs and values.

Notes and Questions:

1. If you were advising a country that is about to implement a comprehensive criminal justice reform as part of a larger political transition to democracy, would you advise that country to introduce plea bargaining? What factors would affect your decision? If you were asked to recommend a particular type of plea bargaining to such a country, what features of the models studied so far would you recommend? Would you advise that the country adopt plea bargaining for all types of crimes? If the country's judicial system is suffering from corruption, how would that affect your recommendations?
2. In your opinion, is the global diffusion of plea bargaining a positive or negative development? Why or why not?
3. Do you believe that criminal procedures will continue to converge toward the same model? Why or why not? What factors are likely to influence convergence in criminal procedure?

COMPARING PLEA BARGAINING IN BULGARIA AND RUSSIA*

Plea Bargaining Feature	Russia ("Special Trial Procedure")	Bulgaria ("Disposing of a Case Through an Agreement")
Legislative Authorization	Yes	Yes
Typical Participants	Defense attorney (required), prosecutor, victim, judge (victim and judge may or may not be involved during negotiations)	Defense attorney (required), prosecutor, possibly victim, judge (victim and judge may or may not be involved during negotiations)
Timing	After charges are filed with the court	Typically after charges are filed with the court, but some agreements are reached when the case is transferred from the police to the prosecutor and before charges are filed with the court
Subject Matter	Defendant does not "plead guilty," but accedes to the charges; may not accede to only some of the charges and contest others; charge bargaining is prohibited; procedure limited to crimes carrying a maximum sentence of up to ten years; sentence discount is at least 1/3 of the statutory maximum; parties' agreement is not binding on the court.	Charge bargaining is prohibited; procedure may not be used for certain serious violent crimes; parties' agreement is not binding on the court; court may sentence below the statutory minimum when the case is resolved through an agreement.

Discovery/Disclosure	Defense has the right to inspect the complete case file at the conclusion of the investigation.	Defense has the right to inspect the complete case file at the conclusion of the investigation.
Cooperation Agreements	Rare	Rare
Conditions for Validity	Accession to charges must be voluntary, informed, and supported by the facts; court relies on case file to establish factual basis; defendant must have consulted with counsel, and counsel must be present at hearing; victims must be allowed to participate at hearing and must consent to motion; defendant must have paid damages arising from the offense; if several defendants are tried jointly, all defendants must agree to the special procedure.	Admission of guilt must be voluntary, informed, and factually based; agreement must not be "contrary to law or morals"; if offense has caused material damages, defendant must pay restitution to the victim before agreement can be approved; counsel must be present during negotiations and at hearing to approve agreement; victims who have joined the case as private prosecutors or civil claimants must consent to agreements reached during trial.
Withdrawal and Breach	No provisions on these questions	If the court rejects the parties' agreement, the defendant's self-incriminating statements made during the hearing may not be used in future proceedings.

* For a broader comparison, see also the chart in Chapter 2, which compares the United States and Germany.

HYPOTHETICALS

Plea Bargaining in a Drug Case in Bulgaria

Ivan Nikolov moved into a new rental apartment in Sofia, Bulgaria, in mid-June 2008. Based on an informant's tip in early July 2008, Bulgarian police searched Nikolov's apartment and found about 25 grams of amphetamine tucked away in a kitchen cabinet behind a water pipe. Nikolov told the police he did not know how the drugs got there and to whom they belonged. He maintained that the drugs must have been there before he moved into the apartment. He said he had never used drugs or even seen amphetamine, but the police and the prosecutor are unconvinced by the story and intend to charge Nikolov with possession of amphetamine and possibly other related offenses. At the same time, the prosecutor wants to avoid a contested trial and would like to find out more about the suppliers of the drug to Nikolov as well as other information that Nikolov might provide about the distribution of amphetamine drugs. Nikolov has no prior convictions.

Consider the following provisions applicable to Nikolov's case and then answer the questions below.

Bulgarian Criminal Code[117]

Article 354a[118]

> (1) Whoever, without due permit, manufactures, processes, acquires, or holds narcotic substances or their analogues with the intent to distribute them, and whoever distributes such substances, shall be punished: for high-risk narcotic substances or their analogues, by imprisonment of two to eight years and a fine of five thousand to twenty thousand levs. [. . .]
>
> [Amphetamine is considered a high-risk substance.—EDS.][119]

[117] Bulg. Crim. Code (2005), *at* http://www.mvr.bg/NR/rdonlyres/330B548F-7504-433A-BE65-5686B7D7FCBB/0/04_Penal_Code_EN.pdf (translation by Ministry of the Interior). The translation in this book partly follows the Interior Ministry's translation, but also edits it for clarity and incorporates more recent amendments. Nakazatelen Kodeks (original version of the Criminal Code, as amended through Jan. 2009), *at* http://lex.bg/bg/laws/ldoc/1589654529.

[118] The crimes listed in Articles 354a and 354b are among the crimes that can be resolved through plea agreements. Bulg. Crim. Proc. Code, *supra* note 63, §381(2).

[119] Drugs and Precursors Control Act of 1999, Schedule 1, *at* http://www.unodc.org/enl/showDocument.do?documentUid=889&node=BUL1970414&country=BUL&cmd=add.

(2) If the narcotic substances or their analogues are in a large quantity, the penalty is imprisonment between three and twelve years and a fine between ten thousand to fifty thousand levs. Whoever, without due permit, acquires in a public place or stores with the intent to distribute, or distributes narcotic substances or their analogues, when the narcotic substances are in a very large quantity or when the act:

1. is committed by a person acting on behalf of an organized crime group;

[. . .] the punishment shall be imprisonment of five to fifteen years and a fine of twenty thousand to a hundred thousand levs.

(3) Whoever, without due permit, acquires or holds narcotic substances or their analogues will be punished:

1. for high-risk narcotic substances or their analogues, by imprisonment of one to six years and a fine of two thousand to ten thousand levs.

[. . .]

(5) In less significant cases falling under Sections 3 and 4 of this article, the punishment is a fine of up to one thousand levs.

Article 55

(1) For exceptional or multiple extenuating circumstances, when even the most lenient punishment stipulated by the law proves to be disproportionately serious, the court shall:

1. determine the punishment under the statutory minimum;
2. replace:
   a) life imprisonment with imprisonment from fifteen to twenty years;
   b) imprisonment, when a minimum is not provided, with probation [. . .];
   c) probation with a fine of one hundred to five hundred levs.

[. . .]

Article 66

(1) When the court imposes a prison sentence of up to three years, it can suspend the sentence for a period of three to five years, if the person has not been sentenced to prison for a crime of

general nature in the past, and if the court finds that the purposes of punishment and, above all, the rehabilitation of the offender, will not be served by the execution of the prison sentence.

(2) The term of probation cannot exceed the prison sentence by more than three years. [...]

Notes and Questions:

1. Based on the Bulgarian Criminal Code provisions above, what kind of offer can a Bulgarian prosecutor make Nikolov to persuade him to cooperate by not contesting the evidence and waiving trial? Is there scope for charge bargaining under the provisions above, given that Bulgarian criminal procedure follows the principle of mandatory prosecution? How could the prosecutor make a more attractive offer so as to encourage Nikolov to reveal information about the drug distribution network?
2. Do you think that Eastern European countries such as Bulgaria and Russia are correct to maintain the principle of mandatory prosecution and to prohibit charge bargaining even as they allow sentence bargaining? Why or why not? What purpose does mandatory prosecution serve?
3. Article 381(4) of the Bulgarian Criminal Procedure Code states that "[b]y virtue of [a plea] agreement, a sentence may be imposed following the provisions of art. 55 [of the] Criminal Code, even in the absence of exceptional or numerous circumstances attenuating the level of responsibility." How much guidance does Article 55 provide to Nikolov and to the prosecutor about the sentence that the court is likely to impose if the parties reach a plea agreement? Could Nikolov receive probation as a result of a plea agreement? Under Article 55, could the discount offered as part of a plea agreement be so large as to potentially coerce an innocent defendant to plead guilty? Does it matter that Article 35 (3) of the Bulgarian Criminal Code states that "[t]he punishment shall be adequate to the crime"?
4. Would a fixed sentencing discount, such as the minimum discount available for the Russian special trial procedure, or the maximum discount available in Italy, be a useful feature to adopt in Bulgaria as well? Why or why not?

Plea Bargaining in a Homicide Case in Bulgaria

Ana Petrova and Nikolay Ivanov were a couple who lived and worked in Sofia. After an argument, Ana stabbed Nikolay with a knife and killed him. The Bulgarian authorities concluded that Ana was responsible and proceeded with her prosecution.

Ana and her defense attorney plan to argue that Nikolay had a history of beating Ana, that on the day of the killing, he hit her several times during an argument and threatened to kill her. They will argue that, fearing for her life, Ana stabbed Nikolay with a kitchen knife that was nearby. Other than Ana, there was only one person who overheard the incident—one of Ana and Nikolay's neighbors. The neighbor claimed he heard nothing to suggest attacks or threats by Nikolay. But the neighbor's credibility will be lessened by the fact that he is a drug addict, has had numerous brushes with the law himself, and has also had disputes with Ana in the past.

Consider the applicable Criminal Code provisions:

Bulgarian Criminal Code

Article 115[120]

Whoever deliberately kills somebody shall be punished for homicide by imprisonment from ten to twenty years.

Article 116

(1) For homicide:

[. . .] 9. committed with premeditation; [. . .] the punishment shall be imprisonment of fifteen to twenty years, life imprisonment, or life imprisonment without parole.

Article 118

For homicide committed in a state of serious disturbance, which was provoked by the victim through violence, grave insult, slander, or another illegal act, which produced or could have produced serious consequences for the offender or his relatives, the punishment is: in the cases of art. 115—imprisonment of one to eight years. . . .

[120] The crimes listed in Articles 115-119 are among the crimes that cannot be resolved through an agreement. Bulg. Crim. Proc. Code, *supra* note 63, §381(2).

Article 119

For a homicide that exceeded the scope of justifiable defense the punishment shall be imprisonment of a maximum of five years.

Article 12

(1) The act of justifiable defense shall not be considered socially dangerous—this includes defense against an imminent illegal attack of state or public interests and defense of the person or the rights of the defender or a third party by proportionate force.

(2) A defense will not be considered justifiable when it obviously does not correspond to the nature and the danger of the assault.

[...]

(4) The perpetrator shall not be punished when he commits the act by exceeding the requirements of justifiable defense if this is due to panic or confusion.

Notes and Questions:

1. Neither the Bulgarian nor the Russian system allows explicit plea bargaining to occur in serious cases, such as this case of alleged homicide. What are the advantages and disadvantages of this approach? Do you believe that the Bulgarian and Russian lawmakers were correct not to allow for plea bargaining in serious criminal cases? Would it be wise for federal and state jurisdictions in the United States to prohibit plea bargaining in such cases? Does it make a difference for your answer that such cases would be decided by a jury in the United States and Russia, but a mixed court of judges and lay assessors in Bulgaria?
2. Although plea bargaining is not available for homicide cases in Bulgaria, another form of summary procedures is—this is the so-called abbreviated judicial inquiry, which is similar to the *giudizio abbreviato* used in Italy.[121] Upon request by the defendant or *sua sponte*, the court may decide to hold a hearing with a view to abbreviating the judicial inquiry. At the hearing, the parties may agree to refrain from examining certain witnesses and experts at trial and allow the court instead to rely on written statements in the investigative file

[121] Marafioti, *supra* note 22, at 90.

as the basis for the final verdict.[122] Alternatively, the accused may admit the facts that form the circumstantial part of the indictment.[123] If the court finds that the admission has a solid factual basis in the investigative file, it can pronounce its verdict without conducting further examination of witnesses or experts.[124] If the court determines that the facts do not support the admission of guilt, it will reject the admission and pronounce the defendant not guilty. It is expected that the abbreviated judicial inquiry, particularly when the defendant offers a confession, would take no longer than one day (the day of the hearing).[125] In return for admitting the facts in the indictment and saving the criminal justice system time and expense, the defendant receives a significantly more lenient sentence—one that falls below the statutory minimum.[126]

In the case above, could Ana benefit from the abbreviated judicial inquiry? How is the abbreviated judicial inquiry different from plea bargaining? Why might Bulgarian legislators have allowed this procedure, but not plea bargaining, for serious violent cases?

---

[122] Bulg. Crim. Proc. Code, *supra* note 63, §371(1).

[123] The circumstantial portion of the indictment includes the following: the offense committed by the accused; the time, place, and manner in which the crime was committed; the name of the victim and the damages suffered; information about the defendant's personal background; evidence used to support the charges; and the legal categorization of the offense committed. *Id.* §232.2.

[124] *Id.* §372(4).

[125] *Noviyat NPK veche e fakt, vliza v sila sled 6 mesetsa*, Oct. 14, 2005, *at* http://www.bgfactor.org/index_.php?ct=1&id=6069.

[126] Bulg. Crim. Proc. Code, *supra* note 63, §373(2). This provision directs the court to apply Article 55 of the Criminal Code "even in the absence of a large number or of exceptional circumstances attenuating liability." It applies only when the defendant has admitted guilt. The sentencing reward is not granted merely for agreeing to refrain from examining witnesses and experts.

CHAPTER

4 Alternatives to Plea Bargaining

China and Japan

INTRODUCTION

The practice of plea bargaining is not yet universal. Exceptions to the global trend can be found in Asia, where governments have been slower to adopt plea bargaining. India introduced the practice in 2006,[1] Taiwan in 2004,[2] and Malaysia and Thailand are considering it at the time of this writing.[3] But countries like China and Japan have addressed the problem of overburdened criminal dockets by pursuing alternatives to plea bargaining, such as simplified trial procedures.[4] This chapter examines some of these alternatives and compares their effectiveness and fairness to the more traditional plea bargaining discussed in earlier chapters.

The chapter focuses on Japan, a country that has adopted several alternatives to plea bargaining as a way of expediting criminal proceedings. Between 2001 and 2004, Japan implemented a broad package of

---

[1] *Plea Bargaining Comes into Force Today*, Times of India, July 5, 2006, *at* http://timesofindia.indiatimes.com/articleshow/1706071.cmsl; *First Plea Bargaining Case in City*, Times of India, Oct. 15, 2007, *at* http://timesofindia.indiatimes.com/articleshow/2458523.cms.

[2] Margaret K. Lewis, *Taiwan's New Adversarial System and the Overlooked Challenge of Efficiency-Driven Reforms*, 49 Va. J. Int'l L. 651, 672 (2009).

[3] V. Anbalagan, *Amendments to Code to Legalise Plea Bargains*, N. Straits Times Online, July 7, 2008, *at* http://www.nst.com.my/Current_News/NST/Monday/National/2287290/Article/pppull_index_html; Department of Justice, Office of Prosecutorial Development, Assistance, and Training, DOJ/OPDAT Asia and Pacific Programs, *at* http://www.usdoj.gov/criminal/opdat/asia-pacific/asia-pacific-prgs.html (noting that OPDAT has worked closely with the Thai government to develop legislation introducing plea bargaining and other criminal procedure reforms).

[4] Randall Peerenboom, China Modernizes: Threat to the West or Model for the Rest? 204-208 (2007).

legal reforms, including a number of measures to expedite the processing of criminal cases. In adopting the reforms, Japanese legislators specifically rejected calls to adopt plea bargaining. Yet Japan is increasingly relying on procedures that hint at the existence of a tacit form of the practice. Prosecutors are willing to suspend prosecution in exchange for cooperation and confession by defendants; judges reward confessions with sentencing discounts; and the system at least indirectly encourages defendants to opt for simplified trial procedures instead of contesting the evidence vigorously. The chapter discusses the advantages and disadvantages of these alternatives to plea bargaining and evaluates the degree to which Japan represents a counter-trend in the global spread of plea bargaining.

After reviewing Japan, the chapter briefly discusses the recent introduction of summary and simplified trial procedures in China. China's summary procedures represent yet another different approach to expediting proceedings, which confirms the diversity of global responses to the same practical need—processing greater numbers of increasingly complex criminal cases. The chapter concludes by discussing the extent to which China's procedures are an effective and legitimate means of expediting the criminal process, particularly given the criticism that has been leveled against the Chinese system with respect to its weak regard for defense rights and the rule of law.

ALTERNATIVES TO PLEA BARGAINING IN JAPAN

Conventional wisdom holds that Japan does not allow plea bargaining in any shape or form. Japanese scholars and practitioners commonly assert that "[t]he Japanese prosecutor does not consult with the defendant or defense attorney and then institute a lesser charge in exchange for a confession."[5] Commentators also reject the existence of any negotiations about sentencing.[6] Indeed, Japan has no statutory provisions allowing for plea bargaining, and like inquisitorial systems, it is committed to the principle of independent investigation by courts.[7] The

[5] Fumio Aoyagi, Nihonjin no Hanzai Ishiki 201 (1986), *cited in* David T. Johnson, *Plea Bargaining in Japan*, *in* The Japanese Adversary System in Context 140, 140 (Malcolm M. Feeley & Setsuo Miyazawa eds., 2002).

[6] *E.g.*, David H. Bayley, Forces of Order: Policing Modern Japan 147 (1991); Daniel H. Foote, *Prosecutorial Discretion in Japan: A Response*, 5 UCLA Pac. Basin L.J. 96, 97 (1986).

[7] Japan. Crim. Proc. Code §1, *at* Ministry of Justice, Translation of Japanese Codes and Regulations, http://www.cas.go.jp/jp/seisaku/hourei/data1.html.

Supreme Court of Japan has specifically held that at least one version of plea bargaining—the grant of immunity in exchange for testimony—is not permitted by the Criminal Procedure Code.[8] Similarly, courts have held that confessions obtained through explicit promises of leniency are involuntary and thus unconstitutional.[9] Finally, public and scholarly sentiment is generally unfavorable to American-style plea bargaining.[10]

But a closer look at Japanese practice suggests that an unspoken exchange of concessions—which some have compared to plea bargaining—may be occurring even here. An empirical study by David Johnson, Associate Professor of Sociology at the University of Hawaii, found that defendants regularly confess and cooperate with the prosecution in exchange for spoken or unspoken promises to recommend a lighter sentence or even to suspend prosecution.[11] Defendants also understand that judges are likely to reward admissions of guilt with a more lenient sentence, and they regularly confess and express remorse to obtain the sentencing benefit.[12]

Although the exchange of such concessions is implicit, some have argued that it falls under a broad definition of plea bargaining, in that defendants are offered sentencing benefits in return for confessing, cooperating with the court and prosecution, and opting for a simpler mode of case processing.[13] This unspoken exchange would not fall under this book's earlier definition of plea bargaining, which presupposes some negotiations and an actual bargain reached by the parties and perhaps

---

[8] Judgment Addressing: (1) the Admissibility of Depositions Obtained Through International Judicial Assistance and (2) the Power and Duties of the Minister for Transport (Supreme Court, Grand Bench, Feb. 22, 1995), 1987(A)No.1351 [Enomoto v. Japan], *at* http://www.courts.go.jp/english/judgments/text/1995.02.22-1987-A-No.1351.html. The Japanese Court holds that evidence obtained in exchange for testimonial immunity cannot be introduced at trial, but it appears that the opinion leaves open the possibility of using the evidence in investigations.

[9] Foote, *supra* note 6, at 101.

[10] Johnson, *supra* note 5, at 141 (noting also that the Japanese translate American-style plea bargaining as *shiho torihiki* or *toben torihiki*).

[11] *Id.*

[12] Joseph Sanders, *Courts and Law in Japan*, *in* Courts, Law and Politics in Comparative Perspective 315, 344 (Herbert Jacob et al. eds., 1996). Anecdotal evidence suggests that defendants' professions of remorse are not always genuine. Johnson, *supra* note 5, at 148-150; Foote, *supra* note 6, at 99.

[13] *Id.* at 142; J. Mark Ramseyer & Eric Rasmusen, Measuring Judicial Independence: The Political Economy of Judging in Japan 98-99 (2003); Foote, *supra* note 6, at 98-99; *see also* Junichiro Otani, The Introduction of Plea Bargaining into Japan, L.L.M. Thesis, Harvard Law School 2, 4-5 (2005) (observing that no explicit plea bargaining exists in Japan, but that "tacit plea bargaining" may exist).

the court.[14] Moreover, while bargaining in other countries occurs primarily to expedite the process, it is debatable whether this is a primary reason for the unspoken exchange of concessions in Japan. It may be that the goals of rehabilitation and reintegration into the community provide an equally compelling reason why the Japanese system provides rewards to those who confess, repent, and cooperate.

As Japan's crime rate increases, its proceedings become more time-consuming, and its criminal procedures become more complex, the importance of expediting proceedings may become more central. Like other countries, Japan may begin to encourage the exchange of concessions primarily to expedite proceedings and obtain information to resolve complex cases. In this sense, Japan is an important country to study. It presently serves as a counter-example to the recent spread of plea bargaining. At the same time, it is possible that in the future it will have to reconsider how to balance increasing pressures to expedite proceedings with its commitment to restorative justice.

THE DEMAND FOR MORE EFFICIENT PROCESS IN JAPAN

In most countries, plea bargaining has been introduced in response to a need for more efficient processing of cases. It may appear initially that in Japan there is no such demand. Japan's crime rate has traditionally been very low compared to that of other developed countries.[15] Japan is also a wealthy country, so one would not expect to find its courts and prosecutor's offices underfunded. But for various reasons, the Japanese criminal justice system is facing increased burdens and has begun to look for ways to expedite proceedings.

One contributing factor appears to be that the government hires relatively few lawyers to prosecute cases. Japan's number of lawyers per capita is generally much lower than that of other developed nations such as France, Germany, the United Kingdom, and the United States,[16] and this holds true for criminal prosecutors and judges.[17] Mark Ramseyer

---

[14] *See* Introduction at 1.

[15] David T. Johnson, *Crime and Punishment in Contemporary Japan*, 36 Crime & Just. 371, 371 (2007).

[16] Whereas the United States has 372 lawyers per 100,000 residents, Japan has only 18.9 per 100,000. Japanese Ministry of Justice, Ensuring That the Results of Justice System Reform Take Root n.5, *at* http://www.moj.go.jp/ENGLISH/issues/justice_system_reform-6.pdf.

[17] In 1998, the last year in which the United States submitted the relevant data to the UN Office on Drugs and Crime, Japan had 1.74 prosecutors and 2.32 judges per 100,000 inhabit-

and Eric Rasmusen report that in the late 1990s, Japan employed about 1,200 prosecutors, whereas the U.S. federal and state governments, with about twice the population, employed about 32,000 prosecutors (about 25 times as many).[18] According to Ramseyer and Rasmusen, this vast discrepancy means that, despite differences in population and crime rate, Japanese prosecutors still end up with a heavier caseload than their American counterparts:

> Each year, police in the United States clear about 14 million crimes by arrest, excluding traffic offenses. Given that there are 32,000 prosecutors, that comes to 438 arrests per prosecutor. In contrast, Japanese police clear about 1.4 million Criminal Code violations per year. This comes to 1,166 crimes per prosecutor.[19]

David Johnson contests the calculations by Ramseyer and Rasmusen and argues that, if traffic offenses are excluded, Japanese prosecutors carry much lighter caseloads than their American counterparts.[20] Johnson also relies on his extensive interviews with prosecutors to argue that a number of Japanese prosecutors are "bored" because they do not have enough cases.[21] But Ramseyer and Rasmusen respond that Johnson's calculations underestimate prosecutorial caseload because they count indictments per prosecutor, not arrests per prosecutor, and thus omit a great number of cases in which prosecutors never file an indictment.[22]

In addition, Johnson seems to rely largely on data from the 1980s (and some data from 1992), and crime rates in Japan have risen significantly since then, without a comparable increase in prosecutorial staff. More recent statistics contradict Johnson's conclusions and suggest that caseloads of Japanese prosecutors are high and continue to grow. For example, the 1998 UN Office on Drugs and Crime Survey suggests that Japanese and American prosecutors carry similar loads, with the rate

---

ants, whereas the United States had 9.45 prosecutors and 10.47 per 100,000 inhabitants. UN Office on Drugs and Crime, Seventh United Nations Survey of Crime Trends and Operations of Criminal Justice Systems, Covering the Period 1998-2002 (2004), *at* http://www.unodc.org/unodc/en/data-and-analysis/Seventh-United-Nations-Survey-on-Crime-Trends-and-the-Operations-of-Criminal-Justice-Systems.html [hereinafter Seventh UN Survey].

[18] Ramseyer & Rasmusen, *supra* note 13, at 105.

[19] *Id.* at 105-106.

[20] David T. Johnson, The Japanese Way of Justice: Prosecuting Crime in Japan 25-26 (2002).

[21] *Id.* at 27.

[22] Ramseyer & Rasmusen, *supra* note 13, at 106.

of recorded crimes per prosecutor in Japan being only somewhat lower than the comparable rate for American prosecutors. In 1998, the ratio of crimes recorded in police statistics to prosecutors was 927.5 in Japan and 944.2 in the United States.[23] As Johnson points out, it is likely that in Japan, the mix of cases included in that number is different and includes fewer violent crimes.[24] Still, given the similar ratio of cases to prosecutor overall, it is also probable that Japanese prosecutors are feeling at least some of the pressure felt by their American counterparts to resolve cases more quickly.

Statistics also show that Japan's crime rate is rising. The overall crime rate has increased from 1,613.93 crimes per 100,000 inhabitants in 1998 to 2,244.39 per 100,000 inhabitants in 2002.[25] David Johnson has argued that this change may be due largely to a broader criminalization of conduct and not to a change of behavior among Japanese residents.[26] But whatever the reason, the number of additional prosecutors and judges appointed by 2002 did not compensate for the increase in crimes. In 1998, the ratio of recorded crimes to prosecutors was 927.5.[27] In 2002, it was 1,233.2.[28]

The important decision to introduce a jury system in Japan has placed additional pressure on prosecutors and courts to expedite proceedings. The Justice System Reform Council, established by the legislature in 1999 to suggest reforms to the Japanese legal system, recommended that Japan return to a system of criminal jury trials. Such trials had existed in a different form for about a decade before World War II, and the Council believed that participation of the general public in the criminal justice system would increase the legitimacy of the system. Jury trials are scheduled to begin in 2009, and they will be used only in cases of serious crimes for which the maximum penalty is death or indefinite imprisonment with hard labor, and crimes where the victim dies due to

---

[23] Seventh UN Survey, *supra* note 17.

[24] Johnson, *supra* note 20, at 22.

[25] UN Office on Drugs and Crime, Eighth United Nations Survey of Crime Trends and Operations of Criminal Justice Systems, Covering the Period 2001-2002 (2005), *at* http://www.unodc.org/unodc/en/data-and-analysis/Eighth-United-Nations-Survey-on-Crime-Trends-and-the-Operations-of-Criminal-Justice-Systems.html [hereinafter Eighth UN Survey]; Seventh UN Survey, *supra* note 17.

[26] Johnson, *supra* note 15, at 386-387.

[27] Seventh UN Survey, *supra* note 17.

[28] Eighth UN Survey, *supra* note 25.

an intentional criminal act.[29] Japan will follow the "mixed jury" model of inquisitorial systems such as Germany. This means that jurors and judges will sit together to hear cases and deliberate about verdicts and sentences.

Jury trials are likely to increase the pressure on judges and lawyers to expedite proceedings in three principal ways. First, the jury selection process, which will include a limited voir dire procedure, is likely to lengthen the proceedings.[30] Second, during the trial itself, the parties will need to read their documentary evidence in court and will likely rely more extensively on witnesses in order to make the evidence more accessible to jurors; jurors will also be able to pose questions to the witnesses.[31] Third, it is likely that the deliberations among professional and lay judges to determine the verdict and sentence will be longer. The professional judges will have to spend more time explaining the applicable law to their lay counterparts, and the greater number of participants will stretch the deliberations further. For all these reasons, observers anticipate a significant increase in judges' workload,[32] even though jury trials will occur in only about 3 percent of all criminal cases.[33]

Jury trials are expected to impose other burdens on the system as well. Japanese citizens have expressed concern about being able to serve on juries if the trials last more than a few days.[34] Policy makers have therefore tried to design the proceedings in a way that would minimize the time that jurors have to serve. The Japanese Justice System Reform Council recommended three specific measures to that end: (1) holding trials in a single session over consecutive days; (2) discussing evidence and resolving disputed issues at pretrial arrangement proceedings; and (3) introducing summary proceedings to dispose of simple and clear

[29] Kent Anderson & Emma Saint, *Japan's Quasi-Jury (Saiban-in) Law: An Annotated Translation of the Act Concerning Participation of Lay Assessors in Criminal Trials*, 6 Asian-Pac. L. & Pol'y J. 9 (2005).

[30] Kent Anderson & Leah Ambler, *The Slow Birth of Japan's Quasi-Jury System (Saiban-in Seido): Interim Report on the Road to Commencement*, 21 J. Japan. L. 55, 64 (2006).

[31] *Id.* at 64-66. Some of these observations are also supported by the author's communications with two Japanese judges.

[32] According to one of the Japanese judges with whom the author communicated, jury trials are likely to lengthen the trial and judgment process from, on average, a few hours, to at least two full days per case.

[33] Matthew Wilson, *The Dawn of Criminal Jury Trials in Japan: Success on the Horizon?*, 24 Wis. Int'l L.J. 835, 845 (2007).

[34] *Id.* at 856-857.

noncontested cases.[35] These recommendations were enacted into law in 2003 and 2004 through amendments to the Criminal Procedure Code and through a special Act on the Expediting of Trial.[36] Consistent with the goals of these laws to keep jury trials short, courts may begin urging the parties to resolve disputed issues consensually during pretrial.

Finally, recent provisions for greater victim participation in certain criminal cases may also encumber the process. Victim participation was introduced in 2007, in response to public demands for broader victim rights.[37] Under the new system, in violent crime cases, victims will have extensive participation rights at trial. They will be able to attend trials and, either personally or through their lawyer, question the defendant and witnesses.[38] In addition, they will be able to file with the court an opinion about the application of the law to the facts.[39] This system has been introduced very recently, so it is not certain how many victims will take advantage of their opportunity to participate. Whatever the number, it will impose additional burdens on the parties and the court and will put pressure on the system to provide shortcuts around ordinary criminal proceedings.

CONFLICT BETWEEN PLEA BARGAINING AND JAPANESE CRIMINAL PROCEDURE

In response to the increasing demands to expedite criminal cases, Japan could have introduced a form of plea bargaining. But this was not one of the recommendations of the Justice System Reform Council.[40] Plea bargaining, at least as practiced in the United States, is seen by

---

[35] Japanese Ministry of Justice, Ensuring That the Results of Justice System Reform Take Root n.4, *at* http://www.moj.go.jp/ENGLISH/issues/justice_system_reform-4.pdf.

[36] *Id. at* http://www.moj.go.jp/ENGLISH/issues/issues01.html; Act on the Expediting of Trials, Act No. 107 of 2003, *at* Ministry of Justice, Translation of Japanese Codes and Regulations, http://www.cas.go.jp/jp/seisaku/hourei/data1.html.

[37] For a fuller history, see Toshihiro Kawaide, Victim's Participation in the Criminal Trial in Japan, Dutch-Japan Law Symposium (2008), *at* http://www.j.u-tokyo.ac.jp/~sota/WelcomeE.html.

[38] *Id.*

[39] *Id.*

[40] The Council considered plea bargaining as a possible measure to expedite proceedings, but it found that plea bargaining "contains problems in terms of whether it is appropriate to let the defendant himself or herself dispose of the case and of the relationship with how the sentencing proceedings should be conducted." Recommendations of the Justice System Reform Council, For a Justice System to Support Japan in the 21st Century (2001), *at* http://www.kantei.go.jp/foreign/judiciary/2001/0612report.html.

many Japanese as a distasteful practice and as incompatible with Japanese criminal procedure.[41] To understand why, it is important to see the potential tension of the practice with certain provisions of the Japanese Criminal Procedure Code and the Constitution.

There are no provisions in the Japanese Criminal Procedure Code that authorize plea bargaining. Indeed, Article 1 of the Code is interpreted by some to preclude the use of plea bargaining because of its emphasis on revealing "the true facts of the case":

> The purpose of this Code, with regard to criminal cases, is to reveal the true facts of cases and to apply and realize criminal laws and regulations quickly and appropriately, while ensuring the maintenance of public welfare and the guarantee of the fundamental human rights of individuals.[42]

Although the search for truth is just one of several goals listed in the Code, many commentators argue that it is in fact regarded as the primary goal of Japanese criminal procedure.[43]

To promote this important goal, Japanese judges examine the facts of each case independently and expect the prosecution to present detailed evidence to support its case. Japanese judges rely extensively on documentary evidence, so much so that some commentators call Japanese trials "trial by dossier."[44] But despite this penchant for written evidence, judges are committed to writing precise and detailed reasoned judgments, laying out all the relevant circumstances of the case. Even in simple cases in which the defendant confesses, judicial opinions may take as many as eight or ten pages to explain the decision; in contested cases, judges "routinely write book-length manuscripts."[45] Accordingly,

---

[41] *E.g.*, Foote, *supra* note 6, at 97; Masahito Inouye, *Witness Immunity and Bargain Justice: A Look at the Japanese Concept of the Adversary System*, *in* The Japanese Adversary System in Context 173, 184 (Malcolm M. Feeley & Setsuo Miyazawa eds., 2002).

[42] Japan. Crim. Proc. Code, *supra* note 7, §1.

[43] *E.g.*, Carl F. Goodman, The Rule of Law in Japan: A Comparative Analysis 387 (2d ed. 2008); Johnson, *supra* note 5, at 144.

[44] Takeo Ishimatsu, *Are Criminal Defendants in Japan Truly Receiving Trial by Judges?*, 22 Law in Japan 143, 143-144 (Daniel H. Foote transl. 1989). Under the law, judges may not render a judgment based solely on the written investigative file, but must entertain oral arguments. Japan. Crim. Proc. Code, *supra* note 7, §43. But the parties often consent to the use of written evidence, and even when they do not, such evidence may be introduced under one of many exceptions to the hearsay rule. Johnson, *supra* note 20, at 39-40 & n.32.

[45] Johnson, *supra* note 20, at 46.

prosecutors know that they need to submit extensive evidence to meet their burden of proof.[46]

One reason why judges demand detailed evidence is that the Japanese Constitution prohibits convictions based solely on the defendant's confession.[47] Accordingly, even in noncontested cases, prosecutors must present physical or other evidence corroborating the confession. Confessions themselves are also expected to be extensive, covering all the circumstances of the crime, including the motive of the offender. These details are considered essential to sentencing, which takes into account the defendant's background and rehabilitation prospects.[48] The insistence on detailed confessions also reflects Japanese judges' reluctance to convict based solely on circumstantial evidence.[49]

Japanese judges also have the authority, where necessary, to conduct additional investigation on their own initiative.[50] They can examine witnesses,[51] order expert testimony,[52] or conduct a search.[53] In practice, judges often defer to the parties with respect to fact-gathering, but their power to conduct or request further investigation serves as an incentive for the parties to do a thorough job. Judges also determine the scope, order, and method of examining the evidence.[54]

In short, while Japanese judges may not be as active in ordering additional fact-gathering as their colleagues in inquisitorial systems such as Germany and France, they expect the prosecution to conduct thorough investigations and to present a detailed account of the case to the court. Their commitment to precision stands in tension with plea bargaining, in which the parties dispose of factual disputes without court involvement and often omit details of the crime for the sake of expediency.

Compared to their American counterparts, Japanese judges also have greater power to oversee prosecutorial charging decisions. When a prosecutor requests that charges be added, withdrawn, or altered after the indictment has been filed with the court, the trial judge will review

---

[46] *Id.*

[47] Constitution of Japan art. 38, *at* http://www.solon.org/Constitutions/Japan/English/english-Constitution.html; Japan. Crim. Proc. Code, *supra* note 7, §319(2).

[48] Daniel H. Foote, *Confessions and the Right to Silence in Japan*, 21 Ga. J. Int'l & Comp. L. 415, 484 (1991).

[49] *Id.* at 472.

[50] Japan. Crim. Proc. Code, *supra* note 7, §298.

[51] *Id.* §143.

[52] *Id.* §165.

[53] *Id.* §128.

[54] *Id.* §§297, 304.

the request to ensure that the proposed modification of charges does not "modify the identity of charged facts."[55] The judge may also "order the public prosecutor to add or alter a count or applicable penal statute when the court finds it appropriate during the course of the proceedings."[56] While prosecutors in Japan have great discretion to decline to prosecute charges before filing them with the court,[57] judges may review charge modifications once the charges have been filed. The ability of judges to influence charging decisions stands as a theoretical obstacle to charge bargaining between the prosecution and the defense. In practice, however, judges rarely object to prosecutorial charging decisions,[58] so it is possible that a limited bargaining practice over charges could develop.

Japanese judges also maintain ultimate authority over sentencing, which could limit the ability of parties to bargain about the sentence. The Japanese Criminal Code provides broad sentencing ranges for individual offenses and gives discretion to judges to depart from the established range. The Code provides that punishment may be reduced in light of "extenuating circumstances"[59] and that "[e]ven if the punishment is aggravated or reduced in accordance with a statute, it may be reduced in light of circumstances."[60] The Code also allows judges, "in light of circumstances," to suspend the sentence of a first-time offender who has received up to three years of imprisonment or a fine of up to 500,000 yen.[61]

In practice, however, judicial discretion is much more limited. Judges are expected to consult prior cases in making sentencing decisions, and they do so regularly. A study conducted by the Japanese Supreme Court found that when career judges were asked to sentence a hypothetical murder defendant, the resulting sentences fell into a narrow range—the average sentence was 11.14 years, and the standard deviation was 2.26. Like judges, prosecutors and defense attorneys are also familiar with the sentencing case law, and they are typically able to predict the sentences imposed by the court.[62]

---

[55] *Id.* §312(1).

[56] *Id.* §312(2).

[57] *See infra* notes 68-76 and accompanying text.

[58] *E.g.*, Johnson, *supra* note 20, at 61, 63.

[59] Japan. Crim. Code §66, *at* Ministry of Justice, Translation of Japanese Codes and Regulations, http://www.cas.go.jp/jp/seisaku/hourei/data1.html. This English translation of the Penal Code has been prepared (up to the revisions of Act No. 54 of 2007 (Effective June 12, 2007)) in compliance with the Standard Bilingual Dictionary (March 2007 edition).

[60] *Id.* §67.

[61] *Id.* §25.

[62] *See* Johnson, *supra* note 20, at 66. Johnson adds that the absence of a jury makes the verdict itself more predictable, further encouraging the parties to settle.

While judges' sentencing discretion does not appear to prevent the development of plea bargaining in practice, a more significant barrier is Japanese courts' interpretation of Article 38 of the Japanese Constitution, which prohibits involuntary confessions. Courts have interpreted this provision to mean that "a confession may be rejected as involuntary if induced by promises of lenient treatment."[63] Therefore, explicit promises of charge reductions or lenient sentence recommendations jeopardize the admissibility of a confession.[64] As will be discussed later, however, this prohibition of explicit exchanges of concessions may have led participants to rely on implicit and unspoken exchanges.

Given the tension between plea bargaining and the principles of Japanese criminal procedure discussed above, it is not surprising that, in the case excerpted below, *Enomoto v. Japan*, the Japanese Supreme Court held that courts may not accept as evidence testimony obtained in exchange for a grant of immunity.[65] In this case, Japanese prosecutors sought to introduce statements that were obtained during depositions in the United States in exchange for promises not to prosecute in Japan. The Court held that it was immaterial that the depositions occurred abroad, given that the evidence itself would be used in a criminal proceeding in Japan.

Judgment Addressing: (1) the Admissibility of Depositions Obtained Through International Judicial Assistance and (2) the Power and Duties of the Minister for Transport (Supreme Court, Grand Bench, Feb. 22, 1995), 1987(A) No. 1351 [Enomoto v. Japan][66]

(Excerpt)

A. (1) The mechanism of testimonial immunity is designed to deal with situations in which the government is unable to obtain testimony

[63] Foote, *supra* note 6, at 101.

[64] *See* Foote, *supra* note 48, at 458 (noting that a confession may be held involuntary where police promise non-indictment in return for a confession).

[65] The decision appears to leave room for the use of such evidence during the investigation, however.

[66] *Official translation available at* http://www.courts.go.jp/english/judgments/text/1995.02.22-1987-A-No.1351.html. The translation in this book has been altered somewhat to enhance its clarity. I thank Daniel Young, Class of 2009, Project Manager, Global Justice Think Tank, University of Utah Law School, for his help with the translation.

necessary to prove criminal charges because one or more suspects are exercising their privilege against self-incrimination. In such a situation, one or more of those suspected of being accomplices in a crime relinquish their privilege against self-incrimination and are compelled to testify in exchange for a grant of immunity from prosecution. The testimony is then used as evidence to prove the charges against the other suspects.

In the United States, [where the depositions in this case were taken,] testimonial immunity is permissible to a certain extent, subject to certain procedural requirements, and it functions as an established procedural mechanism.

A. (2) The Constitution of Japan cannot be construed as rejecting the introduction of testimonial immunity, but the Code of Criminal Procedure has no related provisions. While testimonial immunity serves the practical purposes mentioned above, it is directly related to the interests of persons connected with a crime, and it affects major aspects of criminal procedure. Therefore, the decision whether to adopt the mechanism [of testimonial immunity] should be made with the prudent deliberation about factors such as: whether [practical] circumstances require the mechanism, whether it is consistent with the principle of fair trial, and whether it is compatible with the public's sense of fairness. If testimonial immunity is to be adopted, there ought to be clear statutory provisions concerning its scope, procedural requirements, and effects. Because no such provisions exist in the current Code of Criminal Procedure, we conclude that testimonial immunity is not legal [in Japan] and that testimony obtained in exchange for immunity from prosecution is not admissible as evidence.

A. (3) This holding also applies to evidence obtained in exchange for testimonial immunity in the course of international judicial assistance; there is no reason to treat such evidence differently. The admissibility of evidence [in a Japanese proceeding], even where such evidence is obtained [from abroad,] through international judicial assistance, must be determined pursuant to the applicable laws of Japan, including the Code of Criminal Procedure. Therefore, considering that the Japanese Code of Criminal Procedure does not provide for testimonial immunity, we conclude that the depositions [conducted in the United States in exchange for testimonial immunity] cannot be admitted simply because they were obtained through international judicial assistance.

B. In brief, it is appropriate to exclude the depositions in question because the Japanese Code of Criminal Procedure does not provide for testimonial immunity, and testimony obtained in exchange for immunity from prosecution may not be admitted as evidence.

Notes and Questions:

1. The Japanese Supreme Court has held that a confession induced by promises of lenient treatment is involuntary. What understanding of voluntariness is implied here? Do you think this holding is related to the belief that remorse should accompany a confession? Do you agree with this analysis of voluntariness? Could any form of plea bargaining be reconciled with this holding?
2. The holding of the Japanese Supreme Court in *Enomoto v. Japan* focuses on the practice of granting complete immunity from prosecution in exchange for testimony. To what extent is the Court's reasoning also applicable to the more common practice of plea bargaining, in which the defendant receives a sentence reduction in exchange for confessing or pleading guilty in his own case and perhaps testifying in other cases?
3. How do the powers and responsibilities of Japanese judges compare to the powers and responsibilities of their American, German, and Bulgarian counterparts? To what extent might the different powers and responsibilities explain the absence of plea bargaining in Japan?
4. As in inquisitorial systems, in Japan, plea bargaining is regarded as inconsistent with the pursuit of the truth. How do American courts reconcile the pursuit of truth with plea bargaining? Why hasn't the potential conflict between the search for truth and plea bargaining stood in the way of plea bargaining in the United States?

ALTERNATIVES TO PLEA BARGAINING IN JAPAN

While explicit plea bargaining is not permitted and is seen as inappropriate by many in Japan, several alternative practices are used to encourage confessions and to resolve cases more efficiently. These practices are so prevalent that only about 10 percent of cases are said to be seriously contested in Japan.[67] Consider the degree to which any of these practices resemble plea bargaining. Do they pursue the same objectives? Do they take on similar forms? How do they compare to plea bargaining in terms of their fairness, efficiency, and likelihood to uncover the truth of the case?

---

[67] Nobuyoshi Araki, *The Flow of Criminal Cases in the Japanese Criminal Justice System*, Crime & Delinquency 601, 621 (1985); Ramseyer & Rasmusen, *supra* note 13, at 99.

Discretionary Prosecution. Like their American counterparts, Japanese prosecutors enjoy broad charging discretion. Even when the evidence would support a conviction, under Article 248 of the Criminal Procedure Code, the prosecutor may decide to suspend the prosecution and not file charges after considering a number of factors, including the character, age, and situation of the offender; the gravity of the crime; the circumstances under which the crime was committed; and the conditions subsequent to the crime. Close to half of all investigated cases are disposed of through a decision not to prosecute, whether because of evidentiary insufficiency or because of considerations such as those listed in Article 248.[68] Japanese prosecutors therefore decline to prosecute a higher percentage of arrestees than do their American counterparts.[69]

Although Article 248 does not explicitly allow this, in practice, the decision whether to prosecute is sometimes related to the need to resolve cases more efficiently.[70] Prosecutors may agree to suspend prosecution where the offender cooperates with the prosecution in the investigation of his own case or other future cases.[71] While suspension may be granted when the suspect helps the prosecutor conclude the investigation of that same suspect more speedily, agreements to cooperate in future cases are rare because they are not enforceable.[72]

More commonly, the decision to suspend prosecution depends on the behavior of the accused during the prosecution and his willingness to express remorse and seek the forgiveness of the victim. If he

---

[68] Supreme Court of Japan, Outline of Criminal Justice in Japan, Figure 1, Case Dispositions by Public Prosecutors in 2004, *at* http://www.courts.go.jp/english/proceedings/criminal_justice.html.

[69] J. Mark Ramseyer & Eric B. Rasmusen, *Why Is the Japanese Conviction Rate So High?*, 30 J. Legal Stud. 53, 63 (2001) ("If we use the FBI's definition of "serious crime" arrests as a rough proxy for felony arrests, we obtain a 42 percent prosecution/arrest ratio for felonies. In Japan, by contrast, of the 919,000 people arrested for Criminal Code violations in 1995, prosecutors filed charges against a scant 17.5 percent. [. . .] Again using conviction rates to infer prosecutions from convictions [. . .], we can deduce that prosecutors prosecuted roughly 75 percent [. . .] of all people arrested on murder charges. In Japan, of the approximately 1,800 people processed for 1,300 murders, prosecutors tried only 43 percent.").

[70] Ted D. Westermann & James W. Burfeind, Crime and Justice in Two Societies: Japan and the United States 109 (1991); *see also* Makoto Ida, *Die Beschleunigung des Strafverfahrens: Japanischer Landesbericht*, 37-38 Archivum Iuridicum Cracoviense 261, 267 (2004-2005).

[71] Inouye, *supra* note 41, at 185-186 & n.19; Johnson, *supra* note 5, at 146; *see also* Comments by Shu Sugita, Tokyo District Office Prosecutor, *in* First Joint Canada-Japan Symposium on Crime and Criminal Justice 57 (Boyd & Layton eds. 1991).

[72] *See* Otani, *supra* note 13, at 4, 17.

"acknowledges guilt, asks for pardon, and appears willing to make some restitution to the victim, the prosecutor may suspend court action."[73] The deliberate use of suspending prosecution based on the repentance of the offender has long been a feature of the Japanese system.[74] Some scholars argue that today apology, repentance, and restitution are more common grounds for a decision not to prosecute than evidentiary deficiencies.[75] As a result, defense attorneys will often explore the option of suspending prosecution by emphasizing in conversations with the prosecutor the defendant's good character, remorse, and willingness to cooperate or to pay restitution to the victim.[76]

These practices—the implicit or explicit exchanges of promises to suspend prosecution in exchange for the defendant's cooperation, confession, apology, and reconciliation with the victim—have been compared by some to plea bargaining.[77] Although there are relevant similarities, it is important to note that, unlike plea bargaining in the United States, the primary aim of these exchanges in Japan appears to be to encourage rehabilitation and reconciliation and not so much to expedite prosecutions or obtain information for future cases.

Summary Proceedings. For certain very minor offenses (traffic violations and crimes punishable by fines), the prosecutor may request a summary proceeding if the defendant consents. In summary proceedings, the court may decide the case by examining evidence submitted by the prosecution without conducting a trial. Indeed, even appearance by the defendant, prosecutor, and complainant is typically waived. The highest sentence that the court can impose pursuant to this procedure is 500,000 yen (about $4,500). If either party is dissatisfied with the procedure, that party may apply for a formal trial within 14 days of receiving the judge's decision.[78] About 80 percent of all criminal cases in Japan are disposed of by summary proceedings.[79] Commentators have sug-

---

[73] Westermann & Burfeind, *supra* note 70, at 110 (citing authorities in support).

[74] Shigemitsu Dando, *System of Discretionary Prosecution in Japan*, 18 Am. J. Comp. L. 518, 518-521 (1970).

[75] Westermann & Burfeind, *supra* note 70, at 110.

[76] Goodman, *supra* note 43, at 418; Marcia E. Goodman, *The Exercise and Control of Prosecutorial Discretion in Japan*, 5 UCLA Pac. Basin L.J. 16, 35 (1986); Inouye, *supra* note 41, at 185-186 & n.19; Comments by Shu Sugita, *supra* note 71, at 57.

[77] Goodman, *supra* note 76, at 35; *see also* Johnson, *supra* note 5, at 146-147.

[78] Araki, *supra* note 67, at 619.

[79] Supreme Court of Japan, Outline of Criminal Justice in Japan, *at* http://www.courts.go.jp/english/proceedings/criminal_justice.html.

gested that even cases that might otherwise merit greater punishment are sometimes handled through summary proceedings when the defense agrees not to contest the evidence and the charges, and the defendant confesses.[80]

Pretrial Arrangement Procedure. Under the pretrial arrangement procedure, adopted in 2004, the court and the parties may resolve contested issues and evidence at pretrial hearings. Articles 316-2 to 316-32 govern these proceedings. At the pretrial arrangement proceedings, the parties are asked to cooperate with one another and with the court so as to sort out as many contested issues as possible before trial, thus expediting the ordinary trial itself.[81] Actions that may be taken in these proceedings include clarifying, adding, withdrawing, or altering counts; requesting examination of the evidence; disclosing facts to be proved and other evidence to be examined; deciding on the order and method of examining the evidence; ruling on motions for and against examination of the evidence; and setting trial dates.[82]

The pretrial arrangement procedure is significant in that it allows the defense to obtain discovery at an earlier stage in the process. Under ordinary procedure, the prosecution is merely required to reveal at some point before the first trial date evidence that it plans to use at trial (although under Supreme Court precedent, judges may additionally order the prosecution to reveal evidence material to the defense).[83] As part of the new pretrial arrangement procedure, the prosecution has to disclose evidence that it plans to use at trial and evidence that the defense specifically requests and that either the prosecution or the court determines is material to the defense and will not be abused.[84]

---

[80] *E.g.*, Inouye, *supra* note 41, at 186; Johnson, *supra* note 5, at 146, 151.

[81] Japan. Crim. Proc. Code, *supra* note 7, §316-3(2).

[82] *Id.* §316-5.

[83] United Nations Asia and Far East Institute for the Prevention of Crime and the Treatment of Offenders (UNAFEI), Criminal Justice in Japan 24 (2005), *at* http://www.unafei.or.jp/english/pages/CriminalJusticeJapan.htm.

[84] Japan. Crim. Proc. Code, *supra* note 7, §§316-14; 316-15; 316-20; 316-26. In particular, Articles 316-15 and 316-20 provide that the defense may ask for evidence other than that to be used at trial, but that the prosecution can then decide "when he/she deems it appropriate considering the extent of the connection [to trial], other necessities for disclosure in order to prepare for the defense of the accused, and the contents and extent of abuse which is feared will be caused by the disclosure." Even if the prosecution refuses to disclose certain evidence requested by the defense under these provisions, the court may order such disclosure if it determines that disclosure is appropriate under Articles 316-14, 316-15, or 316-20. *Id.* §316-26.

If the parties fail to disclose on their own the necessary evidence at this stage, the court may enter an order requiring them to disclose it.[85] If one party fails to ask the opposing party to disclose certain evidence for examination during pretrial arrangement, then the first party may not later request that the evidence be examined at trial (unless it can show that the initial failure to request the evidence was unavoidable).[86]

When Japan introduces its mixed jury system in 2009, the pretrial arrangement proceeding will become especially valuable in streamlining the proceedings. If the evidence and other issues discussed at pretrial arrangement hearings are undisputed, the court can appoint a smaller mixed jury than in cases where such issues are contested. In contested cases, three judges and six lay judges will be used; by contrast, when evidence is undisputed during pretrial arrangement, panels of one judge and four lay assessors may be used at trial.[87]

Because the pretrial arrangement procedure is so new and has not yet been used in conjunction with jury trials, it is difficult to assess whether cooperation with the court will bring sentencing reductions or other benefits to the accused. Such exchanges could benefit prosecutors and judges as well as defendants. Judges could conduct jury trials in a more efficient manner, prosecutors and defendants could gain a better grasp of the evidence to be presented at trial, and the defendant could receive a more lenient sentence in exchange for his cooperation. It remains a question, however, whether Japanese courts would be open to rewarding defendants with a sentencing discount simply for their cooperation in expediting the proceedings, apart from any show of remorse or reconciliation with the victim.

Speedy Trial Procedure. In minor cases that carry a sentence of less than one year of imprisonment and in which the evidence is strong, the defendant and his counsel may agree to a speedy trial procedure. The speedy trial procedure was introduced in 2006[88] and is governed by Articles 350-1 through 350-14 of the Japanese Criminal Procedure Code. Under that procedure, the court may examine evidence under simpler rules of evidence and issue a judgment without providing written reasons for it. The speedy trial procedure may be conducted only

---

[85] *Id.* §316-26.

[86] *Id.* §316-32.

[87] Anderson & Ambler, *supra* note 30, at 65.

[88] Supreme Court of Japan, Outline of Criminal Justice in Japan, *at* http://www.courts.go.jp/english/proceedings/criminal_justice.html.

if the defendant is represented by counsel. Under Article 350-14, the execution of any prison sentence imposed under the procedure must be suspended. A defendant therefore has an incentive to consent to the speedy trial procedure because it ensures that he will receive at most a suspended sentence and will be released from detention more quickly. Courts and prosecutors are likely to look favorably upon it because it averts the necessity of a written opinion and enables presentation of evidence in a simpler and less formal manner.

Confession and Cooperation with the Court. Even when a Japanese defendant proceeds to ordinary trial, if he confesses, declines to contest the evidence against him, and expresses remorse, a Japanese court will ordinarily reward such behavior with a lower sentence. As one commentator explains, "Confession, repentance, and absolution provide the underlying theme of the Japanese criminal process. At every stage from initial police investigation through formal proceedings, an individual suspected of criminal conduct gains by confessing, apologizing, and throwing himself upon the mercies of the authorities."[89] As early as the seventeenth century, if a Japanese suspect was willing to confess and cooperate with the police or the court, his punishment was likely to be reduced.[90] By the second half of the eighteenth century, a remorseful confession was a "vital element for obtaining a pardon."[91] Indeed, for a period of time beginning in the late nineteenth century, the Japanese Criminal Code specifically provided for a reduction of punishment for suspects who turned themselves in and confessed.[92]

Although the current Criminal Code does not explicitly provide for a reduced sentence in exchange for a confession, practice follows that rule. In interviews, Japanese prosecutors have stated that they are likely to recommend a lower sentence for a cooperative and remorseful defendant and a harsher sentence for a noncooperative defendant.[93] Importantly, suspects understand that they will be treated with greater lenience if they confess, cooperate, and show remorse.[94] Acting at least in part on that belief, over 90 percent of Japanese defendants confess

---

[89] Westermann & Burfeind, *supra* note 70, at 110 (citing John Owen Haley).

[90] Foote, *supra* note 48, at 419, 420.

[91] *Id.* at 422.

[92] *Id.* at 424.

[93] Johnson, *supra* note 5, at 144-145 (reporting results from a 1994-1995 survey of 231 Japanese prosecutors).

[94] *Id.* at 145; Foote, *supra* note 6, at 99.

to the charges against them.[95] Anecdotal evidence suggests that some defendants do so even though they do not in fact feel remorse.[96] As expected, judges regularly follow prosecutorial recommendations and reward apology and repentance with a more lenient sentence and other benefits.[97] Some judges may even be explicit about these exchanges and tell the defense attorney that her client will receive a concession (release on bail, for example) if he confesses or refrains from objecting to the prosecution's evidence.[98]

There is little doubt that an important reason why Japanese judges reward confessions is that they view remorse as a precondition to the rehabilitation of offenders. Rehabilitation is still a guiding principle of Japanese sentencing law and practice.[99] This is an important explanation for the lenient treatment of those who confess, but it is unlikely to be the only one. It seems probable that judges and prosecutors appreciate the fact that confessions expedite the processing of cases.[100] After a confession, the evidence is not contested, and the courts only need to confirm that the evidence in the investigative file prepared by the police and prosecutors supports the confession.[101] Indeed, when a defendant confesses, in cases punishable by one year of imprisonment or less, the court may examine the remaining evidence under simplified procedures under Criminal Procedure Code Articles 291-2, 307-2, and 320(2) and introduce written evidence that would otherwise be inadmissible under the hearsay rule.

---

[95] Supreme Court of Japan, Outline of Criminal Justice in Japan, Annual Comparison of Rate of the Accused Who Confess (%), *at* http://www.courts.go.jp/english/proceedings/criminal_justice.html (reporting that in 2004, 91.2 percent of the defendants in District Court and 92.4 percent of the defendants in Summary Court confessed).

[96] Johnson, *supra* note 5, at 148-150; Foote, *supra* note 6, at 99.

[97] Westermann & Burfeind, *supra* note 70, at 115 (citing several authorities in support); Foote, *supra* note 48, at 466; Satoru Shinomiya, *Adversarial Procedure Without a Jury: Is Japan's System Adversarial, Inquisitorial, or Something Else?*, *in* The Japanese Adversary System in Context 114, 116 (Malcolm M. Feeley & Setsuo Miyazawa eds., 2002).

[98] Shinomiya, *supra* note 97, at 116.

[99] *E.g.*, Westermann & Burfeind, *supra* note 70, at 115 (arguing that sentencing practice in Japan closely links retribution and rehabilitation); John O. Haley, *Apology and Pardon: Learning from Japan*, 41 Am. Behav. Scientist 842, 852 (1998). *But cf.* Johnson, *supra* note 15 (suggesting that Japanese penal policy has recently become more severe and less focused on rehabilitation).

[100] Makoto Ida reports that judges have actively supported the introduction of measures to expedite criminal proceedings. Ida, *supra* note 70, at 264.

[101] Johnson, *supra* note 5, at 143.

Even under this simplified procedure, the court must examine at least the written evidence gathered by the police and prosecution and ensure that it corroborates the confession of the accused. But this examination does not appear to require more than the inquiry that judges perform upon accepting a bargained-for confession or guilty plea in other jurisdictions such as Germany and Bulgaria. Accordingly, this unspoken exchange of a confession for a reduced sentence has been compared to plea bargaining, even though it does not in fact entail any negotiations or explicit agreements.[102]

EVALUATION OF THE JAPANESE ALTERNATIVES TO PLEA BARGAINING

Although plea bargaining is illegal in Japan, the various procedures above set up a framework in which implicit exchanges of concessions can thrive. Both American and Japanese commentators have therefore argued that a "tacit equivalent of plea bargaining" exists in Japan.[103] This term is used to encompass: (1) offers of a summary prosecution and a fine, rather than a custodial sentence, in exchange for cooperation; (2) offers of suspended prosecution or a recommendation for a lenient sentence in exchange for a confession; and (3) the unspoken exchange of confessions for reduced sentences.[104] Some prosecutors may openly tell the suspect that a confession is in his own interest, but more frequently, the exchange of confessions between the parties (or the parties and the court) is unspoken.[105] As a Japanese journalist summed up the practice to David Johnson, "Plea bargaining in Japan is usually tacit and indirect. This is the main difference. We don't make written records of it."[106]

The illegality of open plea bargaining and the unspoken exchange of concessions carry several important consequences. First, "tacit plea

---

[102] Foote, *supra* note 6, at 98; Goodman, *supra* note 76, at 35, 50; Johnson, *supra* note 5; Otani, *supra* note 13, at 2.

[103] Foote, *supra* note 6, at 98; Goodman, *supra* note 76, at 35, 50; Johnson, *supra* note 5, at 146 (also citing Japanese commentators); *see also* Comments by Shu Sugita, *supra* note 71, at 57 (noting the possibility of bargaining between prosecution and defense about choice of summary vs. ordinary trial procedure in an assault case); Otani, *supra* note 13, at 2, 4-7 (noting other commentators' argument that Japan has "tacit plea bargaining").

[104] Johnson, *supra* note 5, at 146; *see also* Comments by Shu Sugita, *supra* note 71, at 57; Otani, *supra* note 13, at 4-7.

[105] Johnson, *supra* note 5, at 146-147.

[106] *Id.* at 152-153.

bargaining" is less predictable in Japan than in countries where plea bargaining is accepted and regulated. The defendant may expect a lower sentence in exchange for confessing and cooperating, and the lower sentence will be recommended and granted in the vast majority of cases. But a sentence reduction is not guaranteed, and it is not clear in advance how large the reduction will be. The judge may refuse to honor the prosecutor's sentencing recommendation. Similarly, the prosecutor may change her mind about suspending the prosecution or recommending a lower sentence. If a prosecutor fails to honor her promises, the defendant has no legal remedy. There is no evidence of a "deal"; the exchange of concessions is typically unspoken. Plea agreements are illegal and therefore unenforceable.[107] In a real sense, therefore, defendants are not bargaining—instead, they are essentially throwing themselves at the mercy of the authorities, who ultimately decide whether to honor an implicit or explicit "deal."[108]

The Japanese practice differs from American-style plea bargaining in another important respect as well. Apology and remorse are central to the exchange of concessions in Japanese criminal procedure,[109] but not to American plea bargaining. American courts allow guilty pleas that are driven not by remorse, but by purely strategic considerations. For example, a defendant may plead "no contest" and refuse to accept responsibility for his crime. Similarly, he may take an *Alford* plea and protest his innocence, but still receive a reward for waiving trial and expediting the process.[110] This is not to say that remorse is irrelevant to American sentencing law. American courts may and at times do sentence more harshly a defendant who has pleaded guilty, but fails to show remorse.[111] But as a general matter, courts tend to reward guilty pleas with a similar discount, regardless of how repentant a defendant might be.[112]

---

[107] *Id.* at 157.

[108] *See* Foote, *supra* note 6, at 100; Otani, *supra* note 13, at 6-7.

[109] *E.g.*, Goodman, *supra* note 43, at 418-419, 422, 425. On the importance of apology in Japanese law generally, see Hiroshi Wagatsuma & Arthur Rosett, *The Implications of Apology: Law and Culture in Japan and the United States*, 20 Law & Soc'y Rev. 461 (1989).

[110] North Carolina v. Alford, 400 U.S. 25, 37 (1970) (noting that "while most pleas of guilty consist of both a waiver of trial and an express admission of guilt, the latter element is not a constitutional requisite to the imposition of criminal penalty").

[111] *E.g.*, State v. Howry, 896 P.2d 1002 (Idaho Ct. App. 1995); State v. Knight, 701 N.W.2d 83 (Iowa 2005); Smith v. Com., 499 S.E.2d 11 (Va. App. Ct. 1998).

[112] Stephanos Bibas & Richard A. Bierschbach, *Integrating Remorse and Apology into Criminal Procedure*, 114 Yale L.J. 85, 89 (2004).

Moreover, guilty plea hearings in the United States are not structured to encourage defendants to express remorse:

> Right now, guilty plea hearings are often dry recitations of rights and facts. Judges advise defendants of a laundry list of procedural rights they are waiving, and defendants answer "yes" to indicate that they understand each one. After that, defendants provide very brief factual statements explaining what they did, which are often written by their lawyers. Defense lawyers may tell their clients to say that they know they did something wrong and are sorry. These perfunctory, scripted statements are far from full apologies. Plea procedures do little else to encourage remorse or apology, particularly because victims and community members are absent.[113]

By contrast, in Japan, defendants know that they must show remorse in order to receive any of the benefits discussed above. Prosecutors and judges expect defendants to show contrition in court and also to pay compensation to the victim and otherwise seek reconciliation.[114] These expectations are typically unspoken, but well understood by all the participants in the criminal proceedings. As one commentator reports:

> Typically, the suspect not only confesses, but through family and friends also seeks letters from any victims addressed to the prosecutor or judge that acknowledge restitution and express the victim's sentiment that no further penalty need be imposed. So customary are such letters that most Japanese attorneys have some sense of the amounts usually required.[115]

The emphasis on remorse and reconciliation with the victim is part of a broader, "integrated" or restorative approach to justice.[116] The aim of this approach is to rehabilitate and reintegrate the offender into society. Remorse and compensation by the offender and pardon by the victim are expected to facilitate such reintegration.[117]

Because defendants know that a contrite confession and apology and compensation to the victim are preconditions to more lenient treatment, many deliver such confessions and apologies without necessarily

---

[113] *Id.* at 140.

[114] *E.g.*, John Owen Haley, Authority Without Power: Law and the Japanese Paradox 129-133 (1991).

[115] *Id.* at 130.

[116] *Id.* at 133; *see also* Goodman, *supra* note 43, at 388, 396.

[117] Haley, *supra* note 114, at 133.

meaning them.[118] But there is some evidence to suggest that the general emphasis on repentance and restitution to victims still contributes both to defendants' rehabilitation and to the legitimacy of the criminal justice system in the eyes of the victims.[119]

Notes and Questions:

1. To what extent can the Japanese practice be described as "tacit plea bargaining"? Are defendants in the position to bargain, or are they simply hoping for the mercy of the authorities?
2. A large percentage of Japanese defendants confess to receive "lenient" sentences. In your opinion, are these defendants truly receiving leniency, since most confess, or are those who refuse to confess receiving harsher penalties?
3. The most commonly heard argument for allowing open plea bargaining in Japan is that bargaining would permit investigative agencies to obtain information necessary to solve complex crimes. Currently prosecutors have limited ability to obtain the cooperation of defendants in investigating other cases. They are specifically prohibited from bargaining about charges or offering testimonial immunity, and sentencing bargains are unenforceable. Therefore, some commentators have argued that a limited form of plea bargaining should be introduced to deal with complex white-collar and organized crimes.[120] Could plea bargaining be adopted in such a limited form in Japan? Should it be?
4. How does the implicit exchange of concessions in Japan compare to plea bargaining in the United States? Which system is fairer to defendants? Which system is more likely to produce accurate outcomes? Which system is more likely to be acceptable to the general public?
5. In your opinion, why is American criminal procedure less concerned about remorse, apology, and reconciliation with the victim? Should it be? Does the concern with remorse in the Japanese criminal justice system render Japanese procedures qualitatively different from American plea bargaining?

---

[118] Foote, *supra* note 6, at 99; Johnson, *supra* note 5, at 148-150.

[119] Haley, *supra* note 114, at 136-137.

[120] *See, e.g.*, Otani, *supra* note 13, at 17; Remarks by Stuart M. Chemtob, Antitrust Deterrence in the United States and Japan, Conference on Competition Policy in the Global Trading System: Perspectives from Japan, the United States, and the European Union, Washington, DC, June 23, 2000, *at* http://www.usdoj.gov/atr/public/speeches/5076.htm.

6. If Japan were to introduce legislatively a form of plea bargaining, which of the models discussed in this book would be the best fit for the Japanese system? If you believe that one particular model is likely to be the best fit, what adaptations do you think might be necessary to accommodate the Japanese system's emphasis on rehabilitation and reintegration, or some of its other distinctive features?

JAPAN AS A COUNTER-EXAMPLE TO THE GLOBAL SPREAD OF PLEA BARGAINING

While some exchanges of concessions between the parties—or the parties and the court—seem to occur informally in the Japanese criminal justice system, calls for the express introduction of plea bargaining have so far been rejected. Why has Japan resisted the global trend toward explicit plea bargaining?

One possibility is that the practice is "abhorrent to the Japanese legal tradition" and the Japanese public.[121] The criticisms leveled at plea bargaining in other civil-law countries are commonly heard in Japan as well.[122] Yet such criticisms were set aside by legislators in Eastern Europe, so one must ask why Japan has responded differently.

Another possibility is that the Japanese legal system has not been subject to the same level of foreign influence that Eastern European countries have experienced in reforming their criminal procedures. Whereas EU and American advisors were commonly involved in the drafting of new criminal procedure codes in Eastern Europe, the recent reform of the Japanese legal system—while solicitous of comparative insights—was directed by Japanese legal experts. Moreover, Japan is not in transition to a fundamentally new political, legal, and economic system, so a transformation as significant as the introduction of plea bargaining is less likely to be attempted. In Eastern Europe, the adoption of plea bargaining may not have seemed so extraordinary in the context of the larger sweeping reforms of entire legal systems.

Finally, it may be the case that, in light of the mechanisms and understandings already implicit in its system, Japan simply does not need plea bargaining as much as other systems that have adopted the practice.[123]

---

[121] Johnson, *supra* note 5, at 161.

[122] *Id.* at 161 (noting arguments by Japanese commentators that plea bargaining is inconsistent with the search for truth, ignores victims' interests, and frustrates legislative intent).

[123] *See* Foote, *supra* note 6, at 97.

Japan's simplified trial procedures, combined with the tacit exchange of concessions during regular trials, may adequately serve many of the same purposes that plea bargaining does in other countries. Finally, Japan accomplishes greater efficiency in its criminal process by relying on prosecutors to charge very selectively and on police to obtain confessions through long interrogations outside the presence of counsel.

As discussed above, Japanese prosecutors have great discretion to suspend prosecution, and they use it regularly. This results in a significant decrease in caseloads and lessens the need to engage in plea bargaining. This use of prosecutorial discretion to charge more selectively has been proposed by American scholars as a desirable alternative to plea bargaining.[124]

Japan's system of prosecutorial decision making is structured so as to avoid some of the common criticisms of broad discretion—that it may be used arbitrarily or in a discriminatory fashion. Regular supervision by more senior prosecutors ensures consistency across cases, and the system avoids the lack of accountability that is said to pervade plea bargaining.[125]

Still, even senior prosecutors may be selective in the charges they approve, and Japanese prosecutors have been criticized for using their discretion to shield politically powerful figures from prosecution.[126] In particular, commentators have expressed concerns that "politicians, former prosecutors, police officers, and people connected to powerful economic and political organizations" are less likely to be prosecuted than similarly situated suspects who do not enjoy these advantages.[127]

Unprincipled use of prosecutorial discretion is supposed to be countered not only by the prosecutors' supervisors, but also by Prosecutorial Review Commissions (PRCs)—Japan's version of grand juries, which allows randomly selected Japanese citizens to review the appropriateness of prosecutors' non-indictment decisions.[128] But the PRCs have been notoriously ineffective, largely because they can only issue nonbinding recommendations.[129] Accordingly, one of the suggestions of the

[124] Ronald Wright & Marc Miller, *The Screening/Bargaining Tradeoff*, 55 Stan. L. Rev. 29 (2002).

[125] Johnson, *supra* note 5, at 160.

[126] *E.g.*, Goodman, *supra* note 76, at 23, 61.

[127] Hiroshi Furukai, *The Rebirth of Japan's Petit Quasi-Jury and Grand Jury Systems: A Cross-National Analysis of Legal Consciousness and the Lay Participatory Experience in Japan and the U.S.*, 40 Cornell Int'l L.J. 315, 328 (2007).

[128] *Id.* at 323.

[129] *Id.* at 325.

Justice System Reform Council was to strengthen the authority of PRCs by allowing them to issue legally binding recommendations to prosecute. The 2004 Act to Revise the Code of Criminal Procedure enacted the recommendation into law. To the extent that the new PRCs begin to limit prosecutorial discretion to suspend prosecution, they might place additional burdens on the criminal justice system and thereby increase the pressure to find shortcuts such as plea bargaining. But for the moment, the broad discretion to suspend prosecution means that plea bargaining is less needed in Japan than in countries that hew to the principle of mandatory prosecution.

A second reason why Japan has been less tempted by plea bargaining may be the fact that over 90 percent of defendants already confess.[130] This is due, at least in part, to the implicit understanding that defendants will fare better at sentencing if they have confessed to their crimes and shown remorse for them. But the Criminal Procedure Code also enables Japanese police to obtain confessions by authorizing long pretrial detentions during which the suspect can be interrogated in the absence of counsel. The police may continue interrogation for up to 23 days before formal charges are filed.[131] While the suspect does have the right to consult occasionally with counsel during that time, counsel is not present during the interrogations.[132] Nor are the interrogations recorded.[133] The police instead compose narratives of the confession, to which the suspect attests through his signature. These interrogations have been criticized for being coercive and for causing innocent suspects to incriminate themselves.[134]

Japan's broad prosecutorial discretion and its long and secretive police interrogations have both been targets of reform efforts. On the recommendation of the Justice System Reform Council, recent legislation strengthened the authority of Prosecutorial Review Commissions to review decisions to suspend prosecution. At the same time, Japanese lawyers and lawyers' associations have advocated for shorter detention periods, for the recording of police interrogations, and for the right to have counsel present during interrogations.[135]

---

[130] Supreme Court of Japan, *supra* note 95.

[131] International Bar Association, Interrogation of Criminal Suspects in Japan—The Introduction of Electronic Recording 41 (2003), *at* http://www.ibanet.org/images/downloads/HRIJapanIntroOfElectronicRecording.pdf.

[132] *Id.* at 43-44.

[133] *Id.* at 43.

[134] *Id.*

[135] *Id.*

As these suggestions for reform indicate, the prohibition of plea bargaining in Japan does not entirely eliminate concerns about coerced confessions and unequal treatment of defendants. Prosecutorial suspension decisions are effectively free from judicial supervision,[136] and the PRC review process has so far proven to be ineffective. The suspension practice is therefore even less transparent than plea bargaining. In addition, the long detentions and interrogations produce confessions that may be just as involuntary and inaccurate as some of the confessions obtained through bargaining (indeed, prolonged interrogation in custody may be more likely to produce false or involuntary confessions). In the end, the Japanese system presents the difficult question of whether many of the harms often associated with plea bargaining may be less a function of plea bargaining itself, and more a function of the underlying drive for efficiency in criminal justice systems.

ALTERNATIVES TO PLEA BARGAINING IN CHINA

Like Japan, China has so far refrained from introducing plea bargaining and has relied instead on summary trial procedures to deal with an increasing criminal caseload. The introduction of summary trial procedures in China occurred against the backdrop of broader criminal justice reforms beginning in the mid-1990s. In 1996, China amended its Criminal Procedure Code to introduce a number of adversarial elements into its inquisitorial criminal process. The change was a product of both foreign influence and domestic demands.[137] It generally aimed to align Chinese procedure with international fair trial standards[138] and was consistent with the increasing adoption of adversarial features into modern inquisitorial systems. The amended Criminal Procedure Code gave the parties greater responsibilities before and during trial and correspondingly reduced judges' role in the process.[139] In practice, however, these reforms have been difficult to implement:

---

[136] *But see* Goodman, *supra* note 76, at 83-94 (noting a move toward minimal supervision).

[137] Peerenboom, *supra* note 4, at 200, 203 (adding that domestically, it was primarily legal professionals, not so much the general public, that demanded reforms); Wei Luo, The Amended Criminal Procedure Law and the Criminal Court Rules of the People's Republic of China 5-8 (2000).

[138] Luo, *supra* note 137, at 6.

[139] *Id.* at 13-16.

> [L]awyers have been routinely denied access to their clients, the prosecutors have refused to turn over exculpatory evidence or provide defense counsel access to all the information in the dossier, defense counsel have been unable to question key witnesses who often do not show up at court to testify, the high rate of confessions has reduced the role of lawyers to one of seeking leniency, and allegations of torture remain common.[140]

Prosecutors, police, and, to a lesser extent, judges have resisted the loss of power that the adversarial reforms entailed,[141] and the general public has not demanded further liberalization of Chinese criminal procedure.[142] As a result, the reforms have been described as "largely a failure at the basic level of compliance."[143]

Against the background of this broader, but unsteady criminal procedure reform, China introduced "summary" and "simplified" trial procedures to deal with a rising number of criminal cases and overburdened criminal dockets. The 1996 Criminal Procedure Code provided for the application of the so-called summary procedure in minor, uncontested cases. In 2003, the Supreme People's Court, the Supreme Procuratorate, and the Ministry of Justice issued "interpretations" that elaborated on the summary procedure and also regularized the "simplified procedure" that had developed informally in practice.[144]

The "summary procedure" established by Articles 174-179 of the Criminal Procedure Code applies in cases in which the facts are clear, the evidence is sufficient, and the maximum potential punishment is less than three years in prison.[145] In practice, the requirement for clear facts and sufficient evidence means that the defendant has to admit guilt. In such cases, one judge, rather than the usual panel of three, presides over the trial. To apply the procedure, the court must ensure that both the defense and the prosecutor consent.[146] The prosecutor does not need

---

[140] Peerenboom, *supra* note 4, at 200-201; *see also* Luo, *supra* note 137, at 23-24.

[141] Peerenboom, *supra* note 4, at 202.

[142] *Id.* at 201-203.

[143] *Id.* at 203.

[144] *Id.* at 203. These official interpretations are effectively binding on lower-level courts, procuratorates, and public security organs, respectively. Ira Belkin, *China*, *in* Criminal Procedure: A Worldwide Study 91, 94 (Craig Bradley ed., 2007).

[145] Luo, *supra* note 137, at 103, art. 174.

[146] Jeffrey Prescott, *Efficiency and Justice in Summary Criminal Trials*, Legal Daily, July 24, 2003, *at* http://www.law.yale.edu/documents/pdf/Effeciancy_and_Justice.pdf (referring to the 2003 Supreme People's Court interpretation of summary procedures).

to send a representative to appear in court, and the court can dispense with the ordinary procedures for interrogating the accused, questioning fact and expert witnesses, presenting evidence, and conducting courtroom arguments.[147] The defendant does have the opportunity to make statements in his defense.[148]

The "simplified procedure," which was formally established through the 2003 interpretations of the Supreme People's Court and Supreme Procuratorate, applies in more serious cases in which the defendant admits guilt.[149] In these cases, a panel of three judges presides over the trial. The procedure cannot be used in cases in which the death penalty is possible; in which the crime would have a significant social impact; in which the defendant is deaf, blind, or mute; or in which a co-defendant refuses to consent to the application of the simplified procedure.[150] Both parties must consent to the use of the simplified procedure, and the court must agree that the procedure is applicable.[151]

The simplified procedure is different from American plea bargaining in several respects. First, the parties cannot bargain for a specific sentence. Instead, the court has ultimate sentencing discretion, although it may mitigate the sentence for a defendant who has consented to the use of the simplified procedure.[152] Some commentators have suggested that this provision was included to allow the defense to negotiate with the prosecution or the court.[153] Even if some room for negotiation exists, it appears much more limited than in American-style plea bargaining. The parties also cannot bargain over charges. The court has to confirm that the charges to which the defendant pleads guilty accurately reflect the circumstances of the crime.[154] To do so, the court may review the case file and may call for further investigation of the facts.[155] In this sense, at least on paper, the Chinese simplified procedure is closer to plea bargaining in other inquisitorial countries, in which the court continues to be under

---

[147] Luo, *supra* note 137, at 104, arts. 175, 177.

[148] *Id.*

[149] Interpretation of the Procedures Applicable to Cases Involving an Admission of Guilt by the Defendant (test provisions), May 14, 2003 (on file with author) [hereinafter 2003 Interpretation]. For the legal status of these interpretations, see *supra* note 144.

[150] 2003 Interpretation, *supra* note 149, art. 2.

[151] *Id.* art. 3.

[152] *Id.* art. 9.

[153] Prescott, *supra* note 146.

[154] 2003 Interpretation, *supra* note 149, art. 8.

[155] *Id.* arts. 6, 7.

a duty to investigate the truth and has the ability to do so by consulting the file or calling for further evidence-gathering, even when the defendant has admitted guilt. At the same time, as in the United States, the court must confirm that the defendant pleads guilty voluntarily and that he understands the legal consequences of the guilty plea.[156] This allows the defendant to allege coercion by the police and to change his plea,[157] although it is not clear that the voluntariness inquiry is particularly probing in practice.[158] The court must also allow the defendant to make a statement to explain the situation and ask for leniency.[159]

These summary procedures were developed informally in urban courts in response to rising crime and heavier case loads.[160] While they may have been influenced by plea bargaining in other countries, they do not appear to copy a particular foreign model.[161] They were initially considered inconsistent with the Criminal Procedure Code and the inquisitorial tradition, which emphasizes a detailed investigation of the facts by both the prosecution and the court.[162] But the provisions appear to have taken hold for at least three reasons. First, they responded to a clear functional need—to expedite criminal proceedings in the face of overburdened dockets. Second, they are consistent with the emphasis on confessions in the Chinese criminal justice system.[163] Like Japan, China has historically relied extensively on confessions and considered them central to the discovery of truth and the rehabilitation of the defendant. For that reason, it has traditionally rewarded confessions with more lenient sentences. The simplified procedures therefore seem to be a natural outgrowth of this longstanding practice. Finally, key actors in the criminal justice system benefit from summary procedures and have readily embraced them:

> Judges don't have to make tough calls and run the risk of being overturned on appeal. Prosecutors can meet their quotas for cases handled without as much effort, and ensure a conviction. Lawyers, who can

[156] *Id.* arts. 4, 7.

[157] Peerenboom, *supra* note 4, at 208.

[158] Prescott, *supra* note 146.

[159] 2003 Interpretation, *supra* note 149, art. 7; *see also* Peerenboom, *supra* note 4, at 206.

[160] Prescott, *supra* note 146.

[161] Peerenboom, *supra* note 4, at 205.

[162] *See id.*

[163] *Id.* at 206.

rarely charge high fees given the low economic status of most criminals, can rely on volume to generate income, and still claim success in that they are able to obtain a lenient sentence.[164]

A recent Chinese government "white paper" reported that close to 40 percent of criminal cases heard by courts were resolved through the summary procedure.[165] This has eased the burden on local courts; one Beijing court reported that court hearings that would have lasted several hours under the ordinary procedure were cut to less than an hour, and in some cases as short as 20 minutes.[166]

The speed of these proceedings has caused some commentators to question whether the summary procedures are sacrificing justice for efficiency.[167] In particular, anecdotal evidence suggests that courts do not always abide by the procedural requirements laid out by the Supreme People's Court. They often fail to inform defendants of their rights, to explain the consequences of the simplified procedure, or to review evidence contested by the defense.[168] Moreover, some commentators have compared even ordinary criminal trials in China to a "prolonged plea allocution in American criminal procedure" because the courts rarely use their power to investigate the evidence and call witnesses to resolve disputed facts.[169] When the court's responsibility to gather and hear evidence is relaxed even further, there is good reason to worry that justice and truth may suffer.

The summary procedures, as currently structured, may also be unfair to the defense. For example, courts do not appear to have developed procedures to ensure that a defendant who withdraws an admission of guilt does not suffer retaliation in the subsequent ordinary trial.[170] More broadly, when compared to American-style plea bargaining, the Chinese summary procedures appear to offer few benefits to defendants. Defendants do not appear to be able to initiate the proceedings or to negotiate a particular sentence (with either the prosecution or the court); as a result, they are essentially admitting guilt in the hope that the court

---

[164] *Id.* at 206-207.

[165] State Council Information Office, White Paper: China's Efforts and Achievements in Promoting the Rule of Law (2008), *at* http://www.gov.cn/english/2008-02/28/content_904901_15.htm.

[166] Prescott, *supra* note 146.

[167] *Id.*; *see also* Peerenboom, *supra* note 4, at 207.

[168] Prescott, *supra* note 146.

[169] Belkin, *supra* note 144, at 105.

[170] *See* Prescott, *supra* note 146.

will be merciful toward them, but have no protection against frustrated expectations.

The fairness of summary procedures is also likely to be jeopardized because of the broader disregard of fair trial and defense rights in the practice of Chinese criminal procedure. Chinese police often mistreat defendants in custody and coerce confessions.[171] Police prevent defense counsel from meeting with their clients, and prosecutors often refuse to turn over relevant evidence to the defense.[172] The authorities harass and at times imprison defense attorneys for attempting to represent their clients zealously.[173] Finally, courts still lack independence and suffer from corruption.[174] In this climate, it is difficult to believe that summary procedures will consistently offer defendants a fair resolution of their cases. In fact, the more cursory examination of the facts by the court means that many more instances of unfair treatment are likely to remain unaddressed.

Notes and Questions:

1. How would you compare the summary and simplified procedures in China to American-style plea bargaining? How do the responsibilities and powers of the prosecution, defense, and court differ? Which procedure is fairer? Which procedure is more likely to produce accurate results? Which procedure is likely to be more efficient?
2. How is the failure to adequately implement defense and fair trial rights in China likely to affect the functioning of the summary procedures? What is the negotiating power of defendants and defense attorneys in this environment?
3. What institutional, legal, or political factors might explain why China opted for summary procedures rather than American-style plea bargaining?

---

[171] *E.g.*, U.S. Dep't of State, Country Reports on Human Rights Practices—2007: China (includes Tibet, Hong Kong, and Macau), Mar. 11, 2008, *at* http://www.state.gov/g/drl/rls/hrrpt/2007/100518.htm [hereinafter 2007 State Dep't Report].

[172] Peerenboom, *supra* note 4, at 200-201; *see also* Lewis, *supra* note 2, at 723 ("The tremendous scarcity of defense lawyers and glaring power imbalance between lawyers and prosecutors further dampen the prospects for actual adversarial contests. If China continues in this direction where substantive adversarial trials on the books give way to superficial, assembly line proceedings in practice, what appear on the surface to be legitimate, expedited proceedings may fail to provide anything but perfunctory process in the overwhelming majority of cases.").

[173] *E.g.*, 2007 State Dep't Report, *supra* note 171.

[174] *Id.*

4. As an inquisitorial country, China could have adopted plea bargaining practices closer to those recently introduced in Eastern Europe or Germany (see Chapters 2 and 3). But it appears that China did not copy any particular foreign model. Does this mean that criminal procedures around the world are becoming more diverse, rather than more uniform, even as they all increasingly strive for efficiency? In evaluating the different forms of plea bargaining adopted by four inquisitorial countries—Germany, Italy, Argentina, and France, Máximo Langer argues that such diversification is occurring:

   > [T]he adoption of some form of plea bargaining in these [inquisitorial] jurisdictions may produce different transformations or effects in each jurisdiction. Therefore, the potential influence of American plea bargaining on civil law jurisdictions may not be that civil law systems will gradually resemble the American legal system, but rather that they may begin to differ amongst themselves in aspects on which, until very recently, they have been relatively homogeneous. In other words, the paradoxical effect of American influence on the criminal procedures of the civil law tradition may not be Americanization, but rather fragmentation and divergence within the civil law.[175]

   Do you believe China's adoption of summary trials provides additional support for Langer's argument?

[175] Máximo Langer, *From Legal Transplants to Legal Translations: The Globalization of Plea Bargaining and the Americanization Thesis in Criminal Procedure*, 45 Harv. Int'l L.J. 1, 4 (2004).

ALTERNATIVES TO PLEA BARGAINING IN CHINA AND JAPAN

Alternatives to Plea Bargaining	China	Japan
Discretionary Prosecution	No exact equivalent. Chinese prosecutors must generally institute charges when evidence is sufficient, but have the discretion not to charge in certain minor cases; this discretion is used in few cases and is primarily applied to juveniles.*	Prosecutor may decide to suspend the prosecution after considering various factors, including the character of the offender and the conditions subsequent to the crime. Defense attorneys will discuss suspension with the prosecutor by emphasizing the defendant's good character, remorse, and willingness to cooperate or compensate the victim.
Summary Proceedings	(See below—Summary Procedure)	For very minor offenses, the prosecutor may request a summary proceeding if the defendant consents. The court may decide the case by examining evidence submitted by the prosecution without conducting a trial. The maximum sentence is 500,000 yen (= $4,500). If either party is dissatisfied, that party may apply for a formal trial within 14 days of receiving the decision.
Summary Procedure (China)/ Speedy Trial Procedure (Japan)	Applies to cases in which the facts are clear, the evidence is sufficient, and the maximum potential punishment is less than three years imprisonment. The prosecutor need not send a representative to court, and the court can dispense with the ordinary procedures for interrogating the accused, questioning fact and expert witnesses, presenting evidence, and conducting arguments. The defendant may make statements in his defense.	In minor cases that carry a sentence of less than one year of imprisonment and in which the evidence is strong, the defendant and his counsel may agree to a speedy trial procedure. The court may examine evidence under simpler rules of evidence and issue a judgment without providing written reasons for it. Defendant must be represented by counsel. The court must suspend any prison sentence imposed.

(continues)

Simplified Procedure	Applies in more serious cases in which the defendant admits guilt. Cannot be used in certain very serious cases; if the defendant is deaf, blind, or mute; or if a co-defendant refuses to consent. The parties cannot bargain over charges or for a specific sentence, but the court is urged to mitigate the sentence. The court must confirm that: (1) the charges reflect the facts; (2) the defendant admits guilt voluntarily; and (3) the defendant understands the legal consequences of the admission. The defendant may make statements in his defense.	When a defendant confesses, in cases punishable by one year of imprisonment or less, the court may examine the remaining evidence under simplified procedures and introduce written evidence that would otherwise be inadmissible under the hearsay rule. The court must confirm that the confession is supported by other facts.
Confession and Cooperation with the Court	Confessions are very common and are rewarded with leniency. They simplify evidence-gathering in all cases, although the court must confirm that the confession is supported by other facts.	Confessions occur in over 90 percent of cases and are rewarded with leniency. The court needs to confirm that the evidence in the investigative file supports the confession.
Pretrial Arrangement Procedure	No equivalent	Allows the court and the parties to resolve contested charge qualifications, disclosure questions, and other evidence issues at pretrial hearings. Allows and encourages early disclosure of evidence. If all issues are resolved during pretrial arrangement, the court can appoint a smaller mixed jury than in cases where such issues are contested.

* Xiaoyan Hou, *Procuratorial Discretion in China: Formal Rules and Informal Practice*, 33 H.K. L.J. 663 (2003) (discussing decisions not to prosecute and reporting that in 2001, in the Beijing area, only 349 out of 23,474 cases forwarded to the prosecutor's office were ended by a non-prosecution decision).

HYPOTHETICALS

Alternatives to Plea Bargaining in a Drug Case in Japan[176]

Yoshi Suzuki, a Tokyo resident, moved into a new rental apartment in mid-June 2008. Based on an informant's tip in early July 2008, police searched Suzuki's apartment and found about 15 grams of amphetamine tucked away in a kitchen cabinet behind a water pipe. Suzuki told the police he did not know how the drugs got there and to whom they belonged. He maintained that the drugs must have been there before he moved into the apartment. He said he had never used drugs or even seen amphetamine, but the police and the prosecutor are unconvinced by the story and intend to charge Suzuki with possession of amphetamine and possibly other related offenses. At the same time, the prosecutor wants to avoid a contested trial and would like to find out more about the suppliers of the drug to Suzuki as well as other information that Suzuki might provide about the distribution of amphetamine drugs. Suzuki has no prior convictions.

Notes and Questions:

1. What kind of offer can a Japanese prosecutor make to Suzuki to resolve the case more efficiently and to obtain information about the drug distribution ring to which Suzuki might belong? Consider the penal provisions and statistics provided below, as well as the case of *Enomoto v. Japan* and other laws discussed earlier.

Japanese Stimulants Control Law[177]

Article 14, Prohibition of Possession

No person other than a stimulants manufacturer, proprietor and administrator of a stimulants administering institution, medical practitioner engaged in treatment at a stimulants administering institution, stimulants researcher as well as a person who has been supplied stimulants for administering by a medical practitioner engaged in treatment at a stimulants administering institution or by a stimulants researcher shall possess stimulants.

---

[176] The hypothetical is loosely based on a case discussed by David Johnson, *supra* note 5, at 147.

[177] Japan. Stimulants Control Law, *at* http://www.unodc.org/enl/showDocument.do?documentUid=2644&node=docs&country=JPN&cmd=add&pageNum=2. Note that amphetamine is considered a stimulant for purposes of the Stimulants Control Law.

Article 17, Restriction and Prohibition of Transfer and Receipt

1. No stimulants manufacturer shall transfer the stimulants manufactured by him to any person other than a stimulants administering institution or a stimulants researcher.

2. No stimulants administering institution nor stimulants researcher shall receive stimulants from any person other than a stimulants manufacturer.

3. No person shall transfer or receive stimulants except in the cases provided for in the preceding two paragraphs and the case where a medical practitioner engaged in treatment at a stimulants administering institution or a stimulants researcher supplies stimulants for administering.

Article 41-2

1. Any person who unlawfully possesses, transfers or receives stimulants (excluding a person who comes under the provision of Item (5) of Article 42) shall be liable to penal servitude not exceeding 10 years.

2. Any person who commits an offence prescribed in the preceding paragraph for the purpose of gain shall be liable to penal servitude for a limited term not less than 1 year or to both penal servitude of limited term not less than 1 year and a fine not exceeding 5,000,000 yen according to the circumstances.

3. An attempt to commit any of the offences prescribed in the preceding two paragraphs shall be liable to punishment.

Article 41-11

Any person who mediates to transfer or receive stimulants, under the offences prescribed in Article 41-2, shall be liable to penal servitude not exceeding 3 years.

Japanese Criminal Code[178]

Article 25 (Suspension of Execution of the Sentence)

(1) When any one of the following persons has been sentenced to imprisonment with or without work for not more than 3 years or a fine of not more than 500,000 yen, execution of the sentence may, in light of circumstances, be suspended for a period of not less than 1 year but not more than 5 years from the day on which the sentence becomes final and binding:

---

[178] Japan. Crim. Code, *supra* note 59.

(i) A person not previously sentenced to imprisonment without work or a greater punishment.

Article 25-2 (Probation)

(1) In a case prescribed for in paragraph 1 of Article 25, the subject person may be placed under probation through the period of suspended execution of the sentence; and in a case prescribed for in paragraph 2 of Article 25, the subject person shall be placed under probation through the period of suspended execution of the sentence.

Article 66 (Reduction of Punishment in Light of Extenuating Circumstances)

Punishment may be reduced in light of the extenuating circumstances of a crime.

Article 67 (Statutory Aggravation or Reduction and Reduction in Light of Extenuating Circumstances)

Even if the punishment is aggravated or reduced in accordance with a statute, it may be reduced in light of circumstances.

Fig. 1-1-4-14 Number of persons sentenced to imprisonment for Stimulants Control Law violations in the court of first instance by term of imprisonment (1975-2004)

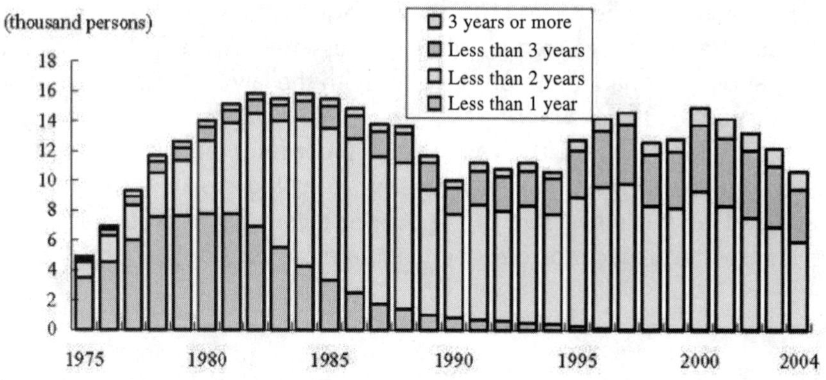

Source: Annual Report of Judicial Statistics[179]

[179] Japanese Ministry of Justice, White Paper on Crime (2005), *at* http://hakusyo1.moj.go.jp/en/53/image/image/h002006002002e.jpg.

2. What can Suzuki and his defense attorney do to increase Suzuki's chances that the prosecutor will suspend his prosecution or at least agree to recommend a more lenient sentence to the judge?
3. How do the procedures available to Suzuki in Japan compare to the summary and simplified procedures available to similarly situated defendants in China? Which system do you believe strikes a better balance between expediency and accuracy and fairness and why?

Alternatives to Plea Bargaining in a Homicide Case in Japan

Yuko Ono and Hiroshi Yamaguchi were a couple who lived and worked in Tokyo. After an argument in their apartment, Yuko stabbed Hiroshi with a knife and killed him. The Japanese authorities commenced investigation and detained Yuko. In response to police questions, Yuko admitted stabbing Hiroshi, but she said that she was merely defending herself. She told the police that Hiroshi had a history of beating her and that on the day of the killing, he hit her several times during an argument, and he threatened to kill her. (Yuko did have some injuries, but the medical examiner could not state with a certainty whether someone else inflicted them or whether Yuko herself did so.) Yuko told the police that, fearing for her life, she stabbed Hiroshi with a kitchen knife that was nearby. Yuko was very regretful for stabbing Hiroshi, and she told the police that she wished she had not done it, but that she had been genuinely concerned for her life.

Upon doing additional investigation, the police found only one person who overheard the incident—one of Yuko and Hiroshi's neighbors. The neighbor claimed he heard nothing to suggest attacks or threats by Hiroshi. But the neighbor's credibility may be lessened by the fact that he is a drug addict, has had numerous brushes with the law himself, and has also had disputes with Yuko in the past.

The police referred the case to the prosecutor, and the prosecutor questioned Yuko, giving her another opportunity to explain the facts. Yuko repeated what she had said to the police officers. Based on the available evidence, the prosecution decided to initiate prosecution for homicide.

Japanese Criminal Code[180]

Article 36 (Self-Defense)

(1) An act unavoidably performed to protect the rights of oneself or any other person against imminent and unlawful infringement is not punishable.

---

[180] Japan. Crim. Code, *supra* note 59.

(2) An act exceeding the limits of self-defense may lead to the punishment being reduced or may exculpate the offender in light of the circumstances.

Article 37 (Averting Present Danger)

(1) An act unavoidably performed to avert a present danger to the life, body, liberty or property of oneself or any other person is not punishable only when the harm produced by such act does not exceed the harm to be averted; provided, however, that an act causing excessive harm may lead to the punishment being reduced or may exculpate the offender in light of the circumstances.

(2) The preceding paragraph does not apply to a person under special professional obligation.

Article 199 (Homicide)

A person who kills another shall be punished by the death penalty or imprisonment with work for life or for a definite term of not less than 5 years.

After Yuko obtained defense counsel, defense counsel contacted the prosecution with a request to review the evidence against Yuko, and the prosecution agreed to show counsel the evidence. Defense counsel quickly discovered the potential problems with the neighbor's testimony and told the prosecutor that she would not consent to the introduction of the neighbor's statement (meaning that the prosecution would have to call him as a witness, giving the defense the opportunity to cross-examine). The trial date was set for six months later.

Notes and Questions:

1. What can Yuko and her defense counsel do increase Yuko's chances for lenient treatment? Could Yuko have convinced the prosecutor to suspend prosecution? Would one of the summary procedures be available for this case? Is there anything that Yuko and her defense attorney can do to persuade the court to acquit Yuko or at least to sentence her leniently?
2. What is the best course of representation for Yuko's attorney? Should she press the self-defense charge aggressively, or is she more likely to be successful if she emphasizes Yuko's remorse for killing Hiroshi? Note that trial and sentencing in Japan are not bifurcated (as they are in the United States), so the parties must bring up evidence related to both guilt/innocence and sentencing during the same proceeding.

3. How does the procedure for resolving this case compare to the abbreviated trials in Bulgaria or the short bench trials in Philadelphia? Which system is likely to produce the most accurate and fair outcomes? Which system is most favorable to defendants, and which is most favorable to victims?

CHAPTER

5 Plea Bargaining at International Criminal Courts

INTRODUCTION

In the aftermath of atrocities committed during ethnic conflicts in the former Yugoslavia and Rwanda in the 1990s, the UN Security Council established the International Criminal Tribunals for the former Yugoslavia and for Rwanda (ICTY and ICTR) to address international crimes arising out of these conflicts. The tribunals have jurisdiction over genocide, crimes against humanity, and war crimes. They are the first international courts since the post–World War II Nuremberg and Tokyo Tribunals to address such crimes.

The law the tribunals apply includes their founding statutes, their rules of procedure and evidence, and standard international law sources (international treaties, custom, and general principles of law recognized by the major legal systems of the world). Because international criminal law and procedure were not well developed when the ICTY and ICTR began their work, the tribunals have had to interpret many of their rules with reference to the laws and practices of domestic legal systems. Both common-law and civil-law countries' procedures have influenced the development of criminal procedure at the ICTY and ICTR, although the common-law, or adversarial, approach has predominated.

Soon after the ICTY and ICTR began their proceedings, in 1998, state delegations from around the world gathered in Rome to negotiate and sign the Rome Treaty establishing the International Criminal Court. As of June 1, 2008, 106 states were parties to the Rome Treaty. The International Criminal Court (ICC) is a permanent court that can try international crimes occurring on the territory of any of its 106 member states or committed by member states' nationals. Its jurisdiction is therefore not limited to a particular conflict or territory, as was the case with all the previous international tribunals. Like the ICTY and ICTR before it, the ICC will apply its own statute and rules of procedure and evidence, as well as international treaties, custom, and general principles of law. The ICC is likely to be influenced greatly by the jurisprudence of the ICTY and ICTR. When it comes to procedure, however, the ICC's Rules are much more aligned with the civil-law or inquisitorial approach. They vest judges with greater control over the proceedings instead of relying on the parties to develop and present the case independently. To that extent, some of the procedural law developed by the ICTY and ICTR—including the law on plea bargaining—may not be applicable to proceedings at the ICC.

The international criminal courts, with their blend of inquisitorial and adversarial procedures, serve as interesting experiments in designing plea bargaining regimes that include features of both approaches. They are also important to study because the use of plea bargaining for international crimes remains very controversial and raises with greater intensity some fundamental questions about the purposes and value of plea bargaining in any criminal justice system. Is it appropriate to offer sentencing concessions to a defendant who pleads guilty to a heinous violent crime involving hundreds or thousands of victims? How can the avoidance of a public trial through plea bargaining be reconciled with some of the professed goals of international criminal law, including the goal of creating a more accurate historical record of the atrocities and that of providing victims with a voice in the process? Conversely, given the very limited resources and enforcement powers of international criminal courts, could these courts achieve any of their goals effectively without the use of plea bargaining? These questions continue to be intensely debated in court opinions and academic commentary.

HISTORY OF PLEA BARGAINING AT INTERNATIONAL CRIMINAL COURTS

Plea bargaining is commonly used by international prosecutors today, but its acceptance in international criminal courts came somewhat slowly. Neither the Nuremberg nor the Tokyo Tribunals made use of plea bargaining in the prosecutions of Nazi and Japanese defendants accused of aggression, war crimes, and crimes against humanity. Half a century later, when the Security Council established the International Criminal Tribunals for the former Yugoslavia and for Rwanda, it did not expressly provide for plea bargaining in the tribunals' statutes. Nor were plea bargaining provisions included in the Rules of Procedure and Evidence adopted by the tribunals. Indeed, the drafters of the ICTY Rules of Procedure rejected a U.S. proposal to include a provision permitting offers of immunity to suspects who provide substantial cooperation to the prosecution.[1] Judge Antonio Cassese, then President of the ICTY, explained the rejection as follows:

> The question of the grant of immunity from prosecution to a potential witness has also generated considerable debate. . . . [A]rrangements such as plea-bargaining could also be considered in an attempt to secure other convictions. However, we always have to keep in mind that this Tribunal is not a municipal court but one that is charged with the task of trying persons accused of the gravest possible of all crimes. . . . After due reflection, we have decided that no one should be immune from prosecution for crimes such as these, no matter how useful their testimony may otherwise be.[2]

For similar reasons, all forms of plea bargaining were initially seen as inappropriate in the context of international criminal prosecutions.[3]

Yet in large part due to American influence, both the Statute and the first ICTY rules of procedure did provide for guilty pleas, a mechanism foreign to civil-law jurisdictions.[4] The availability of a guilty plea—and the waiver of trial rights it entailed—facilitated the later use of plea bargaining by prosecutors. As Judge Cassese explained in his first opinion, "It is apparent from the whole spirit of the Statute and the Rules that, by providing for a guilty plea, the draftsmen intended to enable the accused (as well as the Prosecutor) to avoid a lengthy trial with all the attendant difficulties."[5]

The first guilty pleas tendered by defendants at the ICTY and ICTR were apparently not induced by prosecutorial promises. Defendants like Drazen Erdemović and Goran Jelisić at the ICTY and Jean Kambanda

---

[1] Michael P. Scharf, *Trading Justice for Efficiency: Plea-Bargaining and International Tribunals*, 2 J. Int'l Crim. Just. 1070, 1073 (2004).

[2] Judge Antonio Cassese, President of the ICTY, *Statement by the President Made at a Briefing to Members of Diplomatic Missions*, U.N. Doc. IT/29 (Feb. 11, 1994), *reprinted in* An Insider's Guide to the ICTY 649, 652 (Virginia Morris & Michael P. Scharf eds., 1995).

[3] Nancy Amoury Combs, Guilty Pleas in International Criminal Law: Constructing a Restorative Justice Approach 59 (2007).

[4] *Id.* at 58.

[5] Prosecutor v. Erdemović, Case No. IT-96-22-A, Separate and Dissenting Opinion of Judge Cassese, ¶8 (Oct. 7, 1997).

and Omar Serushago at the ICTR appear to have pleaded guilty on their own initiative.[6] While they may have expected or hoped for a degree of leniency from the court following their guilty pleas, the pleas do not appear to have been made in response to any assurances from the Court or the prosecutors concerning the likely sentence. Two of these four defendants may have received somewhat more favorable treatment in sentencing than they would otherwise have received if they had not pleaded guilty. But at least two, Jelisić and Kambanda, did not receive any sentencing concessions for waiving their right to trial.[7]

While guilty pleas were rare and unsolicited in the early days of the tribunals, by the year 2001, the mounting costs of the prosecutions and the pressure to process cases more quickly encouraged bargaining between the prosecution and the defense. Under the largely adversarial rules of procedure at the tribunal, prosecutors had the authority to dismiss charges and recommend sentences to judges and therefore had the discretion to make promises about these subjects to defendants. While judges were not required to enforce the plea bargains presented to the Court, they felt pressure to complete cases more speedily, and most of them accepted these bargains.[8] As the practice of plea bargaining became more common, the tribunals' rules changed to reflect the development. In 2001, the ICTY adopted Rule 62*ter*, which formalized plea agreement procedures,[9] and two years later, the ICTR adopted essentially the same language in its own Rule 62*bis*.[10]

Even before the ICTY and ICTR rules openly acknowledged the use of plea agreements, the statute for the newly established International Criminal Court recognized the possibility of plea bargaining in its own cases. Articles 64(8) and 65 of the ICC Statute do not use the term "guilty plea." As a concession to member states with inquisitorial traditions[11] (in which the guilty plea, as such, is unknown), the Articles use

---

[6] Kambanda claimed, however, that the prosecution had promised him significant sentencing concessions in return for his cooperation. Combs, *supra* note 3, at 92.

[7] *Id.* at 61-62, 92-95.

[8] *See, e.g.*, Patricia Wald, *Reflections on Judging: At Home and Abroad*, 7 U. Pa. J. Const. L. 219, 246 (2004); Geoffrey R. Watson, *The Changing Jurisprudence of the International Criminal Tribunal for the Former Yugoslavia*, 37 New Eng. L. Rev. 871, 882 (2003).

[9] Prosecutor v. Nikolić, Case No. IT-02-60/1-S, Sentencing Judgment, ¶46 & n.86 (Dec. 2, 2003).

[10] ICTR R. P. & Evid. 62bis (May 26-27, 2003).

[11] Anna Petrig, *Negotiated Justice and the Goals of International Criminal Tribunals*, 8 Chi.-Kent J. Int'l & Comp. L. 1, 9-10 (2008).

the term "proceeding on an admission of guilt." Despite the different phrasing, however, the effect is still to allow negotiations between the defendant and the prosecution about the disposition of the case.

As in the ICTY and ICTR, agreements between the parties at the ICC do not bind the court.[12] This provision presents a compromise between the positions of delegations that opposed plea bargaining at the ICC and delegations that would allow such bargaining. In another compromise between these positions, ICC judges were given a greater role than their ICTY and ICTR counterparts in reviewing plea agreements and were entrusted with the responsibility to ensure that victims' interests are not overlooked in plea negotiations. If judges determine "that a more complete presentation of the facts of the case is required in the interests of justice, in particular the interests of the victims," they may order the production of additional evidence, including testimony of victims, and may even order the parties to proceed to trial. The broader powers of judges to reject plea agreements are likely to discourage some defendants and prosecutors from negotiating such agreements. Yet nothing in the ICC Statute prohibits plea agreements, so it is likely that a limited practice of bargaining will develop, as it did at the ICTY and ICTR, where the parties' agreements are also not binding on the courts.

LAW RELATED TO PLEA BARGAINING AT INTERNATIONAL CRIMINAL COURTS

The first rules of procedure at the ICTY provided no guidance on the conditions for validity of guilty pleas. Article 20 of the ICTY Statute contained only a brief reference to guilty pleas. It simply stated that "the Trial Chamber shall read the indictment, satisfy itself that the rights of the accused are respected, confirm that the accused understands the indictment, and instruct the accused to enter a plea. The Trial Chamber shall then set the date for trial." Similarly, Rule 62 provided for the possibility for entering a guilty or not guilty plea, as is common in adversarial procedure. But neither provision elaborated conditions for the validity of a guilty plea. Therefore, it fell to the Appeals Chamber of the ICTY to set out such conditions in the tribunal's first guilty-plea case, *Prosecutor v. Erdemović*, in which the defendant pleaded guilty to murder as a crime against humanity.

[12] Rome Statute of the International Criminal Court, July 17, 1998, art. 65(5), U.N. Doc. A.CONF/183/9 [hereinafter ICC Statute].

Writing a separate opinion in *Erdemović*, Judges Vohrah and McDonald laid out the standard for valid guilty pleas. They observed that no international authority on the validity of a guilty plea existed, so they turned to national authorities "for guidance as to the true meaning of the guilty plea and as to the safeguards for its acceptance."[13] In particular, the judges relied on common-law authority because they found that ICTY rules reflected the common-law concept of a "guilty plea."[14] In recognizing the common-law roots of the guilty plea, they also noted that the adversarial system of the common law recognizes the advantage that guilty pleas provide to the public "in minimising costs, in the saving of court time and in avoiding the inconvenience to many, particularly to witnesses."[15] They stated that the guilty plea should "find a ready place in an international criminal forum such as the International Tribunal confronted by cases which, by their inherent nature, are very complex and necessarily require lengthy hearings if they go to trial under stringent financial constraints arising from allocations made by the United Nations itself dependent upon the contributions of States."[16]

But the court noted that a guilty plea represents a waiver of important fair trial rights of the accused. Because the accused "forfeits his entitlement to be tried, to be considered innocent until proven guilty, to test the Prosecution case by cross-examination of the Prosecution's witnesses and to present his own case . . . certain pre-conditions must be satisfied before a plea of guilty can be entered."[17] The court therefore set out three minimum preconditions for a valid guilty plea:

> (a) The guilty plea must be voluntary. It must be made by an accused who is mentally fit to understand the consequences of pleading guilty and who is not affected by any threats, inducements or promises.
>
> (b) The guilty plea must be informed, that is, the accused must understand the nature of the charges against him and the

---

[13] Prosecutor v. Erdemović, Case No. IT-96-22-A, Joint Separate Opinion of Judge McDonald and Judge Vohrah, ¶6 (Oct. 7, 1997).

[14] The judges also noted that "Rule 62 reflects substantially Rule 15 of the *Suggestions Made by the Government of the United States of America, Rules of Procedure and Evidence for the International Criminal Tribunal for the Prosecution of Persons Responsible for Serious Violations of International Humanitarian Law Committed in the Former Yugoslavia*." *Id.*

[15] *Id.* ¶2.

[16] *Id.*

[17] *Id.* ¶8.

consequences of pleading guilty to them. The accused must know to what he is pleading guilty.

(c) The guilty plea must not be equivocal. It must not be accompanied by words amounting to a defence contradicting an admission of criminal responsibility. . . .[18]

Applying this standard, the Appeals Chamber concluded that Erdemović's plea was voluntary and unequivocal, but not informed.[19] Consider the Chamber's findings below:

Prosecutor v. Erdemović, Case No. IT-96-22-A, Joint Separate Opinion of Judge McDonald and Judge Vohrah, ICTY Appeals Chamber (Oct. 7, 1997)

[. . .] C. Was the Guilty Plea Voluntary?

10. It is a requirement in all common law jurisdictions that a guilty plea be made voluntarily. Voluntariness involves two elements. Firstly, an accused person must have been mentally competent to understand the consequences of his actions when pleading guilty. [. . .]

Secondly, the plea must not have been the result of any threat or inducement other than the expectation of receiving credit for a guilty plea by way of some reduction of sentence. For instance, in *Brady v. United States*, the United States Supreme Court said:

> [A] plea of guilty entered by one fully aware of the direct consequences, including the actual value of any commitments made to him by the court, prosecutor, or his own counsel, must stand unless induced by threats (or promises to discontinue improper harassment), misrepresentation (including unfulfilled or unfulfillable promises), or perhaps by promises that are by their nature improper as having no proper relationship to the prosecutor's business (e.g. bribes).

The court also stated in that case that guilty pleas could not be treated as involuntary simply because they were

> motivated by the defendant's desire to accept the certainty . . . of a lesser penalty rather than . . . [a trial which might result in] conviction and a higher penalty.

---

[18] *Id.*

[19] The Appeals Chamber was unanimous on the point about voluntariness. Two judges (Judge Cassese and Judge Stephen) dissented from the finding of the plea being unequivocal, and one judge (Judge Li) dissented from the finding that the plea was uninformed.

11. In the Sentencing Judgement, the Trial Chamber examined the voluntariness of the guilty plea under the heading "Formal validity" in the following manner. It noted that it had appointed a panel of psychiatric experts to examine the mental condition of the Appellant, presumably due to his disturbed disposition at the initial appearance. Significantly, it was during this first appearance that the Appellant entered his guilty plea.

The relevant question which the Trial Chamber posed to the panel of experts was:

> Does the examination of the subject reveal that he currently suffers from a psychiatric or neuro-psychiatric disorder or from an emotional disturbance which affects his judgement or his volition? If so, please describe it and indicate precisely to which affections it is related. (Psychiatric Report, 24 June 1996, p.1)

The panel of experts concluded in its report dated 24 June 1996 that the Appellant was not fit to stand trial in his "present condition" because he was suffering from

> post-traumatic shock disorder which took the form of depressions accompanied by a feeling of guilt vis-à-vis his behaviour during the war in the former Yugoslavia.

The Trial Chamber then found that the guilty plea of the Appellant was voluntary for two reasons which appear at paragraph 12 of the Sentencing Judgement. Firstly, the Trial Chamber explained that the second psychiatric report submitted on 17 October 1996 indicated that the Appellant's "conscience was clear" and that he showed "no signs of memory impairment." Secondly, the Trial Chamber stressed that the Appellant reaffirmed his plea of guilty on several occasions, the last at the pre-sentencing hearing of 19 and 20 November 1996 at which time the second psychiatric report had declared the Appellant mentally fit to stand trial.

12. We admit to some difficulty with the proposition that the fact that the second psychiatric report showed the Appellant's conscience was clear and that he was free from memory impairment would somehow dispose of the question whether the Appellant was mentally fit to plead guilty, as the Trial Chamber appears to assert at paragraph 12 of the Sentencing Judgement. Indeed, we find persuasive the Prosecution's submission in reply to the third preliminary question that the psychiatric report focused primarily upon the Appellant's fitness to withstand the

rigours of trial and should not form the sole basis of any conclusions that the Appellant was also unfit to plead guilty. However, if there are any doubts remaining about the mental fitness of the Appellant to plead arising from the conclusions of the report, these doubts are allayed by the fact that the Appellant consistently reiterated his plea of guilty, in particular, after the second psychiatric report found him fit to stand trial. To find the Appellant's plea invalid on the ground of his mental incompetence at the initial appearance, when he clearly affirmed his plea after being declared mentally competent, would defy common sense and require the Appellant to endure another round of lengthy procedures at which he would plead no differently, as clearly evidenced by his subsequent affirmations.

13. Apparently, the Trial Chamber also satisfied itself that the plea was not solicited by any threat or inducement by the following exchange at the initial appearance:

> THE PRESIDING JUDGE: Mr. Erdemović, would you rise again? On behalf of my colleagues and on behalf of the Tribunal, I would like to ask you before you decided to plead guilty or not guilty whether you were threatened or promised anything in order to orientate you in one direction rather than another? Were you told, for example, that you must plead guilty, or you have to do this, you must do that? This is a question I must ask you.
>
> THE ACCUSED ERDEMOVIĆ: No, no one threatened me.

Although it appears that the Appellant did not in his reply address the question whether he was promised anything for his plea, in the absence of any suggestion that the plea was improperly solicited, we would find that the Appellant pleaded guilty voluntarily whilst he was mentally competent to comprehend the consequences of his so pleading.

D. Was the Plea Informed?

14. The fact that the Appellant was mentally competent to comprehend the consequences of pleading guilty does not necessarily mean that the plea was "informed." Indeed, all common law jurisdictions insist that an accused who pleads guilty must understand the nature and consequences of his plea and to what precisely he is pleading guilty. [. . .]

In respect of the present case, an informed plea would require that the Appellant understand

(a) the nature of the charges against him and the consequences of pleading guilty generally; and
(b) the nature and distinction between the alternative charges and the consequences of pleading guilty to one rather than the other.

1. Did the Appellant Understand the Nature and Consequences of Pleading Guilty in General?

15. Before asking the Appellant to enter a plea, the Presiding Judge explained the consequences of pleading guilty in the following language:

> THE PRESIDING JUDGE: Are you prepared to plead, given the fact that the Tribunal would like to recall to you that you can plead either guilty or not guilty? This is the procedure which was adopted in this Tribunal with it being understood, of course, that the consequences are not the same. I will explain them to you.
>
> If you plead not guilty, you are entitled to a trial during which, of course, with your lawyer you will contest the charges and the allegations and the charges presented against you by the Prosecutor, as I will remind you. Alternatively, either one or the other violations, crime against humanity or war crime, violations of laws or customs of war.
>
> If you plead guilty, the trial will continue but completely differently, which I am sure you understand but which I have to explain to you. At that point you will have the opportunity during another hearing at a date which we will set at that point in agreement with everybody, you will plead guilty but you will plead under other circumstances, that is, that there were attenuating circumstances, mitigating circumstances, or aggravating circumstances. Then there will be a discussion between your attorney and the Prosecution which will not be the same.
>
> Having explained this to you, the Tribunal must now ask you whether you are prepared to plead and do you plead guilty or not guilty?
>
> THE ACCUSED ERDEMOVIĆ: Your Honour, I have told my counsel that I plead guilty.

We feel unable to hold with any confidence that the Appellant was adequately informed of the consequences of pleading guilty by the explanation offered during the initial hearing. It was not clearly intimated to the Appellant that by pleading guilty, he would lose his right to a trial, to be considered innocent until proven guilty and to assert his innocence and his lack of criminal responsibility for the offences in any way. It was explained to the Appellant that, if he pleaded not guilty he would have to contest the charges, whereas, if he pleaded guilty he would be given the opportunity of explaining the circumstances under which the offence was committed.

16. Moreover, it appears to us that defence counsel consistently advanced arguments contradicting the admission of guilt and criminal responsibility implicit in a guilty plea. If the defence had truly understood the nature of a guilty plea, it would not have persisted in its arguments which were obviously at odds with such a plea. In his closing submissions during the Sentencing Hearing, defence counsel urged that the uncorroborated evidence of the Appellant alone was insufficient to ground a conviction. He argued:

> Erdemović's plea of guilty and the explanation given by his counsel must be confirmed so that a Court can reach an objective and legally acceptable judgement beyond any doubt. My intention was not to challenge Erdemović's plea on his behalf. However, according to the principle in dubio pro reo, certain questions arose yesterday . . . . [I]f there is any shade of doubt in that answer to that question, then the decision of the Court should go in favour of the accused Erdemović, because regardless of his plea of guilty, if his statement is not corroborated, the alleged crime cannot be proved and the criminal responsibility cannot be established.

From his foregoing statement, defence counsel did not seem to appreciate that a guilty plea had finally decided the issue of conviction or acquittal. Defence counsel was apparently advancing arguments asserting insufficiency of evidence to convict the Appellant and urging for an acquittal during a sentencing hearing after the Appellant had pleaded guilty. Indeed, the Trial Chamber did nothing to dissuade defence counsel from this course of action since it merely said that if the Appellant were to plead guilty, "the trial will continue, but completely differently," and that he would have the opportunity to explain attenuating circumstances. This intricate issue as to whether the defence asserted arguments contradicting a guilty plea is dealt with further when we come to consider the question as to whether the Appellant's plea was equivocal or not. However, it is clear to us thus far that the Appellant did not understand the true nature and consequences of making a guilty plea.

2. Did the Appellant Understand the Nature of the Charges Against Him?

17. During the initial appearance of the Appellant, the Presiding Judge questioned defence counsel regarding the Indictment:

> THE PRESIDING JUDGE: . . . First of all, I would like to turn to Mr. Babić: Mr. Babić, have you received a copy of the indictment in a language which you understand and which, of course, the accused understands? . . .
>
> MR. BABIĆ: Yes . . . . We have received the text of the indictment in Serbo-Croatian and both the accused and myself have understood it.
>
> THE PRESIDING JUDGE: . . . Have you deliberated a long time about the contents of this indictment with the accused and explained what defence strategy can be used, which you are going to use with him?
>
> MR. BABIĆ: With my client, I spent some time, several hours, studying the indictment and studying his rights according to the Statute and Rules of the Tribunal. I think that he had enough time to comprehend what he is charged with by this indictment and to understand his rights on that basis.

The Presiding Judge then addressed questions directly to the Appellant regarding the Indictment:

> THE PRESIDING JUDGE: . . . You have heard what your counsel has just said. On behalf of my colleagues and on behalf of the International Tribunal, I would like to ask you the same question, the one that I asked your attorney: Have you read the indictment, have you had the opportunity, have you had the time, to speak about it with Mr. Babić? Have the facts in that indictment been presented to you, have they been presented to you in a language which you understand, that is, Serbo-Croat?
>
> THE ACCUSED ERDEMOVIĆ: Yes, your Honour. Yes.

The Registrar then read the Indictment and the Presiding Judge continued to question the Appellant:

> THE PRESIDING JUDGE: . . . Mr. Erdemović . . . According to what you said before, you understood what is contained in this indictment as well as the charges against you, those charges which the Prosecution has made against you. Have you spoken about these charges with your counsel, Mr. Babić? I am asking you a question now.
>
> THE ACCUSED ERDEMOVIĆ: Yes.

18. The Trial Chamber has by these exchanges established no more than that the Appellant was advised by his counsel regarding the Indictment before he entered his plea, that the Indictment was available to the Appellant in a language he understood, and that the Appellant understood that the Indictment charged him with two offences. There is no indication that the Appellant understood the nature of the charges. Indeed, there is every indication that the Appellant had no idea what a war crime or a crime against humanity was in terms of the legal requirements of either of these two offences. Our conclusion is supported by what seems to have been some misapprehension on the part of defence counsel himself as to the nature of the charges. [. . .]

Defence counsel's statements would indicate a lack of understanding of the offence of a war crime. We, therefore, hold that the Appellant did not understand the nature of the charges he was facing nor the charge to which he pleaded guilty. Although the Appellant did repeat his plea of guilty on several occasions, he remained on each of these occasions, and probably even to this day, ignorant of the true nature of each of the two charges against him, as it was never adequately explained to him either by the Trial Chamber or by defence counsel.

3. Did the Appellant Comprehend the Distinction Between the Alternative Charges and the Consequences of Pleading Guilty to One Rather Than the Other?

19. It is the answer to this question which, in our view, determines decisively the issue of the validity of the Appellant's guilty plea. Upon the Appellant entering his plea of guilty during the initial hearing, the Presiding Judge of the Trial Chamber asked the Appellant to specify to which count he was pleading guilty:

> THE PRESIDING JUDGE: If you plead guilty, I must also ask you another question. You heard that in the indictment which was drafted by the Office of the Prosecution against you, it provides for a charge which may be one or the other, that [is,] either a crime

against humanity or a violation of the laws or customs of war. The text of our Statute obliges me to ask you whether you are pleading guilty on one of the charges, that is, there are facts, they were read to you, the Tribunal understands that you accept these facts and that they have been classified in a certain way legally.

This is part of international law. It is a bit difficult for you, but I will try to explain it to you in a more simple fashion, that is, there are acts and these are the acts which you have just recognised that, yes, you were at Srebrenica at such and such a moment. I think that the Prosecutor will make things very clear for us. The Prosecutor classifies them, which means that it determines a certain number of conditions from which a criminal violation has been charged. At the stage that we are now in these proceedings, which is at the beginning, the proceedings against you, Mr. Erdemović, given the facts as they are today, that is, the fact that you have recognised what happened, that you were present, the various acts could either be classified as a crime against humanity or what we call violations of the laws or customs of war.

Having said this, if there had been a trial, after the Tribunal would decide what, in fact, you were guilty or not guilty of. In this case, since you have just said that you are pleading guilty, I must ask you if you are pleading guilty to the crime against humanity, that is, the version of the facts which for the Prosecutor would be a crime against humanity, or if it is a violation of the laws or customs of war. I suppose you have spoken about this with your attorney?

Mr. Erdemović, could you answer us on that point which is an important one?

THE ACCUSED ERDEMOVIĆ: I plead guilty for point one, crime against humanity.

With respect, the difference between a crime against humanity and a war crime was not adequately explained to the Appellant by the Trial Chamber at the initial hearing nor was there any attempt to explain the difference to him at any later occasion when the Appellant reaffirmed his plea. The Presiding Judge appears to assume that the Appellant had been advised by his counsel as to the distinction between the charges and that the Prosecution "will make things very clear." From the passage of the transcript previously quoted, it is apparent that defence counsel himself did not appreciate either the true nature of the offences at international law or the true legal distinction between them. It is also clear on the record that the difference between the charges was never made clear by either the Prosecution or by the Presiding Judge.

We have, accordingly, no doubt that the misapprehension regarding the true distinction between the two alternative charges led the Appellant to plead guilty to the more serious of the two charges, that is, the charge alleging the crime against humanity.

(a) Crimes Against Humanity Intrinsically More Serious Than War Crimes

[. . .] 26. [. . .] As has been noted, there is nothing on the record to show that anyone, either defence counsel or the Trial Chamber, had explained to the Appellant that a crime against humanity is a more serious crime and that if he had pleaded guilty to the alternative charge of a war crime he could expect a correspondingly lighter punishment. In light of this, it would not surprise us that the Appellant remains to this day in ignorance of the fact that he could have pleaded guilty to the charge of a war crime under Article 3 of the Statute, that, contrary to the advice of his counsel, a war crime can be committed against a civilian, and that he could accordingly have expected to receive a lighter sentence for this crime. It seems to us that the Appellant reaffirmed his plea solely because he wished to avoid having to undergo a full trial. Had he been properly apprised of the less serious charge and his entitlement to plead to it, we have grave doubts that he would have continued to plead guilty to the more serious charge.

27. We, therefore, hold that the Appellant's plea was not the result of an informed choice. He understood neither the nature of the charges nor the distinction between the two alternative charges and the consequences of pleading guilty to one rather than the other. It thus follows that the Appellant must be afforded an opportunity to replead to the charges with full knowledge of these matters.

E. Was the Plea Equivocal?

28. The question as to whether the Appellant's plea was equivocal or not was examined by the Trial Chamber in the Sentencing Judgement and addressed in the first two of the three preliminary questions put to the parties by the Appeals Chamber in its Scheduling Order of 5 May 1997. For convenience, these two interrelated questions are hereunder re-stated:

(1) In law, may duress afford a complete defence to a charge of crimes against humanity and/or war crimes such that, if the defence is proved at trial, the accused is entitled to an acquittal?

(2) If the answer to (1) is in the affirmative, was the guilty plea entered by the accused at his initial appearance equivocal in that the accused, while pleading guilty, invoked duress?

As is obvious from the formulation of these two preliminary questions, whether the Appellant's plea was, in this case, equivocal depends upon whether duress is a complete defence. We would turn firstly, however, to a consideration of the meaning of the "equivocal" plea.

29. The requirement that a plea must be unequivocal is essential to uphold the presumption of innocence and to provide protection to an accused against forfeiture of the right to a trial where the accused appears to have a defence which he may not realise. This requirement imposes upon the court in a situation where the accused pleads guilty but persists with an explanation of his actions which in law amounts to a defence, to reject the plea and have the defence tested at trial. The courts in common law jurisdictions all over the world, except in the United States, have consistently declared that a guilty plea must be unequivocal. It would appear that in the United States the constitutional right to plead as one chooses outweighs any requirement that a defence be tested on the merits at trial. The validity of a guilty plea turns primarily on the voluntariness of the plea, that it is informed, and that it has a factual basis. If a United States court is satisfied that these conditions are fulfilled, apparently, it will be more willing than courts of other common law jurisdictions to accept a prima facie equivocal plea in recognition of pragmatic considerations relating to the practicality and the reality of plea-bargaining whereby credit is given for pleading guilty by reduction of sentence.

30. It is appropriate at this stage to consider certain strictures emanating from other common law systems for the requirement of an unequivocal guilty plea. Chang Min Tat J. said in *PP v. Cheah Chooi Chuan* that "it is a cardinal principal that any plea of guilty must be completely unreserved, unqualified and unequivocal." The Supreme Court of Malaysia in *Lee Weng Tuck & Anor v. PP* observed: "It is . . . settled practice that where the plea of guilty is equivocal, i.e. where it is not clear, or is doubtful or qualified, the plea must in law be treated as one of not guilty and the court shall proceed to try the case . . . ."

Further, in England it is stated in Blackstone's Criminal Practice that

> [i]f an accused person purports to enter a plea of guilty but, either at the time he pleads or subsequently in mitigation, qualifies it with words that suggest he may have a defence . . . then the court must not proceed to sentence on the basis of the plea but should explain the relevant law

and seek to ascertain whether he genuinely intends to plead guilty. If the plea cannot be clarified, the court should order a not-guilty plea be entered on the accused's behalf.

31. Whether a plea of guilty is equivocal must depend on a consideration, in limine, of the question whether the plea was accompanied or qualified by words describing facts which establish a defence in law. The Appellant pleaded guilty but claimed that he acted under duress. It follows therefore that we must now examine whether duress can constitute a complete defence to the killing of innocent persons.

A majority of the Appeals Chamber, Judges McDonald, Vohrah, and Li, concluded that duress does not afford a complete defense to a soldier charged with a crime against humanity or a war crime involving a killing of innocents. Consequently, it found that the guilty plea of the Appellant was not equivocal. Judges Cassese and Stephen dissented from this view of duress.

Notes and Questions:

1. After reviewing Erdemović's plea hearing, the Appeals Chamber concluded that the hearing fell short of ensuring that his guilty plea was informed. In what ways was the plea hearing inadequate? Would appropriate advice by Erdemović's counsel been sufficient to make Erdemović's plea informed, or was it also necessary that the court provide certain information to the accused before allowing the guilty plea? Would the plea hearing have been considered adequate under Rule 11 of the Federal Rules of Criminal Procedure?
2. What remedy did the Appeals Chamber order for the deficiency in plea colloquy, and was this remedy adequate in your view?
3. The Appeals Chamber imposed a requirement that the guilty plea be unequivocal in order to be valid. What does this requirement mean? Is the Chamber correct in stating that the requirement does not exist in the U.S. criminal justice system? What is the relationship between the requirement that a guilty plea be unequivocal and the requirement that it rest on a factual basis? Does the standard laid out by the Appeals Chamber ensure sufficiently that a conviction resting on a guilty plea will adequately reflect the facts?

The *Erdemović* requirements for valid guilty pleas were later incorporated into the ICTY and ICTR Rules of Procedure and Evidence.[20] Additional amendments clarified the status of plea agreements as well. Importantly, the Rules added a requirement that the guilty plea must rest on a sufficient factual basis to be accepted. Consider the most recent version of the rules:

ICTY Rules of Procedure and Evidence

Rule 62 bis

Guilty Pleas
(Adopted 12 Nov 1997)

If an accused pleads guilty in accordance with Rule 6 (vi), or requests to change his or her plea to guilty and the Trial Chamber is satisfied that:

(i) the guilty plea has been made voluntarily;
(ii) the guilty plea is informed;
(Amended 17 Nov 1999)
(iii) the guilty plea is not equivocal; and
(iv) there is a sufficient factual basis for the crime and the accused's participation in it, either on the basis of independent indicia or on lack of any material disagreement between the parties about the facts of the case,

the Trial Chamber may enter a finding of guilt and instruct the Registrar to set a date for the sentencing hearing. (Amended 10 July 1998, amended 4 Dec 1998)

Rule 62 ter

Plea Agreement Procedure
(Adopted 13 Dec 2001)

(A) The Prosecutor and the defence may agree that, upon the accused entering a plea of guilty to the indictment or to one or more counts of the indictment, the Prosecutor shall do one or more of the following before the Trial Chamber:

[20] ICTY R. P. & Evid. 62bis (Dec. 4, 1998); ICTR R. P. & Evid. 62(B)(iii) (July 1, 1999); Combs, *supra* note 3, at 58.

(i) apply to amend the indictment accordingly;
(ii) submit that a specific sentence or sentencing range is appropriate;
(iii) not oppose a request by the accused for a particular sentence or sentencing range.

(B) The Trial Chamber shall not be bound by any agreement specified in paragraph (A).

(C) If a plea agreement has been reached by the parties, the Trial Chamber shall require the disclosure of the agreement in open session or, on a showing of good cause, in closed session, at the time the accused pleads guilty in accordance with Rule 62(vi), or requests to change his or her plea to guilty.

Rule 101

Penalties

[. . .] (B) In determining the sentence, the Trial Chamber shall take into account the factors mentioned in Article 24, paragraph 2, of the Statute, as well as such factors as:

[. . .]

(ii) any mitigating circumstances including the substantial cooperation with the Prosecutor by the convicted person before or after conviction; [. . .][21]

ICTR Rules of Procedure and Evidence

Rule 62

Initial Appearance of Accused and Plea

[. . .] (B) If an accused pleads guilty in accordance with Rule 62(A)(v), or requests to change his plea to guilty, the Trial Chamber shall satisfy itself that the guilty plea:

(i) is made freely and voluntarily;
(ii) is an informed plea;
(iii) is unequivocal; and
(iv) is based on sufficient facts for the crime and accused's participation in it, either on the basis of objective indicia or of lack

[21] Rule 101(B)(ii) of the ICTR Rules of Procedure and Evidence is identical.

of any material disagreement between the parties about the facts of the case.

Thereafter the Trial Chamber may enter a finding of guilt and instruct the Registrar to set a date for the sentencing hearing.

Rule 62 bis

Plea Agreement Procedure

(A) The Prosecutor and the Defence may agree that, upon the accused entering a plea of guilty to the indictment or to one or more counts of the indictment, the Prosecutor shall do one or more of the following before the Trial Chamber:

(i) apply to amend the indictment accordingly;
(ii) submit that a specific sentence or sentencing range is appropriate;
(iii) not oppose a request by the accused for a particular sentence or sentencing range.

(B) The Trial Chamber shall not be bound by any agreement specified in paragraph (A).

(C) If a plea agreement has been reached by the parties, the Trial Chamber shall require the disclosure of the agreement in open session or, on a showing of good cause, in closed session, at the time the accused pleads guilty in accordance with Rule 62(A)(v), or requests to change his or her plea to guilty.

Compare the Rules of the ICTY and ICTR on guilty pleas to the ICC Statute and Rules on admissions of guilt.

Rome Statute of the International Criminal Court

Article 65, Proceedings on an admission of guilt

1. Where the accused makes an admission of guilt pursuant to article 64, paragraph 8 (a), the Trial Chamber shall determine whether:

(a) The accused understands the nature and consequences of the admission of guilt;

(b) The admission is voluntarily made by the accused after sufficient consultation with defence counsel; and

(c) The admission of guilt is supported by the facts of the case that are contained in:

(i) The charges brought by the Prosecutor and admitted by the accused;

(ii) Any materials presented by the Prosecutor which supplement the charges and which the accused accepts; and

(iii) Any other evidence, such as the testimony of witnesses, presented by the Prosecutor or the accused.

2. Where the Trial Chamber is satisfied that the matters referred to in paragraph 1 are established, it shall consider the admission of guilt, together with any additional evidence presented, as establishing all the essential facts that are required to prove the crime to which the admission of guilt relates, and may convict the accused of that crime.

3. Where the Trial Chamber is not satisfied that the matters referred to in paragraph 1 are established, it shall consider the admission of guilt as not having been made, in which case it shall order that the trial be continued under the ordinary trial procedures provided by this Statute and may remit the case to another Trial Chamber.

4. Where the Trial Chamber is of the opinion that a more complete presentation of the facts of the case is required in the interests of justice, in particular the interests of the victims, the Trial Chamber may:

(a) Request the Prosecutor to present additional evidence, including the testimony of witnesses; or

(b) Order that the trial be continued under the ordinary trial procedures provided by this Statute, in which case it shall consider the admission of guilt as not having been made and may remit the case to another Trial Chamber.

5. Any discussions between the Prosecutor and the defence regarding modification of the charges, the admission of guilt or the penalty to be imposed shall not be binding on the Court.

ICC Rules of Procedure and Evidence

Rule 139, Decision on admission of guilt

1. After having proceeded in accordance with article 65, paragraph 1, the Trial Chamber, in order to decide whether to proceed in accordance with article 65, paragraph 4, may invite the views of the Prosecutor and the defence.

2. The Trial Chamber shall then make its decision on the admission of guilt and shall give reasons for this decision, which shall be placed on the record.

Notes and Questions:

1. What are the main differences between the ICTY/ICTR Rules on guilty pleas and the ICC provisions on admissions of guilt? How do the responsibilities of the court differ in the two regimes? How does the position of the victim differ? Is the difference in the terms used for the procedures—"admission of guilt" versus a "guilty plea"—important? What do you think accounts for all these differences?

PRACTICE OF PLEA BARGAINING AT INTERNATIONAL CRIMINAL COURTS

PARTICIPANTS

As in the United States, plea negotiations at the international criminal tribunals involve only the prosecutor and the defense.[22] There is no prohibition on participation by judges or victims, but in practice, they are not involved.

Although judges are absent from the negotiations, they do play an important role in reviewing the validity of the guilty plea and the plea agreement. First, in a public hearing, a panel of three judges examines the defendant and any evidence related to the case to ensure that the guilty plea is voluntary, informed, unequivocal, and based on the facts of the case. Second, the judges evaluate the agreement. They are not bound by it and may reject any or all of its terms if they believe that it does not further the interests of justice.[23] As the *Nikolić* Trial Chamber explained: "A trial chamber may inquire into the terms of the agreement to ensure that neither party was unfairly treated and particularly that the rights of the accused are respected."[24] Judges may also inquire into the agreement to ensure that it respects victims' interests. ICTY and ICTR judges have in several cases refused to follow the prosecu-

---

[22] Typically, plea discussions are between the defense and the prosecution, but they do occasionally involve the defendant. *See, e.g.*, Prosecutor v. Kunarac, Case No. IT-96-23, Transcript, at 27 (Mar. 13, 1998).

[23] ICTY R. P. & Evid. 62ter(B); ICTR R. P. & Evid. 62bis(B). For an argument that the rules should be amended to make plea agreements binding on the court, except when they are fraudulent or unconscionable, see Thomas W. Pittman, *Making the Case for Binding Plea Agreements at the ICTY*, 3 J. Int'l L. Peace & Armed Conflict 155 (2007).

[24] Prosecutor v. Nikolić, Case No. IT-02-60/1-S, Sentencing Judgment, ¶43 (Dec. 2, 2003).

tor's sentencing recommendations under a plea agreement based upon a determination that these recommendations were too lenient.

At the International Criminal Court, judges may be even more involved in the proceedings on admission of guilt. The ICC Statute gives them greater powers to review agreements between the parties. Under Article 65, "[w]here the Trial Chamber is of the opinion that a more complete presentation of the facts of the case is required in the interests of justice, in particular the interests of the victims," it may order additional evidence-taking or the continuation of trial under ordinary procedures.[25] In addition, as is true for the ICTY and ICTR, prosecutorial commitments to a certain penalty or charges do not bind the court. This vests the court with significant power to review and reject charge bargains—a power available to judges in the German, but not the American system. The ICC has not yet received an admission of guilt, so all of these rules are yet to be tested in practice.

At the ICTY and ICTR, victims are not involved in the plea negotiations, and their interests are not directly represented at that stage. Under the Rules, they may be called to testify at the sentencing hearing following a guilty plea. Because the court is not bound by the plea agreement, victims' statements at sentencing could influence the court's decision whether to accept the sentence agreed upon by the parties. As mentioned earlier, ICTY chambers have rejected plea agreements for being too lenient and therefore not in the interests of justice.[26] But although victims may have this potential source of influence in theory, in practice, they have rarely been given the opportunity to testify at sentencing after a guilty plea.[27] As a result, their actual influence on plea bargaining outcomes appears to have been minimal.

The ICC Statute appears to offer greater opportunities for victims' views to be represented in plea bargaining. It does so in two principal ways. First, as mentioned above, ICC judges are charged with ensuring that agreements between the parties offer a complete presentation of the facts in respect of victims' interests.[28] Judges may therefore order additional testimony, including victims' testimony, to ensure that an agreement

---

[25] ICC Statute, *supra* note 12, art. 65(4).

[26] *Nikolić*, Case No. IT-02-60/1-S, ¶81 n.124; Prosecutor v. Babić, Sentencing Judgment, Case No. IT-03-72-S, ¶101 (June 29, 2004); Prosecutor v. Nikolić, Case No. IT-94-2-S, Sentencing Judgment, ¶230 (Dec. 18, 2003).

[27] No victims had testified at ICTR sentencing hearings until 2007, and "no victim testified at nine of the last eleven sentencing hearings for ICTY defendants who pled guilty." Combs, *supra* note 3, at 191, 202.

[28] ICC Statute, *supra* note 12, art. 65(4).

furthers the interests of justice and the interests of victims. Second, Article 68(3) of the ICC Statute specifically provides that "[w]here the personal interests of victims are affected, the Court shall permit their views and concerns to be presented and considered at stages of the proceedings determined to be appropriate by the Court and in a manner which is not prejudicial to or inconsistent with the rights of the accused and a fair and impartial trial." In recent decisions, ICC pretrial chambers have affirmed victims' ability to present their views to the court, through legal representatives if they so choose, at the pretrial stage. Rule 93 of the ICC Rules of Procedure and Evidence also suggests that the court "may seek the views of victims or their legal representatives" in relation to its decision on admission of guilt. It is likely, therefore, that the ICC will also allow victims to participate in some fashion in plea and sentencing hearings, as long as such involvement is not "prejudicial to or inconsistent with the rights of the accused and a fair and impartial trial."[29]

TIMING

Plea bargains at the ICTY and ICTR may be reached either before or after the charges are filed. Typically, plea bargains occur before trial, but it is possible to reach an agreement during trial.[30] As in the United States, prosecutors typically prefer to make bargains as early in the process as possible, in the interest of saving time and resources. The chambers also appear to offer smaller sentencing rewards to those who plead guilty long after charges against them have been filed.[31]

SUBJECT MATTER

Both charge and sentence bargaining have been used at the international criminal tribunals. As part of the negotiations, the prosecution may agree "to withdraw certain charges or drop certain factual allegations"[32]

---

[29] *Id.* art. 68(3).

[30] *E.g.*, Prosecutor v. Simić, Case No. IT-95-9/2-S, Sentencing Judgment (Oct. 17, 2002); Prosecutor v. Sikirica, Case No. IT-95-8-S, Sentencing Judgment (Nov. 13, 2001).

[31] *E.g.*, Combs, *supra* note 3, at 72; *see also* Prosecutor v. Nikolić, Case No. IT- 02-60/1, Judgment on Sentencing Appeal, ¶¶126-28 (Mar. 8, 2006) (noting that while the timing of the guilty plea cannot be considered an aggravating circumstance at sentencing, it can be considered in assessing the extent to which the guilty plea was motivated by remorse, as opposed to self-interest).

[32] Prosecutor v. Nikolić, Case No. IT-02-60/1-S, Sentencing Judgment ¶48 (Dec. 2, 2003).

and to recommend a particular sentence, a sentencing cap, or a sentencing range. The discretion of the prosecutor to bargain away charges after they have been confirmed by the court is somewhat more limited than that of American prosecutors, but not quite as limited as that of German prosecutors. As the *Momir Nikolić* Trial Chamber explained:

> In the event that the Prosecution seeks to amend the indictment after its confirmation [by a pre-trial chamber] and the assignment of the case to a trial chamber, it must seek leave of the trial chamber pursuant to Rule 50. Such leave is necessary also in cases where the Prosecution seeks to withdraw certain charges following a plea agreement. After hearing the parties, the trial chamber will determine whether to grant the Prosecution's request. In cases of plea agreements where the Prosecution has expressed its intention not to proceed to trial on certain charges, such motions are generally granted; a trial chamber may seek to satisfy itself that the remaining charges reflect the totality of the criminal conduct of the accused.[33]

The *Nikolić* Chamber thus urged the prosecutor to exercise "extreme caution" when agreeing to dismiss or modify charges and suggested that it would reject an agreement that does not adequately reflect "the totality of an individual's criminal conduct" and "the gravity of the offences committed by the accused."[34]

In addition to charging and sentencing concessions, the prosecutor may be able to offer other benefits to the defendant. Prosecutors may offer to recommend a favorable location of imprisonment—this is often sought after by defendants, especially at the ICTR, because the conditions of imprisonment between different locations may be significant. The prosecution may also offer to arrange for protective measures for the defendant's family, particularly when a defendant cooperates with the prosecution. Finally, defendants may plead guilty to avoid referral of their cases to local courts (in the former Yugoslavia or Rwanda), which many defendants perceive to be more likely to convict and possibly to impose harsher sentences.[35]

In exchange for such concessions by the prosecutor, "the accused agrees to waive many of the rights guaranteed to him or her under the Statute and recognized as fundamental rights in human rights law,"

---

[33] *Id.* ¶50.

[34] *Id.* ¶65.

[35] *E.g.*, Prosecutor v. Bralo, Case No. IT-95-17-A, Judgment on Sentencing Appeal (Apr. 2, 2007); Prosecutor v. Zelenović, Case No. IT-96-23/2-S, Decision on Prosecution's Motion to Withdraw the Motion Under Rule 11 Bis (May 8, 2007).

including the right to be presumed innocent, the right to cross-examine adverse witnesses and put on a defense, and the right not to incriminate himself.[36] Defendants, as well as prosecutors, may also waive their right to appeal a sentence imposed within the range agreed upon by the parties.[37] Frequently, defendants also agree to cooperate with the prosecution in providing information and testifying against other accuseds.

Cooperation Agreements. Both the ICTR and ICTY Rules of Procedure provide that, in determining the sentence, chambers should consider in mitigation "the substantial cooperation with the Prosecutor by the convicted person before or after conviction."[38] The trial chamber has the ultimate discretion in deciding whether the defendant has substantially cooperated with the prosecution,[39] although it is encouraged to rely on the prosecution's assessment of the quality and quantity of cooperation. As the Momir Nikolić Appeals Chamber explained, "the Trial Chamber should take into account the Prosecution's assessment of this co-operation because, as noted above, the Prosecution is in a favourable position to make an assessment of it. Moreover, considering that the Trial Chamber has a general obligation to set out a reasoned opinion [. . .], if the Trial Chamber disagrees with the Prosecution's assessment of the accused's co-operation, it has a duty to provide sufficient reasons for not following the Prosecution's assessment."[40] In practice, "in the absence of any information to the contrary," the trial chambers will rely on the prosecution's assessment of the defendant's degree of cooperation.[41] Substantial cooperation can include prior testimony on behalf of the prosecution, the provision of new information helpful to the prosecution, substantiation and corroboration of existing information,

[36] *Nikolić*, Case No. IT-02-60/1-S, ¶48.

[37] Prosecutor v. Sikirica, Case No. IT-95-8-T, Sentencing Judgment, ¶¶17, 25, 31 (Nov. 13, 2001) (noting that the parties had agreed not to appeal a sentence within a set range).

[38] ICTY R. P. & Evid. 101(B)(ii); ICTR R. P. & Evid. 101(B)(ii).

[39] Prosecutor v. Jelisić, Case No. IT-95-10-A, Appeal Judgement, ¶126 (July 5, 2001) (noting that "the determination of whether the cooperation should be considered as substantial and therefore whether it constitutes a mitigating factor is for the Trial Chamber to determine").

[40] Prosecutor v. Nikolić, Case No. IT-02-60/1-A, Judgment on Sentencing Appeal, ¶96 (Mar. 8, 2006).

[41] Prosecutor v. Česić, Case No. IT-95-10/1-S, Sentencing Judgment, ¶62 (Mar. 11, 2004); Prosecutor v. Deronjić, Case No. IT-02-61-S, Sentencing Judgment ¶¶244-245 (Mar. 30, 2004).

and even voluntary surrender to the tribunal.[42] As in the United States, cooperation with the prosecution brings to defendants more significant benefits than a guilty plea alone.[43]

Notes and Questions:

1. As discussed in earlier chapters, some U.S. jurisdictions and a number of civil-law jurisdictions prohibit plea bargaining for serious violent crimes. What might be the reason for such prohibitions? Given that the jurisdiction of international criminal courts covers only very serious violent crimes, should plea bargaining be outlawed altogether at these courts? Should someone charged with genocide or crimes against humanity be allowed to plead to a lesser charge or receive a lesser sentence in return for his guilty plea? Should prosecutors be allowed to bargain away certain facts of the crimes? Should there be any limits on the concessions that can be exchanged between the prosecution and the defense?
2. Judges at the international criminal courts have broad discretion in choosing what punishment to impose. The statutes and rules provide little guidance and few limits on judicial discretion with respect to sentencing. The maximum punishment is life imprisonment; the death penalty is not authorized. At the ICTY and ICTR, judges must consider the gravity of the offense, individual circumstances relevant to sentencing, aggravating and mitigating factors, and the general sentencing practices in the courts of the former Yugoslavia and Rwanda. The statute and rules list no aggravating factors, and the only mitigating factor listed is substantial cooperation with the prosecution. The ICC Statute similarly fails to provide any significant guidance on sentencing.

   Because judges have almost boundless sentencing discretion, charge bargaining by the prosecution is rarely effective. Judges can impose the same punishment, whether the accused is charged with both crimes against humanity and war crimes, or just crimes against humanity, for the same conduct. As is generally the case in civil-law countries, charge bargaining at the international tribunals would be effective only if the parties engage in "fact bargaining" as well—that is, if the prosecutor agrees to limit the facts forming

---

[42] *Deronjić*, Case No. IT-02-61-S, ¶¶242-255; Prosecutor v. Blagojević, Case No. IT-02-60-A, Appeals Judgment, ¶344 (May 9, 2007) (holding that although voluntary surrender is not direct cooperation with the prosecution, it is cooperation with the Tribunal and could be considered in mitigation).

[43] *E.g.*, *Deronjić*, Case No. IT-02-61-S.

the basis of the accusation.[44] Fact bargaining has occurred at the tribunals, but it is still relatively rare and very controversial.[45]

In your opinion, does the limitation on charge bargaining and the broad sentencing discretion by judges make plea bargaining more acceptable or less acceptable at international courts?

3. Another consequence of the broad sentencing discretion of judges is that it is unclear what discount, if any, a guilty plea warrants. Chambers have considered guilty pleas in mitigation, and, on average, defendants who have pleaded guilty have received lower sentences than those who have opted for trial. Ralph Henham and Mark Drumbl report that, as of late 2004, the mean and median sentences for ICTY defendants convicted following a trial were 16.4 and 17 years, respectively (the data excludes the ICTY's single life sentence).[46] By contrast, the mean and median sentences for those who have entered guilty pleas are 13.8 and 11 years.[47] But guilty pleas have typically been accompanied by statements of remorse and cooperation with the prosecution by the defendants. It is therefore unclear to what extent a guilty plea contributes to a sentencing reduction independently of these other mitigating factors.[48]

   Should a guilty plea in international crimes cases warrant a sentencing reduction independently of any remorse expressed by the defendant or cooperation with the prosecution? Why or why not?

CONDITIONS FOR VALIDITY OF A GUILTY PLEA

VOLUNTARINESS AND KNOWLEDGE

In determining whether a guilty plea is voluntary, international criminal courts will examine whether the defendant is mentally competent to understand the consequences of his actions and whether he was threatened or improperly induced into pleading guilty.[49] The test is very simi-

---

[44] Nancy Amoury Combs, *Procuring Guilty Pleas for International Crimes: The Limited Influence of Sentence Discounts*, 59 Vand. L. Rev. 69, 79 (2006).

[45] *Id.*

[46] Ralph Henham & Mark Drumbl, *Plea Bargaining at the International Criminal Tribunal for the Former Yugoslavia*, 16 Crim. L.F. 49, 53-54 (2005).

[47] *Id.* at 54.

[48] *Id.* at 59-62.

[49] As the *Erdemović* Appeals Chamber explained, the plea "must not have been the result of any threat or inducement other than the expectation of receiving credit for a guilty

lar to that established by the U.S. Supreme Court in *Brady v. United States*,[50] which the ICTY cited when developing the test. In *Kambanda v. Prosecutor*, the ICTR Appeals Chamber held that a plea was not involuntary merely because the defendant was "detained and questioned in an unofficial place of detention and during this detention signed the plea agreement while being deprived of chosen counsel."[51] Similarly, the *Erdemović* Appeals Chamber held that, although one psychiatric report had found the defendant unfit to stand trial, this was not sufficient to render the guilty plea involuntary. The Appeals Chamber explained that (1) the psychiatric report "focused primarily upon the [defendant]'s fitness to withstand the rigours of trial and should not form the sole basis of any conclusions that the Appellant was also unfit to plead guilty"; (2) a second psychiatric report found the defendant competent to stand trial; and (3) the Appellant "consistently reiterated his plea of guilty."[52]

In deciding whether a guilty plea is informed, the court will inquire into the defendant's understanding of the nature of the charges to which he is pleading guilty and his awareness of the consequences of the guilty plea. As part of this decision, the court "may inquire into the accused's understanding of the elements of the crime or crimes to which he has pled guilty to ensure that his understanding of the requirements of the crime reflects his actual conduct and participation as well as his state of mind or intent when he committed the crime."[53] In addition, the court must ensure that the defendant understands the rights he is waiving by pleading guilty. Arguably, the court must also inform the defendant of the maximum sentence he may receive, but courts have not done so consistently.[54] Where alternative charges have been preferred against the defendant, the trial chamber must ensure that the defendant understands "the nature and distinction between the alternative charges and the consequences of pleading guilty to one rather than the other."[55] If the chamber

---

plea by way of some reduction of sentences." Prosecutor v. Erdemović, Case No. IT-96-22, Joint Separate Opinion of Judge McDonald and Judge Vohrah, ¶10 (Oct. 7, 1997).

[50] 397 U.S. 742, 755 (1970).

[51] Prosecutor v. Kambanda, Case No. ICTR 97-23-A, Judgment, ¶¶57, 64 (Oct. 19, 2000).

[52] *Erdemović*, Case. No. IT-96-22, ¶12.

[53] Prosecutor v. Nikolić, Case No. IT-02-60/1-S, Sentencing Judgment, ¶12 (Dec. 2, 2003).

[54] *See* Julian A. Cook, III, *Plea Bargaining at The Hague*, 30 Yale J. Int'l L. 473 (2005) (criticizing ICTY plea colloquy procedures as inadequate and arguing that judges ought to ask more questions and provide more information to defendants to ensure that guilty pleas are voluntary and knowing).

[55] *Erdemović*, Case No. IT-96-22, ¶14.

fails to ensure that the defendant understands the nature of the charges and appreciates the difference between alternative charges, the plea will be invalidated and the defendant will be allowed to plead anew.[56]

LACK OF EQUIVOCATION AND FACTUAL BASIS

The requirements that a guilty plea must be unequivocal and factually based are both intended to protect innocent defendants from pleading guilty. Under the first requirement—that a guilty plea be unequivocal—the court must reject a plea when the defendant pleads guilty but persists with an explanation of his actions that amounts to a legal defense. The requirement exists at the ICTY and ICTR, but not the ICC. In determining whether a plea is equivocal, "a trial chamber may question the defence as to its intention to raise any defences."[57] If a defendant invokes a valid defense, the court will enter a "not guilty" plea and order the parties to proceed to trial.

In reviewing the factual basis of a guilty plea, chambers help ensure that the following objectives of the international tribunals are met: (1) that the defendant is pleading to conduct of which he is in fact guilty; and (2) that the charges to which he pleads reflect the totality of his conduct and help establish an accurate historical record of the crimes.[58] The international tribunals have not specified the quantum of proof required to establish a factual basis for a guilty plea. But trial chambers "have increasingly required the submission of statements and documents that support both the acknowledgement of guilt by the accused and the indictment to which he pleaded guilty."[59] It is common practice for the prosecution to submit a document laying out the factual basis for the plea together with the plea agreement between the parties.

WITHDRAWAL OF A GUILTY PLEA AND BREACH OF A PLEA AGREEMENT

The rules of the international tribunals and the ICC do not regulate the procedure following a withdrawal of a guilty plea or a breach

---

[56] *Id.* ¶27.

[57] *Nikolić*, Case No. IT-02-60/1-S, ¶52.

[58] *Id.*

[59] Alan Tieger & Milbert Shin, *Plea Agreements in the ICTY: Purpose, Effects, and Propriety*, 3 J. Int'l Crim. Just. 666, 671 (2005) (citing Prosecutor v. Mrdja, Case No. IT-02-59-S, Sentencing Judgment (Mar. 31, 2004)).

of a plea agreement.[60] The case law also generally fails to address these issues, as they have not arisen before these courts.[61]

It is possible to speculate, however, as Mirjan Damaška does, that the approach to withdrawal and breach will depend on whether the courts view plea bargaining from a more inquisitorial or adversarial perspective. Thus, "when the admission is treated on the analogy to the guilty plea, it resembles a contract and its withdrawal can easily be justified in the contractual mode: one side has performed while the other has not. But the closer an admission comes to a confession, the more difficult it becomes to withdraw or disregard it, because it is in the nature of reliable incriminating evidence."[62] As previous chapters discussed, inquisitorial systems such as Germany's until very recently provided no protection to defendants who wanted to withdraw their admissions of guilt after the court had rejected the terms of their bargain. If international courts adopt a similar approach, withdrawals would be more problematic for defendants at these courts than they are for defendants in adversarial systems.[63] Under this approach, a defendant would not be able to withdraw a guilty plea because courts would treat the plea as an admission of guilt that has important evidentiary value. At the same time, courts would want to deter serious prosecutorial breaches that

---

[60] The ICC Statute does have two provisions relevant to admissions of guilt rejected by the court as invalid. If the court rejects an admission of guilt as invalid or requiring further presentation of facts, it must consider the admission of guilt as not having been made. Further, the court "may remit the case to another Trial Chamber." ICC Statute, *supra* note 12, arts. 65(3), 65(4)(b). These provisions do not, however, address whether a defendant may withdraw an admission of guilt when the court rejects the agreement between the parties or under any other circumstances.

[61] In *Kambanda v. Prosecutor*, the ICTR Appeals Chamber suggested in passing that a defendant could not withdraw his guilty plea after sentencing. Kambanda v. Prosecutor, Case No. ICTR 97-23-S, Appeals Judgment, ¶55 (Oct. 19, 2000). In *Prosecutor v. Kunarac*, the defendant withdrew his plea during the plea hearing, after he was adequately informed about the nature of the charges against him. Prosecutor v. Kunarac, Case No. IT-96-23, ¶892 (Feb. 22, 2001). The subsequent trial continued before the same trial chamber that had heard the guilty plea.

[62] Mirjan Damaška, *Negotiated Justice in International Criminal Courts*, 2 J. Int'l Crim. Just. 1018, 1038 (2004).

[63] The ICTY and ICTR would likely adopt a more adversarial approach to guilty plea withdrawals. One ICTY Chamber has noted in dictum that "nothing an accused says during the [plea] discussions will be used against him at trial should the plea negotiations fail." Prosecutor v. Blagojević, Case No. IT-02-60-T, Decision on Vidoje Blagojević's Expedited Motion to Compel the Prosecution to Disclose Its Notes from Plea Discussions with the Accused Nikolić & Request for an Expedited Open Session Hearing n.25 (June 13, 2003). Given the more inquisitorial features of the admission of guilt procedure at the ICC, it is possible that the ICC would treat withdrawn admissions of guilt differently.

undermine the legitimacy of the tribunals, so egregious breaches would likely entitle defendants to some remedy, including the opportunity to withdraw a guilty plea.

Whatever the legal rules for withdrawal, practical obstacles are likely to prevent defendants from withdrawing their guilty pleas. Because the pool of judges at international courts is very small, once a defendant has pleaded guilty at one of these courts, it will be difficult to find a judge who will be unaware that the defendant has already pleaded guilty.[64] The defendant may therefore reasonably be concerned that, even if a different judge were to preside over his trial, that judge is likely to be influenced by the knowledge of the withdrawn guilty plea. This raises a problem similar to that faced by German defendants, who may have to face the same judge at trial, even after withdrawing their confession.[65]

ARGUMENTS FOR AND AGAINST PLEA BARGAINING AT INTERNATIONAL CRIMINAL COURTS

The arguments in favor of plea bargaining have focused largely on pragmatic considerations—the need to expedite proceedings and to gather evidence of complex organized crimes. As Nancy Combs explains, an important reason to support plea bargaining for international crimes is that it frees up resources for additional prosecutions in a context where prosecutions are the exception, rather than the rule:

> [T]he presumption of prosecution that is so central in the context of domestic crimes simply does not exist for international crimes. . . . Even the wealthiest criminal justice in the world could not hope to provide full-scale trials to the more than one hundred thousand people accused of genocide in Rwanda, say, or even the ten thousand people suspected of committing international crimes in Bosnia. Expeditious alternatives must be found if more than a small fraction of these defendants are to be held criminally accountable. Seen in this light, the use of plea bargaining in the context of international crimes does not constitute an unfortunate dilution of justice but rather presents a potent opportunity to impose justice on those who would otherwise evade it.
>
> [. . .] The "price" that must be paid for guilty pleas is sentence leniency, but in the international context, this price is no cost at all. By enabling more prosecutions to take place, plea bargaining will in most

---

[64] I thank an anonymous reviewer for raising this point.

[65] *See supra* Chapter 2.

cases increase the overall punishment imposed in the context of each mass atrocity.[66]

Although practical considerations drive plea bargaining at the international criminal tribunals, some commentators and judges have rejected such considerations as either irrelevant or inadequate. In the *Momir Nikolić* judgment, excerpted in fuller detail below, the Trial Chamber proclaimed that "while savings of time and resources may be a result of guilty pleas, this consideration should not be the main reason for promoting guilty pleas through plea agreements." Similarly, Mark Drumbl has argued that, whatever its efficiency, plea bargaining as practiced at the tribunals interferes with retribution.[67] Because international criminal law recognizes retribution, but not efficiency, as a goal of punishment, to the extent that plea bargaining conflicts with retribution, it could not be justified.[68]

Some court opinions and academic commentaries have also focused on the potential of plea bargaining to further truth-seeking and reconciliation in post-conflict societies. Both the ICTY and ICTR have acknowledged that a defendant's voluntary recognition of responsibility, particularly when accompanied by statements of remorse, can help reconciliation in the aftermath of a conflict.[69] As Nancy Combs explains, it can do so by preventing denials of the atrocities:

> . . . International crimes . . . are routinely and repeatedly denied. Latin American forced disappearances exemplify the secrecy that can surround international crimes; and even crimes of enormous scale, crimes that cannot possibly be concealed—like the execution of the more than seven thousand Bosnian Muslim men and boys at Srebrenica—can be said never to have happened. Thus, in the context of international crimes, the mere act of pleading guilty—of admitting that a crime occurred and that the defendant is responsible—can have a powerful impact on victims and survivors.[70]

---

[66] Combs, *supra* note 3, at 129-130, 131.

[67] Mark Drumbl, Atrocity, Punishment, and International Law 166 (2007). Drumbl points out that plea bargains have significantly reduced the predictability and consistency of sentencing and have thus undermined the retributive value of punishment at international courts.

[68] *Id.* at 167.

[69] *E.g.*, Prosecutor v. Bisengimana, Case No. ICTR 00-60-T, Judgment, ¶¶139-140 (Apr. 13, 2006); Prosecutor v. Bralo, Case No. IT-95-17-S, Sentencing Judgment, ¶62 (Dec. 7, 2005).

[70] Combs, *supra* note 3, at 130.

While plea bargaining has now been embraced by international criminal courts, judges occasionally express concern about its use at the international level. Reflecting this concern, in several cases, judges imposed higher sentences than those negotiated by the parties. For example, in *Prosecutor v. Momir Nikolić*, the Trial Chamber accepted the guilty plea of the defendant, but after discussing its discomfort with plea bargaining for international crimes, the Chamber rejected the prosecutor's sentencing recommendation. The recommendation, based on a plea agreement with the defendant, was for a sentence of 15-20 years of imprisonment. The Trial Chamber instead sentenced the defendant to 27 years, arguing that the interests of justice required a longer sentence. Consider the opinion's discussion of the appropriateness of plea bargaining in international crimes cases:

Prosecutor v. Momir Nikolić, Case No. IT-02-60/1-S, Sentencing Judgment, ICTY Trial Chamber (Dec. 2, 2003)

[. . .] Are Plea Agreements Appropriate in Cases Involving Serious Violations of International Humanitarian Law?

The Trial Chamber has no doubt that plea agreements are permissible under the Statute and the Rules of the Tribunal.[71] As plea agreements follow discussions or "negotiations" between the Prosecutor and the defence such that the parties agree to which counts or factual allegations an accused will plead guilty, the Trial Chamber does, however, have some concerns about the use of such agreements in cases which come before the Tribunal. These concerns arise from both the nature of the offences over which this Tribunal has jurisdiction and the basis for the establishment of the Tribunal, namely Chapter VII of the United Nations Charter. As seven persons have pled guilty following Momir Nikolić's guilty plea—all of whom pled guilty pursuant to plea agreements—the Trial Chamber finds that it is particularly important at this time to consider how the increased use of plea agreements may affect the Tribunal's ability to fulfil its mandate. Therefore, the Trial Chamber finds it necessary to examine the question of whether plea agreements are appropri-

[71] [Footnote in original] Under Article 20(3) of the Statute, an accused shall enter a plea to the charges contained in the indictment against him—guilty or not guilty. An accused is presumed innocent and shall not be compelled to confess guilt. See Article 21 of the Statute, paragraphs 3 and 4(g). An accused may, however, plead guilty, and thereby avoid a trial; unlike some national systems, a trial—even an abbreviated or expedited trial—will not be held at the Tribunal in cases where an accused has pled guilty.

ate in cases involving serious violations of international humanitarian law brought before this Tribunal.

The United Nations Security Council established the Tribunal in Resolution 808 and adopted the Statute in Resolution 827 pursuant to its powers under Chapter VII of the United Nations Charter, following the Security Council's finding that the situation in the former Yugoslavia constituted a threat to international peace and security. In establishing the Tribunal, the Security Council expressed its determination to "put an end to such crimes and to take effective measures to bring to justice the persons who are responsible for them." The Security Council found the establishment of the Tribunal to be a means for bringing "justice" and "contribut[ing] to the restoration and maintenance of peace."

The Tribunal was to achieve justice through criminal proceedings. The purpose of such proceedings was multi-fold: the primary objective was to convict—and punish—those individually responsible for their crimes. The suffering and loss of the victims of such crimes would thereby be internationally recognised and acknowledged. Furthermore, through criminal proceedings, the Security Council intended to send the message to all persons that any violations of international humanitarian law— and particularly the practice of "ethnic cleansing"—would not be tolerated and must stop. It was further hoped that by highlighting breaches of obligations under international humanitarian law, and in particular the Geneva Conventions, that the parties to the conflict would recommit themselves to observing and adhering to those obligations, thereby preventing the commission of further crimes. Finally, it was hoped that this commitment to end impunity in the former Yugoslavia would promote respect for the rule of law globally.

The Tribunal was further to contribute to the restoration and maintenance of peace through criminal proceedings. The immediate consequence of such proceedings was the removal of those persons most responsible for the commission of crimes in the course of—and even in furtherance of—the armed conflict. Additionally, by holding individuals responsible for the crimes committed, it was hoped that a particular ethnic or religious group (or even political organisation) would not be held responsible for such crimes by members of other ethnic or religious groups, and that the guilt of the few would not be shifted to the innocent. Finally, through public proceedings, the truth about the possible commission of war crimes, crimes against humanity and genocide was to be determined, thereby establishing an accurate, accessible historical record. The Security Council hoped such a historical record would prevent a cycle of revenge killings and future acts of aggression.

When convictions result from a guilty plea, certain aims of having criminal proceedings are not fully realised, most notably a public trial. A public trial, with the presentation of testimonial and documentary evidence by both parties, creates a more complete and detailed historical record than a guilty plea, which may only establish the bare factual allegations in an indictment or may be supplemented by a statement of facts and acceptance of responsibility by the accused.

Furthermore, at a trial, victims or survivors of victims have an opportunity to have their voices heard as part of the criminal justice process. It is rare that victims will be called as witnesses as part of a plea agreement, though witnesses may be called at the sentencing hearing.

Most concerning to this Trial Chamber is that as a result of the negotiations entered into by the Prosecutor and defence, the final plea agreement may include provisions such that the Prosecutor withdraws certain charges or certain factual allegations. The Prosecutor may do so for a variety of reasons. In cases where factual allegations are withdrawn, the public record established by that case might be incomplete or at least open to question, as the public will not know whether the allegations were withdrawn because of insufficient evidence or because they were simply a "bargaining chip" in the negotiation process.

The Trial Chamber notes with interest that at other international criminal institutions, a trial chamber may order that the prosecutor present additional evidence, including the testimony of witnesses "in the interests of justice, in particular the interests of the victims."[72] Additionally, "in the interests of justice," a trial chamber may order that a trial continue before a different trial chamber in order to have a "more complete presentation of the facts of the case" and thereby consider [. . .] the admission of guilt as having not been made.[73]

In cases where charges are withdrawn, extreme caution must be urged. The Prosecutor has a duty to prosecute serious violations of international humanitarian law. The crimes falling within the jurisdiction of this Tribunal are fundamentally different from crimes prosecuted nationally. Although it may seem appropriate to "negotiate" a charge of

---

[72] [Footnote in original] Article 65(4) of the Statute of the ICC provides, "Where the Trial Chamber is of the opinion that a more complete presentation of the facts of the case is required in the interests of justice, in particular the interests of the victims, the Trial Chamber may: (a) Request the Prosecutor to present additional evidence, including the testimony of witnesses; or (b) Order that the trial be continued under the ordinary trial procedures provided by this Statute, in which case it shall consider the admission of guilt as not having been made and may remit the case to another Trial Chamber."

[73] [Footnote in original] *Id.*

attempted murder to a charge of aggravated assault, any "negotiations" on a charge of genocide or crimes against humanity must be carefully considered and be entered into for good cause.[74] While the principle of mandatory prosecutions is not part of the Tribunal's Statute, the Prosecutor does have a duty to prepare an indictment upon a determination that a prima facie case exists. The Prosecutor must carefully consider the factual basis and existing evidence when deciding what charge most adequately reflects the underlying criminal conduct of an accused. Once a charge of genocide has been confirmed, it should not simply be bargained away. If the Prosecutor make[s] a plea agreement such that the totality of an individual's criminal conduct is not reflected or the remaining charges do not sufficiently reflect the gravity of the offences committed by the accused, questions will inevitably arise as to whether justice is in fact being done. The public may be left to wonder about the motives for guilty pleas, whether the conviction in fact reflects the full criminal conduct of the accused and whether it establishes a credible and complete historical record. Convictions entered by a trial chamber must accurately reflect the actual conduct and crime committed and must not simply reflect the agreement of the parties as to what would be a suitable settlement of the matter.

Additionally, the Trial Chamber has a responsibility to ensure that all accused are treated equally before the law. The Prosecutor may seek to make a plea agreement with some accused because of their knowledge of particular events which may be useful in prosecutions of other, more high ranking accused. The Prosecutor may make the terms of such a plea agreement quite generous in order to secure the co-operation of that accused. Other accused, who may not have been involved in the most egregious crimes or who may not have been part of a joint criminal enterprise with more high ranking accused, may not be offered such a generous plea agreement, or indeed any plea agreement.

The Trial Chamber notes that the savings of time and resources due to a guilty plea has often been considered as a valuable and justifiable reason for the promotion of guilty pleas. This Trial Chamber cannot fully endorse this argument. While it appreciates this saving of Tribunal resources, the Trial Chamber finds that in cases of this magnitude, where the Tribunal has been entrusted by the United Nations Security Council—and by extension, the international community as a whole—

[74] [Footnote in original] In this regard, the Trial Chamber recalls that in many national systems where some form of plea agreements exists, such agreements are not permitted in cases of the most serious offences. [. . .]

to bring justice to the former Yugoslavia through criminal proceedings that are fair, in accordance with international human rights standards, and accord due regard to the rights of the accused and the interests of victims, the saving of resources cannot be given undue consideration or importance. The quality of the justice and the fulfilment of the mandate of the Tribunal, including the establishment of a complete and accurate record of the crimes committed in the former Yugoslavia, must not be compromised. Unlike national criminal justice systems, which often must turn to plea agreements as a means to cope with heavy and seemingly endless caseloads, the Tribunal has a fixed mandate. Its very raison d'être is to have criminal proceedings, such that the persons most responsible for serious violations of international humanitarian law are held accountable for their criminal conduct—not simply a portion thereof. Thus, while savings of time and resources may be a result of guilty pleas, this consideration should not be the main reason for promoting guilty pleas through plea agreements.

Having raised some issues of concern in cases where guilty pleas emanated from plea agreements, the Trial Chamber will now turn to some of the possible benefits of guilty pleas, including those resulting from plea agreements, and consider these in light of the purposes and mandate of the Tribunal.

The Tribunal was established to prosecute and punish persons responsible for serious violations of international humanitarian law. Persons who plead guilty are convicted upon the acceptance of the guilty plea. Upon conviction, a trial chamber will determine an appropriate sentence and will take as its principal consideration, as will be discussed below, the gravity of the offence—and not the guilty plea—in determining an appropriate sentence. Thus, a guilty plea leads directly to the fulfilment of a fundamental purpose of this Tribunal.

Because a conviction is based on the accused's acceptance of responsibility and acknowledgement of the crime he committed, there can be no question about the actual guilt of that accused. Denial of the commission of the crime may no longer be an option for those who have convinced themselves that the Tribunal is biased or that its judgements are based on weak or even false evidence. As the guilty plea must be based on a sufficient factual basis, which often will include a statement of facts by the accused person and may be supplemented upon the request of the trial chamber, the underlying facts for each crime will be established. Thus, a purpose of the Tribunal is fulfilled.

As is often highlighted by the Prosecution, guilty pleas can substantially assist in its investigations and presentation of evidence at trials of other accused, including high ranking accused. The Trial Chamber recognises and appreciates the assistance that can be given and the knowledge that can be gained by all organs of the Tribunal from having persons who may have "inside" information testify in other proceedings.

In relation to the Tribunal's mission to assist in restoring peace and bring reconciliation to the territory of the former Yugoslavia, guilty pleas can certainly contribute significantly. Through the acknowledgment of the crimes committed and the recognition of one's own role in the suffering of others, a guilty plea may be more meaningful and significant than a finding of guilt by a trial chamber to the victims and survivors. Without seeking to lessen the impact of a public pronouncement by the Tribunal of guilt following a trial, the Trial Chamber recognises that an admission of guilt from a person perceived as "the enemy" may serve as an opening for dialogue and reconciliation between different groups. When an admission of guilt is coupled with a sincere expression of remorse, a significant opportunity for reconciliation may be created.

The Trial Chamber finds that, on balance, guilty pleas pursuant to plea agreements, may further the work—and the mandate—of the Tribunal. The Trial Chamber further finds, however, that based on the duties incumbent on the Prosecutor and the Trial Chambers pursuant to the Statute of the Tribunal, the use of plea agreements should proceed with caution and such agreements should be used only when doing so would satisfy the interests of justice.

Notes and Questions:

1. The *Nikolić* Trial Chamber observed that "while savings of time and resources may be a result of guilty pleas, this consideration should not be the main reason for promoting guilty pleas through plea agreements." According to the Chamber, what are permissible reasons for promoting plea agreements and what types of plea agreements would be consistent with the mandate of the international tribunals? Do you agree with the Chamber's assessment? Do you believe it is feasible for international courts to reject plea agreements that are driven primarily by the need to save time and resources?
2. The Chamber seems particularly concerned about the practices of charge bargaining and fact bargaining. What is the source of its concern? Can that concern be addressed in any way other than prohibiting charge bargaining entirely?
3. The court also notes that plea bargaining may conflict with the principle of equal treatment under the law. What may a court do

to ensure that the prosecution treats defendants equally in the course of plea bargaining? Would the measures that the court takes in this respect undermine the effectiveness of plea bargaining?

As the *Nikolić* opinion reveals, and Note 2 above highlights, charge bargaining is especially controversial among international judges, because of its potential to distort or omit relevant facts. Consider the following critique of charge bargaining by Judge Schomburg at the ICTY:

Prosecutor v. Deronjić, Case No. IT-02-61-S, Sentencing Judgment, Trial Chamber, Dissenting Opinion of Judge Schomburg (Mar. 30, 2004)

A. Introduction

1. [. . .] I regret that as a member of the bench, for fundamental reasons, I am not able to support the sentence.

2. The sentence is not proportional to the crimes it is based on and amounts to a singing from the wrong hymn sheet. The Accused deserves a sentence of no less than twenty years of imprisonment.

3. There are two main reasons leading me to the conclusion that the imposed sentence, recommended by the Prosecutor is not within mandate and spirit of this Tribunal.

4. First, already the series of indictments, including the Second Amended Indictment, arbitrarily present facts, selected from the context of a larger criminal plan and, for unknown reasons, limited to one day and to the village of Glogova only.

5. Second, even based on these fragments of facts, the heinous and long planned crimes committed by a high ranking perpetrator do not allow for a sentence of only ten years, which may possibly even be a de facto deprivation of liberty of only six years and eight months, taking into account the possibility of an early release.

B. Discussion

1. The Duty of the Prosecutor

6. "Da mihi factum, dabo tibi jus"—give me (all) the facts and I will present you the applicable law (and a just decision). This wise Roman principle unfortunately is not part of our Rules. However, under the mandate of this ad hoc Tribunal the Prosecutor, being part of the Tribunal, is

in principle duty bound to present all the evidence available. The fundament of our Tribunal is the Statute based on Chapter VII of the Charter of the United Nations established as a measure to maintain or restore international peace and security. However, there is no peace without justice; there is no justice without truth, meaning the entire truth and nothing but the truth.

7. The International Prosecutor is not controlled de jure or de facto by independent judges or a government in the selection of suspects to be indicted and in determining the scope of an indictment, as it would be on a domestic level. The state's and the international community's monopoly over the right to exercise force, however, urges the Prosecutor to act in a way that makes victims of crimes and their relatives understand that the Prosecutor is acting on their behalf. When it comes to prosecuting crimes against individuals, a Prosecutor acts with the goal to stop a never-ending circle of "private justice," meaning mutual violence and vengeance. This goal can only be achieved if the entire picture of a crime is presented to the judges.

8. I accept and appreciate that judicial economy and, in concreto, the limited resources of this Tribunal call for a limitation of charges, if only a just judgement remains possible. The test should be, whether individual separable parts of an offense or several violations of law committed as a result of the same offence are not particularly significant for the penalty to be imposed. In those cases the prosecution may be limited to the other parts of the offense or violations of law.

9. However this test has not been met when conducting investigations, prosecution and indicting Miroslav Deronjić.

a) With respect to the events in the Municipality of Bratunac, there was clearly a plan to ethnically cleanse the entire Municipalty, not only Glogova on the 9th of May 1992, with all the accompanying crimes committed in the usual pattern of conduct, observed in other Variant B municipalities. These crimes are of a far more serious nature than those committed in Glogova, if one compares the Second Amended Indictment with what the Accused himself has admitted about events on the following days in the rest of his Municipality.

b) With respect to the Killing/Murder of 64 (?) persons known by name in Glogova, it should be noted that the Prosecutor dropped two charges of murder and deleted the supporting facts from the indictment, already confirmed by an independent judge of this Tribunal. In particular, the deletion of the allegation that Miroslav Deronjić was even present when some of these killings happened (direct intent!), created doubts whether at all he had the dolus eventualis as already accepted by him. This made it incumbent on the Trial Chamber to continue with the Sentencing Hearing. Miroslav Deronjić stated, inter alia,

> — in Blagojević et al., on 21 January 2004: "[. . .] that I did not order, that I did not kill, that I was not present, that I did not know of those events [. . .]."
> — in Krajišnik, on 18 February 2004: "[. . .] I never agreed to that [. . .]."

c) Moreover, the Indictment remains silent about the fate of the other Muslims of Glogova. What about other acts of violence, sexual assaults, or other killings in Glogova? A Trial Chamber cannot enter into speculation or order the production of evidence it is not aware of, even if it is in the possession of the Office of the Prosecutor. The result is that, in the concrete case before us, the Judges have to determine a sentence based on a clinically clean compilation of selected facts by the Prosecution.

d) Finally, having carefully read all the Accused's statements and testimonies, it remains extremely questionable to me, why Miroslav Deronjić was not indicted as a co-perpetrator in the joint criminal enterprise leading to the horrific massacre at Srebrenica in 1995. It transpires on a prima facie basis that there should be enough reason to indict Miroslav Deronjić for his participation in that massacre, based only on his own confession, and leave it finally to a Trial Chamber to decide whether a criminal responsibility can be established beyond reasonable doubt. Apparently Miroslav Deronjić was not afraid that this could happen, as he stated himself:

> [. . .] I was told after all the investigations were completed, that indictments in relation to Srebrenica were being dropped against me. [. . .] [T]he Prosecution stated that [. . .] they have no intention of prosecuting me further for the events in Srebrenica.

10. One might say, under the Rules of this Tribunal, that it is for the Prosecutor alone to decide whom, and under which charges, to indict. In principle, this is correct. However, it is also for the Prosecutor to safeguard that justice is seen to be done and to convince, in particular, those people on whose behalf this Tribunal is working that there is no arbitrary selection of persons to be indicted and no arbitrary selection of charges or facts in case of an indictment. I am afraid that such an unjustified premature procedure has been applied in the proceedings against Miroslav Deronjić.

11. I accept that, in order to break up a circle of silence among perpetrators, some promises can be made by the Prosecutor vis à vis credible and reliable perpetrators. However, these promises shall, proprio motu, be disclosed to the bench by the Prosecutor.

a) Promises, furthermore, cannot result in de facto granting partial amnesty/impunity by the Prosecutor, particularly not in an institution established to avoid impunity.

b) Amnesty can only be granted after an appropriate sentence has been determined.

c) A limited amnesty or early release, if at all, can only be granted by those to whom this power is or will be vested, based on a sentenced person's entire post-crime conduct, or in order to restore peace.

12. There is no legal basis in the Statute or the Rules for the Prosecutor to promise in the beginning of each statement that information provided by the Accused would never be used against him. Such promise has been made in this case by the Prosecutor, formulated in the "Understanding of the Parties," paragraph 7 of which states: "The Prosecutor agrees that anything said by Mr. Deronjić during the interview will not be used as evidence in legal proceedings against him before the Tribunal." This "Understanding of the Parties," for unknown reasons, did not form part of the Plea Agreement presented to this Trial Chamber, even though this should have been the case according to the Prosecutor's own statement. I believe that this promise has also been a prerequisite for the Accused's guilty plea, contrary to the submissions given by the Prosecutor. Furthermore, it was a misleading promise, amounting to unfairness to the Accused, as this understanding cannot be binding upon other courts also having jurisdiction over these crimes. Additionally, it was not combined with a warning that the Accused has to tell the truth when called as a witness before this Tribunal (consequences otherwise to be read in Rule 91 and being not under the control of the Prosecutor).

2. The Appropriate Sentence for the Crimes to Which the Accused Has Pleaded Guilty

13. The gravity of the crime before us cannot be better defined than by the words of the Prosecutor:

> [. . .] the crime for which Miroslav Deronjić is to be sentenced is precisely the type of crime about which the Security Council expressed its grave alarm in Resolution 808. The events in Glogova on the 9th of May 1992 are a classical case of ethnic cleansing, and precisely the

reason why the Security Council established this Tribunal. The attack on Glogova was not an isolated or random event, but a critical element in a larger scheme to divide Bosnia and Herzegovina and create Serb-ethnic territories.

14. A perpetrator deserves a proportional sanction for his crime, primarily defined by its gravity. The mitigating weight of any post-crime conduct in general is, if at all, limited. In particular, in this concrete case the mitigating factors are extraordinarily limited.

(a) Guilty Plea

a) An analysis of various national legal systems shows that a guilty plea is generally accepted as a mitigating factor leading to a reduction of the sentence. Reasons justifying such mitigation include the willingness of an offender to co-operate in the administration of justice, the showing of remorse, acknowledgment of responsibility, sparing the victims from testifying and being cross-examined, the stage of proceedings at which the offender pleads guilty, and the circumstances in which the plea is tendered.

b) It becomes evident from the analysis, however, that in the majority of the countries under survey a guilty plea is given only little—if any—weight in relation to serious crimes. In Australia, Canada, China, England, and Germany, first degree murder attracts a mandatory sentence of life imprisonment that cannot be altered by the acceptance of the guilty plea or confession of the accused. In Poland, a plea bargain is only possible in relation to misdemeanours, but not crimes. Similar provisions on guilty pleas or plea bargaining exist in other countries, e.g. Argentina, Brazil, and Chile.

c) In the light of this analysis, and taking into consideration that a guilty plea cannot derogate from the gravity of a crime, I believe that the guilty plea of Miroslav Deronjić only warrants little weight in sentencing.

(b) Co-operation with the Tribunal

15. The forensic value of his statements and testimonies is extremely limited, until the Accused is prepared to clarify which details are true and which are not. The Accused himself admitted:

> So I did not give an entirely truthful statement [. . .]. But I do not agree that those statements are completely untrue. They are partially untrue [. . .].

I can not attach any mitigating weight to such an unsound mixture of truth and lies, creating more confusion than assistance in the Tribunal's search for the truth.

(c) Remorse

17. The remorse shown by the Accused is hardly credible, inter alia, because from testimony to testimony given after his guilty plea, he wants to minimize his guilt.

a) On his responsibility for the killings, on 18 February 2004, he testified:

> [. . .] I agreed to certain things, which I did, but I never agreed to that, nor did I ever order or wish that people are killed.

On the 19 February 2004 in the same testimony, he stated:

> Later, after that period, different information reached me about the events in Glogova.
>
> [H]e continued that: "[. . .] I had the opportunity to read a book whose author is a man from Bratunac, and he mentioned in this book that a certain number of people had been killed in Glogova."
>
> [T]hen he stated that: "Some inquiry was done by my lawyers [. . .]."
>
> [A]nd finally he concluded: "[. . .] I accepted the allegation of the Prosecutor [. . .]."

b) On his responsibility for triggering the attack, on 30 September 2003, he pleaded guilty to the fact that:

> Miroslav Deronjić urged Captain Reljić to fire a tank shell into a house at the initial stage of the attack in order to sow panic among the Muslim residents of Glogova.

[T]hen he confirmed it in his testimony on 27 January 2004:

> Judge Schomburg: [. . .] you yourself urged Captain Reljić to fire a tank shell into a house at the initial stage of the attack in order to sow panic amongst the residents of Glogova. [. . .]
>
> A.: Yes, Your Honour.

[I]n Blagojević et al., on 21 January 2004, he testified: "I told them to shoot at the roof using, if possible, a lighter weapon. I didn't say they had necessarily to shoot at the house itself. I said they could shoot at an auxiliary structure."

[F]inally, out of the blue, he stated: "This grenade shell was not fired."

If this were the truth, why would he not mention this in all his prior testimonies?

18. I need not repeat the aforementioned advantages Miroslav Deronjić has already received.

C. Conclusion

19. The crime before us, limited as it is described, has, however, all of the ingredients of one of the most heinous crimes against humanity. Therefore, the appropriate sentence can only be found in twenty years of imprisonment or higher, thereby adequately acknowledging the fate of the victims and their relatives. Everything else could be seen as an incentive for politicians, who might in future find themselves in a similar situation as Miroslav Deronjić was as of December 1991, to act in the same manner. Even if this person were brought before criminal court he/she would believe that he/she could buy him/herself more or less free by admitting some guilt and giving some information to the then competent prosecutor.

20. As no victim or relative of a victim has been given the opportunity to address this Trial Chamber in person, I should like to give the last word to one of them:

> I saw Miroslav Deronjić plead guilty on the television. The Bosnian Muslims in the community that I have spoken to, felt relieved because he admitted his guilt. This is a positive thing and can heal the wounds of the community provided that he is punished adequately. A mild punishment however would not serve any purpose; he does not deserve any compassion as he did not show any, not only to people of Glogova but also to the other Muslim Bosnians of Bratunac and Srebrenica.

Notes and Questions:

1. On what grounds did Judge Schomburg object to the charge bargain between the ICTY prosecutor and Miroslav Deronjić? Was he concerned that the charge bargain omitted relevant facts and distorted the truth, or that it prevented the imposition of a proportionate sentence? Based on his opinion in *Deronjić*, do you think that Judge Schomburg would accept any charge bargain at the ICTY? Do you agree with his position? Why or why not?

PLEA BARGAINING IN INTERNATIONAL CRIMES CASES AT "HYBRID" COURTS

Plea bargaining for international crimes has also occurred in the so-called hybrid courts, such as the UN-sponsored Special Panels for East Timor and the Bosnian State Court War Crimes Chamber. These courts are located on the territory where the crimes occurred, but they were established with the help of the international community, include international judges and lawyers in their ranks, and follow a mix of international and domestic criminal law and procedure.

The Special Panels for East Timor, which operated between 2001 and 2005, resolved about half of their cases through guilty pleas.[75] But the guilty plea process experienced various problems and was much criticized by commentators. Many of the defendants pleaded guilty without a clear understanding of the meaning or consequences of their guilty pleas.[76] As Nancy Combs reports, defendants commonly pleaded guilty while also insisting that they committed the crime under duress or superior orders.[77] The following colloquy exemplifies the problem. In response to a question from the court as to whether he was prepared to plead guilty, Defendant Romeiro Tilman responded as follows:

> I agree. This is not because of what I wanted, but because those in charge forced me. I did it. It is not that I used a knife, or a machete to kill. I didn't. The commander of militia forced me. I was scared of death. My colleague did it. And I have been in jail for over 3 years. This wrong is not mine. The person who did this is not here. And I, have come to accept my wrong. . . . I feel that I am wrong because I held with my hands.[78]

Defense attorneys at the Special Panels have also expressed concerns with the plea bargaining process. They have argued that, as the date for the completion of the Special Panel trials was set, defendants were pressured to plead guilty to expedite the process. As the Head of the Defense Lawyers United noted, "[c]lients often have no choice but to

---

[75] Combs, *supra* note 3, at 117.

[76] *Id.*

[77] *Id.* at 115-118.

[78] Special Panels for Serious Crimes, Prosecutor v. Sarmento et al., Court Record, at 11 (June 30, 2003), *quoted in id.* at 118.

enter into a plea agreement" and are subject to "a highly coercive technique to elicit a plea of guilt and avoid trial and get a lesser sentence."[79]

Throughout their operation, the Special Panels also suffered from a serious lack of resources. This underfunding affected the defense most severely, leading many commentators to criticize the lack of adequate defense.[80] These broader problems likely affected the fairness of plea bargaining as well.

Another hybrid court, the War Crimes Chamber of the State Court of Bosnia and Herzegovina (War Crimes Chamber), has also recently begun using plea bargaining to resolve international crimes cases. The War Crimes Chamber was created with international support, includes national and international judges and officials in its ranks, but operates on the territory of Bosnia and Herzegovina, applies Bosnian law, and will gradually become a fully domestic court.[81]

The possibility for conducting plea bargaining at the War Crimes Chamber has existed since the beginning of the Chamber's work in 2005. The Bosnian legislature had introduced plea bargaining provisions as part of a more comprehensive overhaul of the Bosnian Criminal Procedure Code in 2003.[82] But prosecutors at the War Crimes Chamber were reluctant to use these provisions, even though their colleagues in the Organized Crime Chamber had begun using them regularly to resolve complex organized crimes.[83] As the International Center for Transitional Justice reports, several reasons helped explain this reluctance:

> According to a Bosnian prosecutor, the prosecutors were concerned that the more lenient sentences often resulting from such agreements would provoke negative public reaction, a risk they were unwilling to take. When such agreements have been reached at the ICTY, some in

---

[79] Ramavarma Thamburan, Defense Lawyers United Head, *quoted in* David Cohen, *"Justice on the Cheap" Revisited: The Failure of the Serious Crimes Trials in East Timor*, 80 Asia Pac. Issues 4 (May 2006).

[80] Cohen, *supra* note 79, at 2, 4-5.

[81] The transition is supposed to be complete by the end of 2009. Bogdan Ivanišević, The War Crimes Chamber in Bosnia and Herzegovina: From Hybrid to Domestic Court 5, 7 (Int'l Center for Transitional Just. 2008), *at* http://www.ictj.org/images/content/1/0/1088.pdf.

[82] *See* American Bar Association, Judicial Reform Index for Bosnia and Herzegovina 21 (2006), *at* http://www.abanet.org/rol/publications/bosnia-jri-2006-eng.pdf. For an excellent study of the plea bargaining practice in ordinary Bosnian courts under the new Code, see Organization on Security and Cooperation in Europe, Plea Agreements in Bosnia and Herzegovina: Practices Before the Courts and Their Compliance with International Human Rights Standards (2d ed. 2006).

[83] Ivanišević, *supra* note 81, at 14.

> Bosnia have negatively perceived them and considered them an affront to victims. The potential benefits of plea agreements—including clearing the backlog of lower level cases and obtaining evidence to allow higher-level prosecutions—have been largely absent from public debate in Bosnia. There had also been concerns that defendants who pled guilty and pledged to testify in other cases, or at least to provide information about undiscovered mass graves, might avoid fulfilling this obligation, leaving the prosecutors without legal means to compel them or revoke the reduction of sentence. Defense counsel, for their part, hesitated to suggest to their clients to plead guilty in the absence of clearer sentencing practice or guidelines.[84]

Overcoming this initial reluctance, in 2008, the Special Department for War Crimes in the Bosnian State Prosecutor's Office changed its policy to encourage bargaining by its prosecutors.[85] In 2008, the War Crimes Chamber accepted six guilty pleas and plea agreements.[86] This means that a quarter of the 24 verdicts handed down since the beginning of the Chamber's operation in 2005 were based on guilty pleas.

Victims have generally opposed the use of plea bargaining at the War Crimes Chamber, and one victims' group staged a demonstration in front of the court to protest a particular plea agreement.[87] Some legal commentators have also expressed skepticism and argued that plea agreements "do not contribute to fulfillment of justice, because the rights of injured parties have been marginalized, while the purpose of the agreements is unclear."[88] Others have recommended that victims at least be consulted before plea agreements are approved.[89]

Notes and Questions:

1. Is plea bargaining likely to be more acceptable or less acceptable when it is conducted in a hybrid court on the territory where the

---

[84] *Id.*

[85] The Special Department is responsible for prosecuting cases before the War Crimes Chamber. *See id.* at 5.

[86] The following six individuals pleaded guilty: Veiz Bjelić, Dušan Fuštar, Paško Ljubičić, Idhan Sipić, Slavko Šakić, and Vaso Todorović. *See* Court of Bosnia and Herzegovina, Cases Completed by a Final Decision, *at* http://www.sudbih.gov.ba/?jezik=e.

[87] Ivanišević, *supra* note 81, at 15 (noting protests by victims over plea agreements); Aida Alić, *A Year of Progress over War Crimes*, BalkanInsight.com, *at* http://www.balkaninsight.com/en/main/analysis/15763 (noting that one victims' group considered that the agreements "represent some form of a betrayal of victims").

[88] Alić, *supra* note 87.

[89] Ivanišević, *supra* note 81, at 15.

crimes were committed? If you had to decide whether to propose the introduction of plea bargaining at such a hybrid court, what factors would you consider in making the recommendation?

THE FUTURE OF PLEA BARGAINING IN INTERNATIONAL CRIMES CASES

Some authors have taken the debate beyond the question of whether plea bargaining should occur at international courts and have suggested ways in which the practice can be structured to align more closely with the goals of international criminal justice.

Nancy Amoury Combs, for example, has argued for a guilty plea system that follows restorative justice principles.[90] Such a system would require defendants who plead guilty "to provide a full and complete accounting of their crimes as part of a guilty plea."[91] This full accounting would promote the truth-seeking function of international criminal law and would benefit victims and family members of victims by bringing a sense of closure. The restorative justice approach would also promote greater victim involvement in the guilty plea process. It would allow victims to confront and question the defendants and to provide information relevant to sentencing. Finally, a restorative justice guilty plea system would require defendants who plead guilty to provide reparations to victims or their families. The reparations could be monetary or symbolic, including apologies and service in the community victimized by the defendant's crimes.[92] For a fuller explanation of how restorative justice principles can be applied in the plea bargaining context, see Nancy Amoury Combs, Guilty Pleas in International Criminal Law: Constructing a Restorative Justice Approach 141-147 (2007).

Another author, Julian Cook, has argued that it is important for international criminal courts to strengthen procedural protections during plea hearings.[93] In particular, courts must develop clearer standards to ensure that defendants understand the various rights and consequences of pleading guilty, that they are pleading guilty voluntarily, and that the evidence supports the guilty plea. Cook argues that international courts

---

[90] Combs, *supra* note 3, at 141.

[91] *Id.* at 141-142.

[92] *Id.* at 144-147.

[93] Cook, *supra* note 54, at 502.

ought to require more thorough explanations from defendants on these questions to ensure the fairness of the plea bargaining process.[94]

Finally, Mirjan Damaška has argued for using the continental approach to negotiated justice at international criminal courts. Under that model, the defendant confesses guilt, and the court conducts a thorough inquiry not only into the voluntariness and knowingness of the confession, but also into the facts supporting it. The procedure he proposes is akin to a summary trial upon confession and is closer to the German rather than the American model of negotiated justice.

Mirjan Damaška, *Negotiated Justice in International Criminal Courts,* 2 J. INT'L CRIM. JUST. 1018, 1037, 1038-1039 (2004)

Which Model Is Best Suited to International Proceedings—The Continental In-Court Confession or the Anglo-American Guilty Plea?

. . . [A] judicial inquiry into the factual basis and voluntariness of a guilty plea is only part of the court's properly understood responsibility. It is true that the objection to asking the defendant a question which is ultimately a legal one is primarily a matter of juridical elegance, motivated by the desire to enhance the law's coherence. It is not deprived of practical value, however. Abstaining from asking the defendant questions with both factual and legal components underscores the need that the judge, prior to accepting negotiated admissions of guilt, should carefully inquire into the legal issues flowing from the facts admitted by the defendant. This is particularly important where, as in international criminal law, these issues are often uncertain and can easily remain unnoticed or ignored in admission agreements.

Another already adduced reason for preferring the confession model is that confession-like acts hold greater promise of advancing the pedagogical goals of international justice or even its ambition to bring about reconciliation of groups involved in a crime-generating conflict. As previously suggested, it is easier to read remorse into confessions than into formal declarations of guilt or refusals to contest charges. Manifest contrition, especially by superiors in movements responsible for human rights violations, can have a cathartic effect on the movement's victims

---

[94] *Id.*

and shake the belief system of the movement's participants. There is yet another reason, unmentioned before, for the preference for the confession model. If an act of self-conviction is treated as analogous to a confession, then that analogy suggests to the court that admitted facts, being evidence, must be stated in considerable detail and included into the reasoning part of the judgment. The resulting material grows more abundant for historians and the court's objective to create a historical record can be advanced: less information is lost in the catacombs of the past.

[. . .] But the closer an admission comes to a confession, the more difficult it becomes to withdraw or disregard it, because it is in the nature of reliable incriminating evidence. It will be said that there is nothing unfair about using evidence prompted by prosecutorial promises that the judges choose to disregard. After all, they did not participate in negotiations. However, this is not really satisfying. Judges and prosecutors are interacting organs of the same institution, perceived as forming a sort of unity.

[. . .] If the defendant's admission does not conclusively establish his guilt and a degree of judicial oversight is necessary, how is this oversight to be structured? Because docket-pressures are the primary reason for departing from the full adjudicative process, it is clear that such oversight must involve a substantial simplification of ordinary trial procedures. Pulling in the opposite direction, however, are the special needs of international justice. As we have seen, the transparency of proceedings is a more pressing need than in domestic courts and the multiple audiences of international criminal courts generate more than ordinary interest in the public airing of the full facts of cases. The challenge is then to develop a model of judicial oversight that steers a mid-way course between the Scylla of being too cumbersome and the Charybdis of being too informal.

Notes and Questions:

1. Based on your review of the practice of plea bargaining at international criminal courts, which of the above proposals do you believe is most needed at this time? Does your answer depend on your view about the primary goals of international criminal law?
2. Which of the proposals above do you believe is most likely to be adopted at the International Criminal Court? At future hybrid courts?
3. Can you think of other ways in which the fairness and legitimacy of plea bargaining at international criminal courts could be enhanced?

COMPARING PLEA BARGAINING AT THE INTERNATIONAL CRIMINAL COURTS

Plea Bargaining Feature	ICTY and ICTR	ICC ("proceeding on an admission of guilt")
Legislative Authorization	Yes	Yes (although no specific authorization for negotiations)
Typical Participants	Defense attorney and prosecutor; (judges review guilty plea and impose sentence)	Defense attorney and prosecutor; (judges review admission of guilt and impose sentence)
Timing	After charges are filed with the court; timing of guilty plea considered at sentencing	After charges are filed with the court
Subject Matter	Sentence and charge bargaining; parties' agreement is not binding on the court; may be used in war crimes, crimes against humanity, and genocide cases; may waive right to appeal	Arguably both sentence and charge bargaining are permissible, but the parties' agreement is not binding on the court; may be used in war crimes, crimes against humanity, genocide, and possibly aggression cases
Discovery/Disclosure	The prosecution must disclose potentially exculpatory evidence "as soon as practicable." Evidence to support the indictment and prior statements of the accused are disclosed within 30 days of the accused's initial appearance. Witness statements are disclosed later, on a schedule determined by the pretrial judge.	The prosecution must disclose potentially exculpatory evidence "as soon as practicable." Before charges are confirmed, the prosecution must disclose all the incriminating evidence on which it will rely to argue that charges should be confirmed.
Cooperation Agreements	Yes	Possible
Conditions for Validity	Guilty plea must be voluntary, informed, unequivocal, and supported by the facts.	Admission of guilt must be voluntary, informed, and factually based.
Withdrawal and Breach	No provisions on these questions	If the court rejects an admission of guilt as invalid, it must consider the admission of guilt as not having been made and "may remit the case to another Trial Chamber." No provisions address whether a defendant may withdraw an admission of guilt when the court rejects the agreement between the parties. No provisions address the consequences of a breach of the agreement.

HYPOTHETICALS

Guilty Plea, Remorse, and Cooperation in a Genocide Case at the ICTR

Jean Nikindi

Jean Nikindi was a colonel in the Rwandan Armed Forces (FAR) and an officer in the Ministry of Defense from 1990 to 1994. He managed day-to-day affairs in the absence of the Defense Minister. In 1999, the ICTR prosecutor charged Nikindi, together with other high-ranking officers of the FAR, with crimes against humanity, genocide, and conspiracy to commit genocide for devising and implementing a plan to exterminate the civilian Tutsi population and eliminate members of the opposition in 1994. According to the indictment, this plan included the training of and distribution of weapons to militiamen as well as the preparation of lists of people to be eliminated. In executing the plan, Nikindi helped organize and ordered massacres against Rwandan Tutsis and moderate Hutus.

In the course of negotiations with the prosecution, Nikindi agreed to plead guilty and cooperate with the prosecution, in exchange for a recommendation of a more lenient sentence and the dropping of the genocide charge. Although Nikindi would likely face life imprisonment if convicted of the original charges after a contested trial, the prosecution agreed to recommend 15 years pursuant to the plea bargain.

Consistent with the plea agreement, Nikindi cooperated fully with the prosecution, revealing important and detailed information about the operations of the FAR and the Ministry of Defense at the time of the genocide and providing the prosecution with original documents that inculpated at least eight other defendants. Nikindi also testified for the prosecution in the trials of two other defendants and then pleaded guilty himself. At sentencing, however, Nikindi failed to show any remorse for his actions. Instead, while confirming his guilty plea to crimes against humanity and conspiracy to commit genocide, he refused to apologize for his actions. He stated that he had acted to defend his country against the Tutsi-led Rwandan Patriotic Front, which had been attacking Hutus and trying to overthrow the Hutu-led government. He had not made this argument at the plea colloquy, where his guilty plea had been accepted as voluntary, informed, unequivocal, and resting on a factual basis.

Despite Nikindi's failure to show remorse, the prosecution still recommended that he receive 15 years for his crimes, emphasizing that he had cooperated substantially with the prosecution and had offered valuable information and testimony that had helped prosecute many other ICTR defendants. The prosecution declared that by pleading guilty, Nikindi helped preserve the resources of the Tribunal and develop the historical record about atrocities committed in Rwanda in 1994. In this way, his guilty plea advanced the goal of reconciliation in post-conflict Rwanda.

The Trial Chamber refused to follow the prosecutorial recommendation and instead imposed a 25-year sentence on Nikindi. The court was troubled by his lack of remorse and felt that 15 years was insufficient for one who showed so little regret for his heinous actions.

Joseph Biziligi

Joseph Biziligi was a colonel in the FAR and one of Jean Nikindi's co-defendants. He was also charged with crimes against humanity, genocide, and conspiracy to commit genocide for devising and helping implement a plan to exterminate the civilian Tutsi population and eliminate members of the opposition in 1994. Like Nikindi, Biziligi had helped train and distribute weapons to militiamen who exterminated Tutsis, and he had provided lists of people who were to be eliminated. He had also ordered and participated in massacres against Rwandan Tutsis and moderate Hutus.

After negotiations with the prosecution, Biziligi received a deal similar to Nikindi's. He agreed to plead guilty and cooperate with the prosecution, in exchange for a recommendation of a more lenient sentence and the dropping of the genocide charge. Although Biziligi would likely face life imprisonment if convicted of the original charges after a contested trial, the prosecution agreed to recommend 20 years pursuant to the plea bargain (the bargained-for sentence was higher than Nikindi's because of Biziligi's more direct involvement with the massacres and because of the lesser value of his anticipated cooperation with the prosecution).

Biziligi pleaded guilty and cooperated with the prosecution by revealing information about two of his accomplices that had been unknown to the prosecution and by testifying at two other trials. When the time came for him to testify in the trials, he was often evasive and inconsistent. But most of the points on which the testimony was evasive or inconsistent were collateral, so Biziligi's testimony ultimately helped the prosecution secure convictions in the two cases.

As a result, the prosecution still dismissed the genocide charge and recommended a sentence of 20 years, as agreed upon by the parties. At sentencing, Biziligi showed remorse for his actions and apologized to the victims. However, the judges decided that Biziligi's testimony was evasive and contradictory on a number of occasions and that he had not cooperated fully and substantially with the prosecution. As a result, the judges ignored the prosecutor's recommendation and sentenced Biziligi to 30 years in prison.

Notes and Questions:

1. Was it appropriate for the *Nikindi* Trial Chamber to ignore the plea agreement and the prosecutor's sentence recommendation because Nikindi had not expressed remorse at his sentencing hearing? What is the relationship between pleading guilty and expressing remorse, and what is the relevance of each to sentencing? How do national jurisdictions such as the United States and Japan approach this question?
2. Should the trial chamber on its own initiative be able to determine that the cooperation provided by Biziligi was not substantial? Who is in a better position to make this determination—the prosecution or the court? Can you think of circumstances in which judges should make such determinations? Would this be permitted in the U.S. federal system? In the German system?

Guilty Plea in a War Crimes/Crimes Against Humanity Case at the ICTY

Goran Nikolić and Dragan Simić were Bosnian Serb lieutenants and deputy commanders of the Dvornik Brigade, which was a unit of the Trina Corps of the Army of Republika Srpska (VRS). The VRS was the military force of the Bosnian Serbs during the armed conflict in Bosnia and Herzegovina.

After the conflict erupted in Bosnia and Herzegovina in the spring of 1992, Bosnian Serb military and paramilitary forces attacked and occupied cities, towns, and villages, including Dvornik, in the eastern part of the country, and participated in an ethnic cleansing campaign that resulted in an exodus of Bosnian Muslim civilians to enclaves such as Tebnica.

In July 1995, the Trina Corps commander, Milen Ivanović, ordered that the Tebnica enclave, which numbered about 1,000 citizens, be attacked and its citizens forced to leave. Forces from the Dvornik Brigade entered Tebnica and, in the process of forcibly transferring Bosnian Muslims out of the enclave, summarily executed 50 civilian men and boys.

The prosecution charged both Goran Nikolić and Dragan Simić with war crimes and crimes against humanity committed during the attack on Tebnica. Each of the accused asserted that he had not given orders to attack Tebnica and that he was not aware of any war crimes or crimes against humanity that occurred during the attack. Because Nikolić and Simić were the only two officers in the Trina Corps who would have given direct orders to soldiers, prosecutors felt that they could prove beyond a reasonable doubt that at least one of the two defendants—Nikolić or Simić—ordered the attack and should have known about the war crimes and crimes against humanity committed by subordinates. The prosecution considered it highly likely that both were responsible. But on the evidence available, the prosecution felt unsure of its ability to prove either defendant guilty beyond a reasonable doubt. In plea negotiations, the prosecution made the following offer to both of them: If they pleaded guilty to war crimes, the prosecution would drop the crimes against humanity charges and would recommend a sentence in the range of 10 to 15 years. In the absence of the agreement, the defendants would likely face at least 25 years of imprisonment if convicted.

Both defendants accepted the deal and pleaded guilty. But at the plea hearings of both Nikolić and Simić, the Trial Chamber refused to accept the guilty pleas, noting that the pleas lacked the required factual basis.

Notes and Questions:

1. Was it appropriate for the prosecution to enter into plea bargains with Nikolić and Simić given the uncertainty in the evidence? Should the prosecution have agreed to drop the crimes against humanity charges? Should it have offered to recommend a more lenient sentence? Were these actions consistent with the goals of international criminal law?
2. Assume that the trial court, based on its review of the facts, concluded the following: (1) It was clear beyond a reasonable doubt that at least one of the two defendants was guilty; and (2) excluding the evidence of the guilty pleas and examining only the independently gathered evidence, it was likely by a preponderance of the evidence that both defendants were guilty; but (3) the evidence would likely not support a finding that either defendant was guilty beyond a reasonable doubt. Assuming that these were the court's conclusions, did the Trial Chamber act properly in rejecting the guilty pleas? How would American, German, and Japanese courts approach this issue?
3. Suppose that, after the chamber rejected the guilty pleas, the prosecution decided to proceed with ordinary trial proceedings against Nikolić. Would statements that Nikolić or his attorney made during the negotiations with the prosecution, or the fact of the guilty plea itself, be admissible evidence in the trial? Should they be?

Conclusion

The Global Future of Plea Bargaining

The spread of plea bargaining around the world in the last few decades illustrates several different ways in which criminal procedure practices in different legal systems can converge. Introduction and adoption of plea bargaining has occurred through the influence of informal networks, through law-reform movements, and in response to the practical needs of each system. Plea bargaining first developed on a large scale in the United States. In Germany, despite a number of formal barriers, plea bargaining has recently gained acceptance in response to the pressure for greater efficiency in the criminal justice system. Eastern European nations like Russia and Bulgaria have been more directly encouraged and prodded to introduce the practice in the context of law-reform movements. China and Japan remain two major criminal justice systems that have so far resisted the express adoption of plea bargaining, but which seem to tolerate an implicit and limited form of it. Finally, the adoption of plea bargaining in international courts signals its true global reach.

As the preceding chapters have shown, however, to say that criminal justice systems have tended to converge toward plea bargaining is not to say that the systems are now identical. When plea bargaining has been incorporated in new systems, it has taken on characteristics reflecting its new environment. As Máximo Langer has written, it is more appropriate to speak of a process of "translation," rather than "transplantation," as each new country adapts the practice to its own needs and values.[1]

---

[1] Máximo Langer, *From Legal Transplants to Legal Translations: The Globalization of Plea Bargaining and the Americanization Thesis in Criminal Procedure*, 45 Harv. Int'l L.J. 1 (2004).

The adaptation to local conditions has created worldwide laboratories of experimentation that help countries develop models best suited to their needs. It has given policy makers valuable new information on which to base proposals for reforms. Consider the following different features of plea bargaining rules and arrangements that are now adopted by one or more jurisdictions across the world:

- Plea bargaining is limited to less serious offenses: *Italy, Germany, Bulgaria, Poland, and Russia*
- Judges are actively involved in the plea negotiations: *Germany and some American jurisdictions*
- Lay judges (jurors) must approve the outcome of plea bargaining: *Germany*
- The defense is entitled to review the prosecutor's evidence before plea negotiations: *Germany, Russia, Bulgaria, and international criminal courts*
- Defendant must be represented by counsel to plead guilty: *Bulgaria and Russia*
- Victims may testify at the sentencing hearing following a guilty plea: *United States (some jurisdictions) and international criminal courts*[2]
- Defendants receive a set (minimum or maximum) sentencing discount for pleading guilty: *England and Wales, Italy, and Russia*
- Judges have broad discretion to reject plea agreements: *Italy, Bulgaria, and international criminal courts*
- Prosecutors who refuse to accept a defendant's request to plea bargain must explain and justify their reasons for doing so, and defendants may renew their application for a reduced sentence before the court: *Italy*
- Judges must provide reasons for accepting or rejecting sentence agreements between the parties: *Italy, Bulgaria, and the International Criminal Court*
- Defendants cannot plead "nolo contendere" or protest their innocence while pleading guilty: *Germany, Bulgaria, Russia, Poland, and international criminal courts*

---

[2] In practice, this has occurred in very few cases at the International Criminal Tribunals for the former Yugoslavia and for Rwanda. Nancy Amoury Combs, Guilty Pleas in International Criminal Law: Constructing a Restorative Justice Approach 191, 202 (2007). The International Criminal Court has yet to accept a guilty plea, so it is unclear whether victims will be testifying at sentencing, even though the rules provide for such testimony as needed.

- The Constitution prohibits a conviction based solely on confession: *Japan, Bulgaria, and Russia*
- Defendants must pay restitution to victims before a plea agreement can be approved by the court: *Bulgaria*
- Victims must approve the plea agreement: *Russia and (for some cases) Bulgaria and Poland*
- Judges may award a sentencing discount for cooperation with the prosecution up until a year after defendants are sentenced: *United States*
- Judges ultimately decide what sentencing reduction is appropriate for a defendant's cooperation with the prosecution: *Germany and international criminal courts*
- If either the prosecution or the defendant breaches a plea agreement, the opposing party is entitled to rescission or specific performance of the agreement: *United States*
- After the court has accepted a guilty plea, the defendant may withdraw the plea if the court has rejected the plea agreement between the parties, or if the defendant shows a fair and just reason: *United States*
- If defendants make incriminating statements during the plea hearing, these statements may not be introduced into evidence at a subsequent trial: *United States, Bulgaria, Bosnia and Herzegovina, and Germany (as of May 2009)*
- Statements made by defendants during plea negotiations may not be used as evidence in subsequent proceedings: *United States and Italy*
- Charge bargaining is prohibited or strictly limited: *Bulgaria, Russia, Poland, Germany, Japan, and Italy*

Plainly, plea bargaining is not a "one size fits all" practice. Yet among this diversity of approaches, it is possible to discern general features shared by countries that favor inquisitorial models of criminal justice, and general features shared by those that have a stronger adversarial tradition. Consistent with their greater insistence on independent investigation of truth by judges, inquisitorial systems are likely to give judges greater authority to oversee plea agreements and guilty pleas. They are also more likely to require a stronger factual basis for guilty pleas—with some countries even expressly prohibiting in their constitutions a conviction based solely on the suspect's confession. Finally, inquisitorial systems are more likely to involve victims at plea hearings.

The strong commitment to judicial investigation of the facts does not always fit easily with plea bargaining. When a plea negotiation is not successful, a defendant in an inquisitorial system is more likely to be prejudiced by statements made in the course of plea negotiations or at plea hearings. In these systems, a confession often continues to have probative value even after the defendant attempts to retract it. Moreover, because the court in inquisitorial systems has greater powers to review a plea agreement, the court's potential interference with the agreement may discourage the parties from negotiating in the first place. Some countries, like Germany, have involved judges in the negotiations to alleviate the problem of uncertainty, but such involvement increases concerns about coerced admissions of guilt. For all these reasons, the approach to plea bargaining in some civil-law countries, while perhaps more faithful to the objective of truth-seeking, raises concerns of fairness. Yet even in adversarial systems, plea bargaining is hardly without its critics, as Chapter 1 discussed in detail.

From an American perspective, an additional benefit of comparing different systems of plea bargaining is the opportunity to consider whether certain practices from other jurisdictions might be tried with success in the United States. For example, the United States can study the ways other countries have sought to reduce the coerciveness of plea bargaining. While coercion has been identified as a serious problem in American plea bargaining regimes, at least so far, it does not appear to be a systemic problem in inquisitorial countries like Germany, Bulgaria, and Italy. This may be due in large part to the more limited application of plea bargaining to less serious crimes, the generally milder sentences, the lower sentencing discounts for pleading guilty, the broader pre-plea discovery available to the defense, and the near absence of charge bargaining. Of course, it may also be too early to conclude that coercion is not a serious problem in these countries and that innocent defendants are not pressured to plead guilty. Anecdotal evidence suggests that such pressure does occur, so the question will not be answered fully until further empirical research attempts to uncover whether erroneous convictions have occurred as a result of plea bargains. But to the extent that it seems that coercion of defendants is less frequent in these countries, American jurisdictions may consider adopting some of these features as a way to reduce coerciveness.

American scholars and policy makers may also consider the various simplified trial procedures used in Eastern Europe and Asia as an alternative or complement to plea bargaining. If properly structured and implemented, such procedures have the potential to expedite proceedings while maintaining a concern for fairness, accuracy, transparency, and victims' interests. Transparency may also be promoted by requiring prosecutors to give written reasons for their plea bargaining decisions, and by requiring judges to justify in writing their decisions to accept or reject a plea agreement. Finally, American legislators can learn from civil-law countries about different ways of involving victims in plea bargaining. They may also wish to consider, in light of Japan's experience, the importance of integrating remorse and apology into the guilty plea process.

Other countries can also continue to learn from the American model. Areas in which American plea bargaining law is more developed include provisions for withdrawal of guilty pleas, remedies for breach of plea agreements, and the regulation of cooperation agreements between the defendant and the prosecution. Certain inquisitorial countries have already begun to import some of these provisions. The Bulgarian Criminal Procedure Code, for example, provides that if a plea agreement is rejected by the court, self-incriminating statements made by the defendant during the plea hearing have no probative value in future trials.[3] Similar provisions could be adopted by other inquisitorial countries. While such provisions may occasionally appear in tension with the focus on independent judicial investigation of the truth, they are essential to ensuring a fair process. Other features of American plea bargaining that could be usefully adopted by other countries include procedures related to cooperation agreements. For example, inquisitorial countries such as Germany and Bulgaria could benefit from a separation of the plea and sentencing hearings to allow the defendant to complete his cooperation with the government before he receives the appropriate sentence reduction. Such reform would make cooperation agreements fairer and more effective.

These examples illustrate how the diffusion of plea bargaining across borders can encourage a fruitful transnational dialogue on "best practices" in plea bargaining. This dialogue should occur not only when countries that are new to the practice consider what plea bargaining model to adopt, but also when countries with established plea bargaining practices contemplate reform. It is too early, at the date of this writing, to assess all the advantages and disadvantages of plea bargaining practices and innovations introduced since the year 2000. But as more studies examine their effects on victims, defendants, and the public, a global dialogue on best approaches to plea bargaining will continue.

---

[3] Bulg. Crim Proc. Code §382 (8), *translated at* http://www.legislationline.org/documents/section/criminal-codes.

Two positive trends emerge from the review of plea bargaining regimes around the world. One is that countries tend to adapt practices suited to their own distinct needs and values. The other is that these countries are serving as sources of empirical data from which scholars and policy makers will be able to glean useful information about diverse approaches to plea bargaining. One may hope that through a process of careful comparison and adaptation, countries that are converging toward plea bargaining will choose procedures that are not only efficient, but also fair and legitimate.

Index